ST. MARY'S COLLEGE OF MARYLAND LIBRARY
ST.

W9-AQR-240

STUDIES IN HISTORY, ECONOMICS AND PUBLIC LAW

Edited by the

FACULTY OF POLITICAL SCIENCE
OF COLUMBIA UNIVERSITY

NUMBER 341

HERDER AND GERMAN NATIONALISM

BY

ROBERT REINHOLD ERGANG

34652

HERDER AND THE FOUNDATIONS OF GERMAN NATIONALISM

BY

ROBERT REINHOLD ERGANG

1966

OCTAGON BOOKS, INC.

New York

Copyright 1931 by Columbia University Press

Reprinted 1966
by special arrangement with Columbia University Press

OCTAGON BOOKS, INC.
175 Fifth Avenue
New York, N. Y. 10010

Library of Congress Catalog Card Number: 66-19732

Printed in U.S.A. by
NOBLE OFFSET PRINTERS, INC.
NEW YORK 3, N. Y.

To
M. M. E.

PREFACE

NATIONALISM is a phenomenon of such breadth and depth that one cannot do justice to it in a short definition. At best one can but point out some of the chief tendencies which make up this complex phenomenon. Nationalism may be regarded as the historical process of transforming petty states and polyglot empires into national states, but it may also be regarded as the intensification of national sentiment or the cultivation of group consciousness either before or after the establishment of a national state. In the latter meaning it rests more commonly on cultural factors. After all, is not nationalism largely a complex cultural phenomenon, despite patriotic reverence for the political state? It is with the cultural phase of nationalism that this study is chiefly concerned.

The word nationality, when used in this study, designates " a group of people who speak either the same language or closely related dialects, who cherish common historical traditions, and who constitute, or think they constitute, a distinct cultural society ".[1] It is most nearly in this sense that Herder used the words *Volk* and *Nation*. " Every *Volk* ", he wrote, " is one people having its own national culture as well as its language ".[2] Since Herder's idea of culture was organic, the cherishing of common traditions was necessarily involved. The word nation is used in this study in the sense

[1] Hayes, C. J. H., *Essays on Nationalism* (New York, 1926), p. 5.
[2] Herder's *Sämmtliche Werke*, Suphan edition (Berlin, 1877-1913), vol. xiii, p. 258. Unless otherwise indicated, all references to Herder's works are from the Suphan edition and will be cited simply by the number of the volume and of the page.

7

of a political union of a group of people and may embrace one nationality or more.

The author welcomes this opportunity to acknowledge his indebtedness to Professor Carlton J. H. Hayes at whose suggestion this study was undertaken and under whose guidance it was completed. He is also deeply grateful to Professor Camillo von Klenze of the University of Munich who read the manuscript and offered most welcome criticism. To Professor Jonathan F. Scott of New York University the author owes much for his personal interest, encouragement and helpful suggestions. He also wishes to thank Professor Henry L. Schulze of Columbia University for numerous suggestions and corrections. To Professor William L. Langer of Harvard University who has been kind enough to read the proofs the author's gratitude is due for many emendations.

The author is also under a host of obligations to the staff of Columbia University Library, especially to Miss Constance M. Winchell and Mr. Charles Claar, for courtesies shown and assistance rendered. Grateful acknowledgment is made to the libraries of Princeton University, Harvard University and the University of Michigan, to the Library of Union Theological Seminary, to the Library of Congress and to the Boston Public Library for the loan of books in the preparation of this study.

ROBERT R. ERGANG.

NEW YORK CITY, AUGUST, 1930.

TABLE OF CONTENTS

CHAPTER I

National Feeling in Eighteenth-Century Germany

During the early part of the sixteenth century it seemed as if a vigorous national life was about to blossom forth in Germany. In Luther, it seemed, the German people had a Moses who was about to lead them out of the wilderness of impotence and disunion to the promised land of strength and unity. Luther, it is true, did not revolt for national reasons; yet in his writings he appealed to the German national sentiment. Immediately preceding the activity of Luther such writers as Konrad Celtis (1459-1508), Jacob Wimpheling (1450-1528) and Heinrich Bebel (1472-1516) had deplored the decline of national unity. With infinite pride they had pointed to the German heroes of the past, to the magnanimity of the German princes, to the great military exploits of the Germans, and to the fidelity and valor of the ancient Germans which they regarded as national virtues. Likewise the writings of Ulrich von Hutten (1488-1523) breathed a vigorous, hopeful spirit. Hutten desired to make the princes independent of the papacy which he regarded as a foreign power.[1] In Luther he saw the standard-bearer in the national battle against Rome. His national enthusiasm rose to such heights that he did not hesitate to resort to force in attempting to carry out his plans. Also Franz von Sickingen (1481-1523), who after 1517 gave his support to Hutten's schemes, was to some extent actuated by national motives.[2]

[1] See Hutten, *Opera*, edited by Münch (Berlin, 1825), vol. v, p. 59 *et seq.*
[2] In general, see Tietz, J., *Die geschichtliche Entwicklung des deutschen*

But by the end of the sixteenth century the dreams of the German patriots had been dispelled and their hopes crushed. The religious movement which had bidden fair to usher in a new era of national life had effected the direct opposite; it had dismembered and disrupted Germany. As a result Germany saw itself divided into several hostile religious camps. After several years of mutual vitriolic attacks and endless petty disputations, the pent-up feelings which had gradually become more heated burst forth into physical combat in the Smalkald War. In giving each prince the unconditional right to prescribe the religious beliefs of his subjects the Peace of Augsburg, which ended the war, further divided Germany. From this time on the Reformation was the most important means of strengthening the centrifugal power of the princes. The intellectual life of Germany which had held out so much promise earlier in the century gradually declined. Whilst England had such names in literature as More, Marlowe, Spenser, Hooker, Shakespeare, Bacon and Jonson, and France such literary lights as Rabelais, Ronsard, Montaigne and Bodin, Germany, excepting Hans Sachs and Fischart, had hardly a noteworthy name between Hutten and the Thirty Years' War. Soon French, Spanish, English and Italian customs and language began to make their appearance at the German courts, among the nobility generally, and even among the upper middle class. In general, while England rose to a high position in the age of Elisabeth, and France became the cultural dictator of continental Europe, Germany sank from its high place and was drifting rapidly into that long, bloody conflict, the Thirty Years' War.

Nationalbewusstseins (Hanover, 1880), pp. 45-53; Erhard, H. A., *Geschichte des Wiederaufblühens wissenschaftlicher Bildung*, 3 vols. (Magdeburg, 1827-32), vol. iii, p. 141 *et seq.*; vol. ii, p. 1 *et seq.*; vol. i, p. 428 *et seq.*

Although a general deterioration had set in before the hostilities broke out, the effect of the Thirty Years' War upon Germany was so terrible that it is difficult to find an analogous chapter in modern history.[1] The gap which it made in the national development of Germany was so large that it required several centuries to repair it. When the treaties of peace were concluded, millions of people, it is true, still lived in the territory which we call Germany, there were still towns and cities which had been only partially destroyed; but the healthy prosperity, the vigorous intellectual life, and the military power which in the sixteenth century had given Germany a place beside the other nations had practically been wiped out by the unsparing deluge. Instead of uniting the people of Germany against the foreigner, the Thirty Years' War had finished the disruption started by the Reformation and continued by the Counter-Reformation. Upon this territorial and confessional dismemberment the peace treaties put their stamp of approval.

At the opening of the eighteenth century, conditions, in general, had changed very little since the Thirty Years' War. One glance at the political map will show that Germany was a masterpiece of partition, entanglement and confusion. It comprised approximately eighteen hundred separate territories of various sizes and forms of government, over which an equal number of sovereigns ruled. Each of these territories was practically a distinct sovereignty. The theory uniting them rested not upon a feeling of German nationalism, but rather upon the idea of universality. The sum of the possessions of the 1475 knights of the empire was only

[1] For a fuller account of the effects of the Thirty Years' War on Germany see Biedermann, K., *Deutschland im achtzehnten Jahrhundert*, 6 vols. in three (Leipzig, 1867-80), vol. ii, pt. i, p. 36 *et seq.* or *Deutschlands trübste Zeit oder der dreissigjährige Krieg in seinen Folgen* (Berlin, 1862) by the same author.

two hundred square miles, so that on the average each knight had about an eighth of a square mile of territory. Besides the small territories of the knights there were the Free Cities and more than three hundred states of the empire. For purposes of administration and unity this agglomeration of small and smaller states was gathered into ten circles, but of the ten only two, the Swabian and the Franconian, had a somewhat systematic organization. Petty quarrels and dissensions between the circles were never lacking and the arrangement which was to make unity of action possible most often achieved the contrary.[1]

The Holy Roman Empire, the only tie which still held the small sovereignties together, was hardly more than a name. Though embracing, at the beginning of the eighteenth century, a population of approximately twenty-five millions, it was so weak and powerless that the Germans were ashamed of it and foreigners derided it.[2] At the head of the empire we still find the Emperor, the imperial diet, the imperial army and the imperial courts; but they retained only the name of institutions whose real power had passed away. The members of the House of Habsburg were so involved in European politics that they considered the imperial crown to be merely a means of protecting their personal property.[3] After the Peace of Westphalia the general diets of the empire were changed to a permanent diet, held at Regensburg. Instead of making the welfare of Germany and the German people the subject of discussion, the envoys spent their time mainly in bickering over the vainest formalities. Such questions as who was to be honored by being addressed as " His

[1] Biedermann, *Deutschland im achtzehnten Jahrhundert*, vol. i, pt. i, p. 6; Boehn, Max, *Deutschland im achtzehnten Jahrhundert* (Berlin, 1922), vol. i, p. 4 *et seq.*

[2] Biedermann, *op. cit.*, vol. i, pt. i, p. 4 *et seq.*

[3] *Ibid.*, vol. i, pt. i, p. 22.

Excellency " and in what sequence they were to drink to the health of the envoys occupied much of their attention. The Imperial Chamber of Justice still pretended to be the highest court in the empire, but because of the endless ceremony and official red tape its decisions were rare, and then often met with disregard on the part of the princes, especially the more powerful. The imperial army, a motley assemblage of small contingents from the petty states, was characterized by a lack of harmony. Composed of the lowest type of recruits, for the various states kept the better ones for their own military forces, and equipped with diverse weapons, the army became the object of ridicule. In 1667 Pufendorf called the Holy Roman Empire a *Monstrum*,[1] and one might add to this comment that in the eighteenth century it was not only a monstrosity, but a moribund monstrosity. Its former dazzling visions of world-wide dominion shattered, the empire was slowly sinking into unconsciousness.[2]

Moreover, the German people did not desire to restore to the empire its former power. With few exceptions, the idea of national unity on the basis of the empire was opposed alike by the sovereigns and by the people. Instinctively some of the people still clung to the idea of *Kaiser und Reich,* but for the most part only in the sovereignties in which the conditions were such that the subjects looked above their government to the emperor for protection. For certain parts of western Germany the empire still seemed a necessity. Some of the states were so small and so weak that it was at times necessary for the officials of the empire to lend support to the officials of a state in matters of law

---

[1] Jastrow, I., *Geschichte des deutschen Einheitstraumes,* 4th ed., (Berlin, 1891), p. 77.

[2] See Biedermann, *op. cit.,* vol. i, pt. i, p. 22 *et seq.*; Herder, J. G., *Sämmtliche Werke,* vol. iv, p. 466; Moser, F. K. von, *Neues patriotisches Archiv für Deutschland,* vol. i (1792), p. 140 *et seq.*

and justice.[1] Justus Möser, renowned as a German patriot, gives us a hint in a book which he wrote in 1781 as to how low the empire had fallen in the popular estimation. " At the most ", he wrote, " we have but native towns and a fatherland of learning, and these we love as citizens or as men of learning. There is among us no Curtius who will cast himself into the abyss for the preservation of the Holy Roman Empire ".[2] Already in Goethe's earliest extant version of *Faust* (*Urfaust*), probably written in 1773 or 1774, one of the students in the drinking scene in *Auerbachs Keller* says,

> " The dear old holy Roman realm,
> How does it hold together? " [3]

The general tendency, then, was not toward strengthening the empire, but in the opposite direction. It seemed to please especially the ruling classes of .the several states when the imperial power met with reverses. The possession by the Habsburgs of large non-German territories fostered a feeling of particularism, for, to some, opposition to the power of the Habsburgs was a movement in the direction of the freedom of Germany from a power largely non-German.[4] In some circles the division of Germany into many petty states was extolled as an undisguised blessing. Many centers rather than one, it was believed, permitted a free and natural development of the individual and of the local community. As late as 1791 Wieland wrote:

[1] Biedermann, *op. cit.*, vol. i, pt. i, p. 56 *et seq.*; Wenck, W., *Deutschland vor hundert Jahren* (Leipzig, 1887), vol. i, p. 130.

[2] Möser, J., *Ueber die deutsche Sprache und Litteratur*, edited by C. Schüddekopf (Berlin, 1902), p. 7.

[3] *Faust*, edited by G. Witkowski (Leipzig, 1908), vol. i, p. 328. (Bayard Taylor's translation).

[4] Biedermann, *op. cit.*, vol. i, pt. i, p. 22 *et seq.*; Moser, *op. cit.*, vol. i, p 301.

One often hears the division of the German empire into several hundred larger and smaller, nay chiefly very tiny . . . . states mentioned as the reason why Germany, as long as it retains this system of government, never will reach the maximum of inner strength, never attain the florid prosperity, the esteem, and the importance among the European powers to which it might lay claim under another form of government. One can, I believe, attach as much value to this reproach as it deserves and yet, notwithstanding, assert with good reason that the advantages which on the whole accrue for us from this division outweigh the disadvantages considerably, or rather that it is to the division that we are indebted for these advantages.[1]

Concerning the sectionalism and localism of eighteenth-century Germany, Wenck wrote, " Today it is difficult for us to conceive how widespread this optimistic satisfaction with the political multiplicity was and how great the aversion to any project which might alter these conditions ".[2]

Economically Germany was as disunited as it was politically. It had not shared in the invigorating acquisition of oversea colonial possessions which had done so much to knit the bone and harden the muscle of England, France and Holland. Germany as a whole was too busy repairing the ravages of the Thirty Years' War within her own territories to engage in colonial enterprises. Moreover, the political division, and the narrow provincialism which it fostered, would have rendered concerted action for purposes of colonization impossible. Under the guidance of Frederick William, the Great Elector, Brandenburg had embarked upon oversea colonization by establishing in 1681 a trading station on the Guinea coast and by organizing the Brandenburg-Africa Company. But the venture was not very successful. The ruler and his subjects directed their energies toward the

---

[1] *Sämtliche Werke*, Hempel ed., vol. xxxv, pp. 251-52.
[2] *Op. cit.*, vol. i, p. 124.

aggrandisement of their native state in Europe and they therefore did not give to the undertaking the necessary support. The unfortunate enterprise terminated in 1717 when Frederick William I, king in Prussia, sold his rights on the Guinea coast to the Dutch East India Company for seven thousand guldens.[1]

In general, there was no unity of action in Germany regarding policies of commerce and industry. The Hanseatic League which in spite of the political disunion had upheld the honor of German trade for centuries had broken up during the Thirty Years' War (1632). The Peace of Westphalia had theoretically dissolved all internal customs and had decreed the removal of all hindrances to commerce in an effort to establish " complete freedom and security of trade ". Furthermore, every emperor upon his election had to promise to do all in his power to " guard the freedom of commerce ". But in spite of these promises, assurances and laws Germany was a checker-board of clashing economic interests. Each petty ruler did just about as he pleased regarding custom duties. Many of them rigidly applied the mercantile theory to their respective states. The network of tariff frontiers which resulted not only covered the land, but also cut up the rivers of Germany. On the Rhine, for example, there were from Strassburg to the national frontier of Holland no less than thirty custom stations. Trade was further cramped by nearly threescore laws regarding bills of exchange. The standards of silver coinage numbered no less than ten, of which five were in general use. In addition, innumerable coins of small denomination were issued by those who had limited rights of coinage. In 1660 and again in 1738 attempts were made to establish monetary unity in the empire, but those who enjoyed the rights of coinage were

---

[1] For a fuller account of the Brandenburg-Africa Company see Lewin, E., *The Germans and Africa* (New York, 1915), p. 7 *et seq.*

opposed to the measures and the emperor was powerless to do anything. Besides the tariff divisions and the monetary confusion state and gild monopolies on the manufacture and sale of certain wares handicapped the free development of industry and commerce. In short, the most antiquated and absurd regulations shackled the industry and trade in Germany, preventing both the free development of trade and industry and the growth of economic unity.[1]

The sectionalist spirit which prevailed also manifested its discordant character in the religious feuds which absorbed a good deal of public attention and served any purpose but that of German unification. Patriotic Christians who had the welfare of Germany at heart and who saw in the religious factions a cause of the weakness of Germany attempted to effect a reconciliation between the confessions. Thus Friedrich von Logau (1604-1655), the celebrated epigrammatist and patriot, worked for religious unity in Germany. In one of his epigrams, for example, he wrote, "Lutheran, Papist, Calvinist, these three faiths exist; yet there is reason to doubt where Christianity is to be found ".[2] In 1677 Karl Ludwig von der Pfalz sought to make a beginning toward religious unity by building a church in which he hoped both Protestants and Catholics would worship. He was, however, disappointed in his expectations.[3] Endeavors such as that of Georg Calixtus during and after the Thirty Years' War to unite the confessions on the basis of dogmatic concessions contributed but little toward the cause of religious unity.[4] Even the efforts of Leibniz who

[1] See Dietze, H., *Geschichte des deutschen Handels* (Leipzig, 1923), p. 83 *et seq.*; Day, C., *History of Commerce* (New York, 1916), p. 392; Biedermann, *op. cit.*, vol. i, p. 222 *et seq.*

[2] Logau, F. von, *Sinngedichte* (Leipzig, 1870), no. 232.

[3] Biedermann, *op. cit.*, vol. ii, pt. i, p. 275.

[4] See *Realencyklopädie für protestantische Theologie und Kirche* (Leipzig, 1897), vol. iii, p. 644 *et seq.*

attempted to heal the great schism of the West by means of
a reconciliation between the Catholics and the Protestants
were doomed to disappointment.[1]   Not until the fruits of
Pietism and Rationalism ripened were the outstanding differences pushed into the background.

During a large part of the eighteenth century the German
language seemed as much neglected as the interests of the
empire.   As the Holy Roman Empire grew more and more
impotent, the learned classes of Germany had reluctantly
abandoned their hope of establishing the Latin tongue as the
universal language of Christendom.   But for a long time
after the abandonment of this hope, Latin still continued to
be used in Germany itself.   Leibniz (1646-1716) was the
last great German thinker to write his major works in Latin.
But the unreadiness to use German as a vehicle of expression did not die with Leibniz.   For from Latin the upper
classes of Germany turned to French, which came to be used
freely not only for literary purposes, but also as the medium
of conversation in polite society.   Soon the French language
was regarded as essential for anyone who wished to make
any claim to refinement and culture.   The German language
was relegated to the common people and its use considered
vulgar.   Gottsched, the arbiter of literary taste in early
eighteenth-century Germany, stated that French was the only
respectable medium of correspondence.[2]   Konrad Friedrich
Uden wrote in *Ueber die Erziehung der Töchter des Mittelstandes* which was published in the last quarter of the
eighteenth century, " The speaking of German is for the

[1] See Schmidt, J., *Geschichte des geistigen Lebens in Deutschland*
(Leipzig, 1862-64), vol. i, pp. 137-151.   For a fuller account of the efforts of Leibniz in behalf of reconciliation see Kiefl, F. X., *Der Friedens-
plan des Leibniz zur Wiedervereinigung der getrennten christlichen
Kirchen* (Paderborn, 1903).

[2] Weise, O., " Die deutsche Sprache ", in Meyer, H., *Das deutsche
Volkstum*, 2nd rev. ed. (Leipzig, 1903), pt. i, p. 258.

daughters of burghers, for the maids. The little *mademoiselle*, however, must rather know how to say *bon jour* and *bon soir* and *je vous souhaite une bonne nuit* than to call God her greatest benefactor." [1] In many of the common schools the study of foreign languages was also given preference over the study of the German tongue. [2] In the choice of state officials a thorough knowledge of French was regarded as essential whilst a knowledge of German was passed over as a minor matter. Side by side with the old Latin and the new German periodicals, French periodicals were published in Germany and a not inconsiderable part of the books published were also in French. The Academy of Sciences in Berlin, which was founded in 1700, adopted French as its official language. Almost sixty years later Goldsmith found that the proceedings of the academy were still carried on in French and that the transactions were published in the same language. [3] In his Venetian epigrams of 1790 Goethe wrote, "Long have the great spoken the language of France and respected but half the man from whose mouth it did not flow. Enraptured, all the people now babble the language of the Franks. Be not angry, O mighty ones. What you demanded has come to pass." [4] Many of those who of necessity had to use the German language felt that the addition of French and Latin terms would give it the appearance of elegance and therefore padded it with foreign terms until it was hardly recognizable by the lower classes. This tendency became so common and so widespread that even patriotic zealots for the purity of

[1] 2nd ed. (Stendal, 1796), p. 148.

[2] See Weise, O., *Unsere Muttersprache*, 2nd ed. (Leipzig, 1895), p. 191; Biedermann, *op. cit.*, vol. ii, pt. i, p. 73.

[3] Goldsmith's *Works* (London, 1908), vol. iii, p. 486; Robertson, J. M., *The Germans* (London, 1916), p. 172.

[4] *Sämmtliche Werke*, Cotta ed., vol. i, p. 218.

the mother-tongue were guilty of it in their own writings.[1]
Early in the eighteenth century the German poet Burkard
Menke (1675-1732) had written in a spirit of ridicule:

> Da heisst das andre Wort gloire, renomée,
> Massacre, bel esprit, fier, capricieux;
> La précieuse hat das Deutsche gar verschworen,
> Es klingt ja zu paysan in ihren zarten Ohren
> Und kommt nach ihrem goût zu canailleux heraus;
> Ein Wort französisch ziert den ganzen Menschen aus.[2]

This padding of the German tongue with foreign words
because they were considered more elegant, and, in general,
the contempt which the upper classes showed toward the
mother tongue, did not augur well for the development of a
national consciousness.

German literature of the first half of the eighteenth century had little in form or subject matter or inspiration
that might be styled national. Like most of the literature of the preceding age it was a copy of French, Italian,
Spanish and English models. These imitations were characterized by an utter lack of originality and a complete de-
tachment from the life of the time. Hans Sachs, Fischart
and Sebastian Brandt had in the sixteenth century written
popular poetry and prose, but during the seventeenth century
the separation between literature and the life of the people
had become almost complete. Foreign ideas, characters and
manners had gradually monopolized the literature of Germany. Opitz had aped Tasso, Ronsard and Ben Jonson;
Gottsched not only adopted the rules of the French classic
authors which he regarded as authoritative, but he also

---

[1] For examples see Hirt, H., *Geschichte der deutschen Sprache* (Munich,
1919), p. 226.

[2] Cited in Weise, " Die deutsche Sprache ", *op. cit.*, p. 259.

recommended to the German writers the imitation of French models as the most successful way of developing a literature comparable to that of France and England. In short, the German literature of the first half of the eighteenth century was, generally speaking, divorced from German life.[1]

Since about the middle of the sixteenth century the life and culture of the upper classes, in general, had gradually taken on a foreign impress. The achievements of Molière (d. 1673), Corneille (d. 1684), Racine (d. 1699), Descartes (d. 1650), Pascal (d. 1662) and Bayle (d. 1706) had, generally speaking, been far superior to those of the Germans of the same age. The contrast between the polished and brilliant court of France and the rusticity of German court life was so great that it is easy to understand why the attractions of a superior culture were almost irresistible to many Germans, especially to the nobility. Many who had studied or traveled in France had brought back French ideas and customs, and the ever-growing French influence in Germany had been increased not a little by the French immigration which had resulted from the revocation of the Edict of Nantes in 1685. Despite the strict prohibition many Huguenots had left France and had been received most cordially in Germany. The Great Elector of Brandenburg had made a special effort to induce them to settle in his provinces. Hesse, Hanover, Brunswick, Saxony, and several Free Cities had also held out inducements to them.[2]

[1] See Hillebrand, J., *Die deutsche Nationalliteratur seit dem Anfange des achtzehnten Jahrhunderts*, 2 vols. (Hamburg and Gotha, 1850-51), vol. i, p. 38 *et seq.*; Francke, K., *A History of German Literature as Determined by Social Forces* (New York, 1911), p. 172 *et seq.*; Hillebrand, K., *German Thought from the Seven Years War to Goethe's Death* (New York, 1880), p. 49 *et seq.*

[2] See Rühs, F., *Historische Entwicklung des Einflusses Frankreichs und der Franzosen auf Deutschland und die Deutschen* (Berlin, 1815), p. 203 *et seq.*; Biedermann, *op. cit.*, vol. ii, pt. iv, p. 81 *et seq.*

Thus gradually French influence had become predominant in the life of the upper classes in Germany. This *Gallomania* or, as it was also styled, French *influenza* held sway during the larger part of the eighteenth century. Whatever was not of foreign importation or, as it was called, *à la mode* was regarded as barbarian and fit only for the rabble.[1] Many of the rulers were so enamored of French ways and manners that they lost touch almost wholly with whatever remained of German culture. Frederick the Great, whose own court was far removed from being German in spirit, though today he is honored in Germany and elsewhere as a great German national hero, commented ironically on the tendency of the smaller princes to imitate the life of the French court. " There is not a younger son of a side line ", he wrote, " who does not imagine himself to be something like Louis XIV. He builds his Versailles, has his mistresses, and maintains his armies." [2] Versailles was the model upon which the eyes of the princes and the nobility were fixed and it was the height of ambition of almost every German princeling to copy the buildings, the gardens and parks of Versailles, and to mirror its festivities. Almost every princeling also held a levee even though only the riding-master and the steward appeared for it. The German noble-man imported French maids, French governesses and French teachers for his children. His viands were prepared by French cooks and the coiffure of the noble dame was ar-ranged by a French hairdresser. French dancing and fenc-ing masters instructed the younger nobility in French grace. The clothes of the noble were French and much of the money which he extorted from his subjects found its way to France for the latest styles in French clothing. In 1680

[1] In general see Rühs, *op. cit., passim.*
[2] Cited in Hillebrand, K., *op. cit.,* p. 46.

Johann von Horneck had derided the love of French wares
by the upper classes in Germany in a book entitled *Ueber die
Manufacturen in Deutschland.*

Things have gone so far concerning French goods in Germany
[he wrote] that for us Germans hardly a piece of clothing is
proper unless it was made in France; nay even the French
razors cut our German beards better than any others, the French
scissors manicure the nails better, and French tweezers pull out
the hairs better than ours. The clocks run better if they were
made by the Germans in Paris. The coiffures, garnitures,
ribbons, chains, shoes, stockings, nay even the shirts are much
better when perfumed by the French air. In no other carriage
does one ride better than in one that is French. The French
perruque is more befitting to German heads than the German
hair; so also French hair cannot be combed with any but a
French comb or powdered with any but French powder. German gold can be gambled away only with French cards and can
be kept only in French purses or caskets. French plasters
adhere better to German faces than ours, and so it is with a
thousand other things.[1]

To be a person of fashion it was necessary that one visit
Paris at least once. The example of Augustus the Strong
whom nothing pleased more than to hear Mlle. Duparc, a
French dancer and one of his numerous mistresses, say,
"Vous êtes tout Français", shows the predilection for
French culture, in fact, for everything that was French.[2]

This predilection for French culture, French customs and
French products spread from the gentry to the wealthy
bourgeoisie in the towns and cities. Since it was comparatively easy to procure French teachers, many of the middle-
class burghers soon followed the example of the upper classes
and either employed French tutors for their children or else

---

[1] Cited in Biedermann, *op. cit.*, vol. i, p. 286.
[2] *Ibid.*, vol. ii, pt. i, p. 118.

sent them to French schools.[1] In the words of a German
writer, " Only he who lived in straightened circumstances
denied himself the pleasure of being able to count a [French]
governess as a member of his family. In Catholic districts
this mania was not so prevalent, for there the convents were
held in high regard as educational institutions for girls ".[2]
Briefly, anything that was French was regarded as fashionable by the princely and noble classes and from them the
contagion spread to the townspeople.

But not only the nobility and the middle classes were infected with *Gallomania*. The great Frederick who occupied
the throne of the Prussian state was himself, as has already
been indicated, strongly prepossessed in favor of French
culture. He read French works almost exclusively, spoke
and wrote French, and associated with French men of learning. He is said to have confessed to Gottsched, " Since the
days of my youth I have not read a German book and I
speak German no better than a coachman ".[3] In 1773
Friedrich Nicolai wrote to Herder from Berlin, " I know
only too well that the king reads nothing that is German ".[4]
While at the court of Frederick, Voltaire wrote, " I am in
France here. Only our language is spoken. German is for
servants and for horses. One has need for it only on jour-
neys ".[5] Frederick's knowledge of German literature was
meager and his interest still less. All attempts to interest

---

[1] Rühs, *op. cit.*, p. 206 *et seq.*; Herder, *Werke*, vol. xviii, p. 333.

[2] Stephan, G., *Die häusliche Erziehung in Deutschland während des
achtzehnten Jahrhunderts* (Wiesbaden, 1891), p. 107.

[3] Cited in Scherer, W. and Walzel, O., *Geschichte der deutschen Literatur*, 3rd ed. (Berlin, 1921), p. 322.

[4] *Von und an Herder*, edited by Düntzer, 3 vols. (Leipzig, 1861-62),
vol. i, p. 348.

[5] *Germanische Wiedererstehung*, edited by H. Nollau (Heidelberg,
1926), p. 535.

him in German literature were in vain. The German literary works of his time and also the German writers he regarded as much inferior to those of France. Of the German men of letters living during his age he seems to have had a kind word only for Gellert.[1] Only about a fifteenth part of the thirty volumes which comprise the edition of the *Oeuvres de Frédéric le Grand* [2] consists of statements of the king written in the German language.

In addition to these factors the cause of unity was further impeded by the sharp division of classes in Germany. An almost impassable gulf separated the upper from the lower classes at the beginning of the eighteenth century. At this time the English already had their Magna Charta, Bill of Rights and Habeas Corpus Acts which granted important rights not only to the great barons, but to all, irrespective of social status. In Germany the upper classes were the sole possessors of important rights. The nobility considered it a duty to separate themselves as widely and rigidly as possible from the other classes. They buttressed their position with the statement that God had decreed the separation of classes, and many people, it seems, really believed the myth that the blood which coursed through the veins of the nobleman was different from that which filled the veins of the commoner or peasant.[3] Even Justus Möser who worked zealously for the welfare of all classes desired a further division of the nobility into an old and a new nobility.[4] About the middle of the century the Prussian minister von

---

[1] See Suphan, B., *Friedrichs des Grossen Schrift über die deutsche Litteratur* (Berlin, 1888), p. 20 *et seq.*; Mentz, G., " Friedrich der Grosse und die deutsche Sprache ", in *Zeitschrift für deutsche Wortforschung*, vol. i (1901), p. 194 *et seq.*

[2] Berlin, 1847-57.

[3] See Biedermann, *op. cit.*, vol. i, p. 4.

[4] Wenck, *Deutschland vor hundert Jahren*, vol. i, p. 34.

Zedlitz advocated the introduction of a system of education which would divide the youth of Prussia into groups according to their social status.[1] In Prussia and also in some of the other states even the holding of land was regulated according to classes and the land of one class could be transferred to a member of another class only by a special dispensation of the ruler. The members of the upper class were forbidden to engage in occupations which by law were reserved for the citizens, neither could a citizen perform work which the law regarded as peasant labor. " In no other period of German history ", Biedermann writes, " was the separation of classes so striking and in its effect so tragic." [2]

As early as the first quarter of the seventeenth century a few of the members of the upper classes had felt the lack of a patriotic German spirit and had seen danger for the German people in the adoption of foreign customs and languages. They had, therefore, set themselves the task of effecting a change in spirit among their countrymen. To that end they had founded patriotic societies for the avowed purpose of putting a stop to the conquest of Germany by foreign culture. As an antidote they had desired to awaken an interest in the German language, in German customs and in German literature. In 1617 the *Fruchtbringende Gesellschaft* had been organized and the century which followed had seen the establishment of many other societies of the same sort. Although individuals belonging to these societies, as for example Opitz, Moscherosch, Logau and others, had been instrumental in purging the German language of foreign words and in arousing some interest in German culture, the societies as such had accomplished little. Their

[1] *Ibid.*, p. 33.
[2] *Op. cit.*, vol. i, p. 3.

original purpose had soon been forgotten and they had occupied themselves with trivial matters which in many instances hindered rather than encouraged the development of a national culture. Herder said concerning these societies, " Of the many German societies, only two or three have shown that they have been able to produce anything ".[1] There had also been no lack of opponents of these societies. Hardly eight weeks, for example, after the organization of the *Fruchtbringende Gesellschaft* a society bearing the name *L'Ordre de la palme d'or* had been organized to counteract the influence of the former group. The by-laws of the latter society were written in French and its stated purpose was the establishment and protection of French culture in Germany.[2]

Of German patriotism, that is of a patriotism which embraced the whole of the German people either as a cultural or as a political group, there is little evidence either among the people at large or in the writings of the time until near the end of the eighteenth century. An indifference to problems affecting the weal or woe of the German people as a whole had permeated all classes. According to the *Teutsche Merkur* of June, 1786, " We no longer have a fatherland " was the slogan of the day.[3] In *Ueber die Liebe des Vaterlandes* which was published in Vienna in 1771 Sonnenfels stated that of the love of the fatherland which was one of the most powerful motives in history " only the name has come down to our times and the amazement as to how it could possibly stimulate the imagination to such an extent that for a patriot nothing was so dear that he would have

---

[1] i, 148.

[2] See Schultz, H., *Die Bestrebungen der Sprachgesellschaften des achtzehnten Jahrhunderts* (Goettingen, 1888), p. 19; Biedermann, *op. cit.*, vol. ii, pt. i, p. 96 *et seq.*; vol. ii, pt. ii, p. 81 *et seq.*; vol. ii, pt. i, p. 24 *et seq.*

[3] p. 80.

hesitated to leave it, nothing so precious that he would not have sacrificed it gladly ".[1]   Wieland wrote in 1793, " I was told much in my youth concerning different duties, but of the duty of being a German patriot so little was said that I do not remember ever having heard the word German mentioned in an honorable connection.   *Deutschheit* was then an entirely unknown word." [2]   In the same essay he wrote:

There are doubtless patriots of Brandenburg, Saxony, Bavaria, Württemberg. Hamburg, Nuremberg, Frankfort, etc., but German patriots who love the whole German empire as their fatherland, love it above anything else, and are willing to make considerable sacrifices not only for its preservation and protection against a common enemy, but also, after the danger has passed, for its prosperity, for the strengthening of its weaknesses, for its outward respect—where are they?   Who will show them to me or at least name them?   What have they done and what can still be expected of them? [3]

The German people, then, generally speaking, were either provincial or cosmopolitan.   The knowledge and desire of the ordinary citizen engrossed in his simple everyday life did not go far beyond the boundaries of the state in which he lived.   His interests, habits and memories nourished a particularist feeling.   Even in the independent and semi-independent cities of the empire where one might expect to find a wider interest in politics and culture, German patriotism had sunk to a nadir.[4]   As a reaction against the provin-

---

[1] Cited in Wenck, *op. cit.*, vol. i, p. 129.

[2] *Sämmtliche Werke*, Göschen ed., vol. xxxi, p. 247.

[3] *Ibid.*, p. 252.

[4] See Wenck, *op. cit.*, vol. i, p. 115. Among the writings aiming to stimulate local patriotism were Thomas Abbt's *Vom Tode fürs Vaterland* (1761), Gleim's *Preussische Kriegslieder* (1758), Josef von Sonnenfels' *Ueber die Liebe des Vaterlandes* (1771) and Christian Ludwig Hahnzog's *Patriotische Predigten zur Beförderung der Vaterlandsliebe* (1785).

cial tendencies of the time there had sprung up among certain groups of people a cosmopolitan attitude which knew no fatherland. The words *Cosmopolit* and *Weltbürger* seem to have been the favorites among the so-called intellectual classes during the second half of the eighteenth century. As they were used in the eighteenth century both words were in direct contrast to the idea of patriotism. The whole world was the fatherland of the cosmopolite.[1] In a discussion of the cosmopolitanism of his time Wieland wrote, " That which was regarded as patriotism in the old Greek republics and by the proud citizens of that state which believed that it was founded to rule the world is a passion incompatible with the cosmopolitan principles, ideas and duties. No Roman could be a cosmopolite and no cosmopolite a Roman ". [2]

In harmony with the cosmopolitan attitude many of the leading men of eighteenth-century Germany were convinced that patriotism placed a limitation upon the mind and that cosmopolitanism alone accorded the necessary freedom. Wieland opened his *Kosmopolitische Adresse* by styling himself a citizen of the world (*Weltbürger*).[3] Lessing wrote to Gleim in 1758, " Perhaps the patriot in me has not been smothered entirely although the honor of being a zealous patriot is according to my mode of thinking the last which I should covet; especially of a patriotism which would teach me to forget that I must be a citizen of the world ".[4] In another letter in the following year, also to Gleim, he

---

[1] See Feldmann, W., " Modewörter des achtzehnten Jahrhunderts ", in *Zeitschrift für deutsche Wortforschung*, vol. vi (Strassburg, 1904/5), p. 345 *et seq.*

[2] *Op. cit.*, vol. xxx, p 413.

[3] *Ibid.*, vol. xxxi, p. 31. See also Wieland's *Ausgewählte Briefe* (Zürich, 1815), vol. i, p. 235.

[4] *Sämmtliche Schriften*, Lachmann-Muncker ed., vol. xii, p. 125.

wrote, " I have no conception of love of the fatherland and, at best, it appears to me a heroic weakness with which I can gladly dispense ".[1] Schiller proudly stated in the announcement of the *Rheinische Thalia* in 1784, " I write as a citizen of the world who serves no prince. At an early time I lost my fatherland in order to trade it for the whole world ".[2] He felt that it was " a miserably small ideal to write for one nationality ".[3] In the *Xenien* we read, " You Germans are hoping in vain to become a *Nation* ". Schiller advised the German people to develop themselves as individuals instead of trying to become a *Nation*.[4] Also Goethe was a cosmopolite excepting perhaps during the short time in which he was under the influence of Herder. *Faust,* his greatest work, carries no national message. In 1772 Goethe published a review of Sonnenfels' *Ueber die Liebe des Vaterlandes* in the *Frankfurter gelehrte Anzeigen* and in it wrote:

Have we a fatherland? If we can find a place in the world where we can rest with our possessions, a field to sustain us, a house to cover us, have we not there a fatherland? And do not thousands and thousands have that in every state? And are they not living happily within these confines? Why then this striving for a feeling which we neither can have nor wish to have, which was and is to be found only with certain peoples in certain places and is the result of many happily coordinating circumstances?[5]

If, then, despite the fact that there was little national

---

[1] *Ibid.*, p. 127.

[2] *Werke,* edited by Bellermann, 14 vols. (Leipzig, 1895-97), vol. xiii, p. 223.

[3] *Schillers Briefe,* edited by F. Jonas (Stuttgart, 1893), vol. ii, p. 343.

[4] Saupe, E. J., *Die Schiller-Goetheschen Xenien* (Leipzig, 1852), p. 117.

[5] *Sämmtliche Werke,* Cotta ed., vol. xxxvi, p. 67.

patriotism in eighteenth-century Germany, the words *Vaterland* and *Vaterlandsliebe* are to be found in the literature of the time, they probably refer either to one of the many states of Germany or they are a part of patriotic phrases which were taken from the Greek or Latin classics. In the former meaning they might have been used by some sycophantic court poet who was attempting to "immortalize" as a fatherland the "square mile" of his sovereign. In the latter sense writers used the words without attaching any deeper meaning to them. Only in exceptional cases do they refer to the Holy Roman Empire or to Germany as a whole.[1] Wieland wrote of the word patriotism:

Perhaps to most people who have enjoyed a certain education it is but the aggregate of all the impressions made upon their then still impressionable and unprejudiced minds by the maxims and examples concerned with the love of the fatherland which they read in their youth in the ancient writers.[2]

During the last half of the seventeenth and the first half of the eighteenth century when it seemed as if German culture was to give way entirely to the imported culture of France among the upper classes there were some among the writers of Germany who opposed the adoption of foreign customs and ideas, advocating instead that the German people develop their own latent genius. Worthy of mention in this respect is Friedrich von Logau (1604-1655).[3] In

[1] Jastrow, *Geschichte des deutschen Einheitstraumes*, p. 82.

[2] *Werke*, Göschen ed., vol. xxxi, p. 253.

[3] Others who opposed the domination of foreign culture among the upper classes were Hans Michael Moscherosch (1601-1669), Johann Jakob von Grimmelshausen (1624-1676) and Samuel Pufendorf (1632-1696). See Preuss, G. F., *Die Quellen des Nationalgeistes der Befreiungskriege* (Berlin, 1914), p. 6; Mitscherlich, W., *Der Nationalismus Westeuropas* (Leipzig, 1920), p. 165 *et seq.*; Tietz, *Die geschichtliche Entwickelung des deutschen Nationalbewusstseins*, p. 63 *et seq.*

his collection of epigrams and short poems numbering more than three thousand which were published in 1654 under the pseudonym Salomon von Golaw there were many biting satires upon the manners of his age. In some he deplored the division among the German people and the degeneration which had resulted from the Thirty Years' War, and in others he preached against the contempt of the German language, at the same time pointing out the wealth of the German language and urging that its purity be guarded. A favorite butt of his satire were the à la mode customs, language and dress of the upper classes. His hatred of the *Gallomania* was so intense that he preferred to see the Germans give themselves up to immoderate drinking rather than to the imitation of the French.[1] The great need of his age, as he saw it, was above all a revival of the old German customs and manners. But, though many of Logau's epigrams and short poems were forceful, the collection seems to have been received somewhat indifferently by the German people. In 1759 Ramler and Lessing resurrected Logau from oblivion by publishing a selection of about twelve hundred of his epigrams.[2] Logau's influence in Germany virtually dates from this time.[3]

Prominent in the latter half of the seventeenth century

[1] Logau, F. von, *Sinngedichte* (Leipzig, 1870), no. 994. See also nos. 106, 127, 281, 293, 379, 463, 643, 737, 236, 273, 401, 427, 736, 750, 770, 778, 439, 449, 753. No. 401, for example, reads,

> *Wer nicht französisch kann*
> *Ist kein gerühmter Mann,*
> *Drum müssen wir verdammen*
> *Von denen wir entstammen,*
> *Bei denen Herz und Mund*
> *Alleine deutsch gekunnt.*

[2] *Sinngedichte*, edited by Ramler, C. W. and Lessing, G. E. (Leipzig, 1759).

[3] See Lessing's *Werke*, Lachmann-Muncker ed., vol. viii, p. 75; Hempel, P., *Die Kunst Friedrichs von Logau* (Berlin, 1917), p. 9.

as one who labored for national improvement in Germany was Gottfried Wilhelm Leibniz (1646-1716). In his efforts in behalf of betterment he always considered the interests of Germany as a whole. Even when he was occupied with the particular interests of the Duke of Brunswick, Leibniz did not lose sight of the common German fatherland. For him the interests of the particular state and those of Germany as a whole were identical. He saw the evils from which Germany was suffering—political feebleness and torpor, economic exhaustion, the decline of national sentiment under the dominant influence of neighbors richer and more cultured—and for the evils which he saw Leibniz proposed remedies.[1] In the treatise *Bedencken von der Securität des deutschen Reiches*[2] (1670) he opposed the policy of joining the triple alliance which England, Holland and Sweden had formed to curb the ambitions of Louis XIV. The proposed alliance of the German princes with the opponents of France he regarded as foolhardy, especially for those German states along the Rhine which were exposed to the attacks of the French monarch. Instead he urged the formation of a league of the Rhine (*Rheinbund*) among the princes themselves. Excluding foreign powers, every state of the empire irrespective of religion was to be eligible for membership in this league. At the head of the league there was to be a directory of alternating membership. The emperor was to enter the league not as emperor, but as hereditary ruler of the states of Austria and Bohemia. Each member of the

---

[1] See Pfleiderer, E., *Gottfried Wilhelm Leibniz als Patriot, Staatsmann und Bildungsträger* (Leipzig, 1870), p. 432 *et seq.*; Lévy-Bruhl, L., *L'Allemagne depuis Leibniz* (Paris, 1890), p. 12 *et seq.*; Huber, J., *Das Verhältniss der deutschen Philosophie zur deutschen Erhebung* (Berlin, 1871), p. 6 *et seq.*

[2] *Die Werke von Leibniz*, edited by Klopp (Hannover, 1854), vol. i, pp. 179-327.

league was to furnish one thousand men for the protection of the league as a whole. A league of this type, Leibniz believed, would give Louis XIV no cause for enmity, and would be powerful enough to give to the empire the necessary security. Furthermore, Leibniz believed that such a league would give to the empire the importance in Europe which he thought it deserved.

> Then also [he wrote] many other important questions regarding the welfare of the empire and of common peace could be solved, the disputes between the states settled, the administration of justice—irregular, uncertain laws and wearisome proceedings—improved, energetic resolutions could then be passed for the organization of commerce and of the police, nay in time for provincial or even national synods and voluntary conventions and toleration in religious matters . . . . Germany is the ball which those who wished to gain rule over it tossed to and fro; Germany is the field of battle on which they fought for the mastery of Europe. In short, Germany will not cease to be the cause of its own and foreign bloodshed until it awakes collects itself, unites itself and the hope of winning it is definitely crushed for every wooer.[1]

It seems, however, that the idea fell on deaf ears.

In general Leibniz viewed with alarm the ambitious policy of Louis XIV. He saw the dangers to which Germany would be exposed if the French monarch succeeded in carrying out his plan of crushing Holland. Leibniz therefore immediately put himself to the task of devising a plan which while still offering an outlet for the military propensities of the French king would divert his attention from the vicinity of Germany. In conjunction with Johann Christian von Boineburg he drew up several papers proposing to Louis as a substitute for the contemplated campaign against Holland the conquest of Egypt and the disruption of the Turk-

[1] *Ibid.*, pp. 245-46.

ish empire.[1] The Turks had been troublesome neighbors to
the Holy Roman Empire and the disruption of their empire
would probably have given to Germany a greater degree of
security. If the plan had been carried out it would have
occupied at least for a time the attention of the two powers
from which Germany had most to fear. Owing to a change
in the affairs of Europe, however, neither of the papers were
sent to the *Grand Monarque*. But the idea was not given up.
In January of 1672 Boineburg briefly presented the plan in
a letter to Louis, proposing to send Leibniz in person to explain the details.[2] In consequence of a favorable reply[3]
which the French ruler sent through Arnauld de Pomponne,
one of his ministers, Leibniz set out for Paris in March of
the same year. Little more is known concerning this political mission of Leibniz than that the plan was rejected. Further efforts on the part of Leibniz through the medium of
the Elector of Mainz to induce Louis to undertake the expedition proved equally fruitless.[4] Leibniz also protested
energetically against the disastrous treaties of Nijmwegen
(1678), Ryswick (1697) and Utrecht (1713-14). He dis-
approved especially of the treaty of Ryswick which gave to
France Strassburg and the territories annexed by the *Cham-
bres de réunion*. Leibniz demanded the addition to this
treaty of a clause which specified that Strassburg was to be
returned to the empire in case the treaty was violated by
France.[5]

[1] The entire second volume of Klopp's edition of the writings of Leibniz is devoted to documents concerning the Egyptian expedition. The
introduction to the volume gives the historical background of the plan.
See also Guhrauer, G. E., *Gottfried Wilhelm, Freiherr von Leibniz*,
2 vols. (Breslau, 1846), vol. i, p. 92 *et seq.*

[2] Boineburg's letter in *Werke*, vol. ii, p. 108.

[3] *Ibid.*, p. 115.

[4] Guhrauer, *op. cit.*, vol. i, p. 108 *et seq.*

[5] *Werke*, vol. vi, p. 161; Guhrauer, *op. cit.*, vol. ii, p. 142 *et seq.*

But above all Leibniz worked for the awakening of the German mind. The imitation of the French irked him and in the *Unvorgreifliche Gedanken* [1] he wrote:

France has, so to speak, been set up as a model for everything that is elegant and our young people, even the young lords themselves, do not know their own homeland and therefore admire everything that is French. They have not only brought it about that their fatherland is for foreigners the object of contempt, but have also helped despise it themselves.[2]

In 1688 Leibniz asked permission to publish the *Semestria*, a bibliographical review of everything that had been written and published in Germany. From this idea he passed over to the idea of an encyclopedia, but the princes were indisposed to use a part of their funds to encourage science and learning.[3] Beyond this it was the greatest desire of Leibniz to establish a learned society which was to serve the twofold purpose of aiding the progress of the arts and sciences in Germany and of limiting foreign influence. In his *Bedencken von Aufrichtung einer Academie oder Societät in Deutschland* he wrote: " It is by no means praiseworthy that since we were in many respects the first in the invention of mechanical, natural and other arts and sciences, we are now the last in increasing and improving them. Just as if the reputation of our forefathers was sufficient to maintain ours." [4] He urged his countrymen to regain the leadership in the domain of practical knowledge and to lead the other nationalities instead of following them. Only a small part of his plan was to become a reality. Leibniz finally suc-

---

[1] Not published until 1717, the year after his death.

[2] *Unvorgreifliche Gedanken*, edited by Schmarsow (Strassburg, 1877), pp. 53-54.

[3] *Werke*, vol. i, p. 11 *et seq.*; Lévy-Bruhl, *op. cit.*, p. 22.

[4] *Werke*, vol. i, p. 133.

ceeded in winning the support of Sophia Charlotte, wife of Frederick III of Brandenburg, for the founding of an academy in Berlin which was to further the cultivation of science. In 1700 with the sanction and support of the Elector of Brandenburg an observatory was erected and a society was founded with Leibniz as its first president. Because of the War of the Spanish Succession which broke out soon after, the society, to the great disappointment of Leibniz, achieved but little during his lifetime. When he died in 1716 the Society of Berlin was the only one of his many projects that was active, and even this was barely functioning.[1]

Noteworthy also in the reaction against the French customs and manners were the so-called *Moralische Wochenschriften* which first appeared in the first half of the eighteenth century and of which more than five hundred made their appearance before the end of the century. Written professedly in imitation of such English journals as *The Tatler, The Spectator* and *The Guardian*, the *Moralische Wochenschriften* were destined to wield for a time a far-reaching influence over the German people. The most important of these periodicals were perhaps *Discourse der Mahlern* and *Der Patriot*. The former, which appeared in 1721, was written and published by Bodmer and Breitinger, later famous as the heads of the so-called Swiss school, and the latter was first issued in 1724 in Hamburg by the members of the *Patriotische Gesellschaft*. Among other things these periodicals stressed the necessity of the ennoblement of the family life of Germany, they sought to purge the German language of foreign words and to give it a place of honor in German life and, in general, they opposed the foreign imitation of the time.[2]

[1] See Merz, J. T., *Leibniz* (Edinburgh, 1884), p. 80 *et seq.*
[2] Tietz, *op. cit.*, p. 69; Biedermann, vol. ii, pt. i, p. 431.

Towards the end of the seventeenth century two movements—Pietism and Rationalism—took up the task of religious compromise and intellectual liberation, thereby preparing the ground for the seeds of a national culture and the growth of a national spirit. Turning from outward authority to inner feelings, Pietism stressed love and godliness to the neglect of arbitrary dogmas and external religious ordinances. Brotherly love, active piety and submission to the will of God replaced traditional dogmas as the means of salvation. By bringing together the members of all classes and confessions in its gatherings Pietism contributed its bit toward making the outstanding religious differences less severe. By recognizing personal differences it contributed toward the emancipation of the individual from the religious forms in which the state-ecclesiasticism of the seventeenth century had merged all individuality. The German *Realgymnasium* or *Realschule* as it was formerly known also owes its origin to the pietist movement, and the schools of August Hermann Francke (1663-1727), the best known pedagogue of the movement, were the first to be founded in Germany by national subscription.[1]

Rationalism did much to wipe out the outstanding differences between the Catholics, the Jews and the Protestants which barred the path to the rise of a national feeling and of a national culture. The rationalistic deism which arose won an ever-increasing following among the adherents of both Protestantism and Catholicism through the Freemason lodges in Protestant Germany and the Order of the

[1] See Kaemmel, O., *Der Werdegang des deutschen Volkes*, 4th ed. (Berlin and Munich, 1921), vol. iii, p. 54 *et seq.*; Richard, E., *History of German Civilization* (New York, 1911), p. 366; Hillebrand, *Die deutsche Nationalliteratur*, vol. i, p. 4 *et seq.* A study by Koppel S. Pinson of the influence of Pietism on the development of modern German nationalism is now in preparation.

Illuminati, founded in 1776, in Catholic Germany. The latter flourished especially in Bavaria. Although the members of these societies did not sever their connections with the existing churches in order to found a church of the Enlightenment, many of the members learned to overlook to some extent the religious differences. This aided in ushering into controversy-ridden Germany a period of peace between the confessions and in creating an atmosphere of common culture. The influence of Christian Wolff (1679-1754), perhaps the greatest teacher of the German *Aufklärung*, whose books were eagerly read by the public of his day, was immense. If we can believe Wolff's own statement, even peasants read his works.[1] Through his writings he contributed perhaps more than anyone of his time toward freeing the intellectual life from theological dogmatism.[2]

Furthermore, there were several noteworthy exceptions to the statement that there was little national patriotism in eighteenth-century Germany. Such was Johann Jakob Moser (1701-1785), and more particularly his son Friedrich Karl von Moser (1723-1798) who might be regarded as the outstanding imperial patriot in the eighteenth century. For him the word *Nation* included all the citizens of the empire.[3] In 1759 he published a treatise entitled *Der Herr und der Diener* which scored the political conditions in the small states, the moral laxity at the courts, the favoritism of the princes, their senseless squandering of the money of their subjects, in general, their abuse of the power which they wielded over their subjects. This work, which Hettner

[1] See Steinhausen, G., *Die deutsche Kultur vom achtzehnten Jahrhundert bis zum Weltkrieg* (Leipzig, 1920), p. 6.

[2] See Kaemmel, *op. cit.*, vol. iii, p. 96; Joachimsen, P., *Vom deutschen Volk zum deutschen Staat* (Leipzig, 1916), p. 46.

[3] See Renner, B., *Die nationalen Einigungsbestrebungen F. K. von Mosers* (Königsberg, 1919), p. 48.

styled "without contradiction one of the most important writings of the entire German literature of the Enlightenment "[1] was read widely. In a short time about ten thousand copies were sold and it was also translated into French and Russian.[2] In consequence Moser became the most celebrated patriot in Germany.[3] Herder openly commended him for being the first of his time to criticize publicly the abuse of power on the part of the petty sovereigns.[4]

It is striking that the writings of Moser which have as their central theme his national ideas and aspirations were all written in the short space of the three years from 1765 to 1767. The burning enthusiasm for the empire which characterizes Moser's life and writings during these years seems to have been evoked by the coronation of Joseph II in 1764. During the coronation festival Moser had come into personal contact with Joseph and the impression which the new regent had made upon him was favorable, to say the least.[5] Moser's hopes for a strong empire under the rule of Joseph now ran high. Working to make his hopes a reality, he issued a number of works in rapid succession during the next three years. Early in 1765 his *Neujahrswunsch an den Reichstag zu Regensburg* appeared in print. In a pithy and impressive manner it sketched the deplorable condition of the empire and then closed with a plea for unity.[6] After the sad experience of the Seven Years' War the German people,

[1] Hettner, H., *Geschichte der deutschen Literatur im achtzehnten Jahrhundert*, edited by Witkowski (Leipzig, 1929), pt. ii, p. 215.

[2] See Rosenstein, I., " Friedrich Karl von Moser ", in *Preussische Jahrbücher*, vol. xv (1865), p. 239.

[3] See *Allgemeine deutsche Biographie*, vol. xxii (Leipzig, 1885), p. 770.

[4] xviii, 258.

[5] Renner, *op. cit.*, p. 26.

[6] Published separately in 1765 and reprinted in *Neues patriotisches Archiv*, vol. i (Leipzig, 1792), p. 293 *et seq.*

he said in effect, must learn to harvest the fruits of peace by uniting for their common welfare and by cultivating "a true and common German national interest ".[1] For the past three decades, he continued, foreign nations have succeeded in fostering discord among the people of Germany with the consequence that the German people have sought and desired to limit the power of the emperor whenever they could.

The German empire in itself [he wrote] can be great, powerful, quiet and happy if the interference of the foreigner is eliminated. . . . Who would dare to attack Germany if Germany were united? We must begin here if we expect to receive advice and help. This is the foundation and corner-stone upon which the whole structure of our welfare can rest securely and immovably. For a structure, harmony and ability in making a plan, and care, zeal and faithfulness in carrying it out, are necessary. No member of the state is excluded hereby. He who lacks the strength may substitute for it a larger measure of determination. No German citizen is too small or too weak to contribute his share of counsel and encouragement. I am joining your ranks and although I may not be able to perform deeds, permit me at least to hope, to pray and to wish.[2]

Moser had three earnest wishes for the new year. He wished, first, that "there might be unity and faith among the head and the members" of the empire. "Only one name", he wrote, "only the honorable name of patriot must designate the good, honorable, law-conforming, thinking German . . . and it must be the disgrace of one dishonored, of one who has disowned his fatherland, not to be a patriot." [3] Secondly, he wished for "concord among the religions ".

[1] p. 301.
[2] p. 303 *et seq.*
[3] p. 304.

O that in the new year [he wrote] the blissful days would begin for Germany in which the honorable men of both religions would make up their minds .... to overlook with noble magnanimity the hatred and the reproaches of the blind, zealous party spirit, and would not tire in preaching everywhere gentleness, love of peace, love of man, Christian love, respect for the laws of both parties. . . . Finally, with a strong conviction of the dignity and excellence of the German name I wish for my beloved fatherland the uninterrupted preservation of that precious treasure, the freedom granted by the laws.[1]

Summing up his wishes in the words, " O that a spirit of peace and of concord, a burning enthusiasm for the welfare of the fatherland might gain mastery over us all ", he closed his short treatise with a plea to the members of the diet to work for the common welfare, so that posterity in looking back might point to them and say, " Those were the men through whom God blessed our fatherland ".[2]

In the same year he also published a treatise entitled *Von dem deutschen Nationalgeist* which is built around the idea of strengthening the power of the emperor at the expense of the power of the petty despots. The work opens with the forceful words:

We are one people [*Volk*], have one name and language, are under one common head, under one body of laws which determines our form of government, our rights and our duties, are united in one great common interest of freedom, are united for this purpose on the basis of a national assembly more than a century old, in internal power and strength the first empire in Europe, whose royal crowns scintillate on German heads, and as we are, so we have been for centuries, an enigma of political organization, the prey of our neighbors, the object of their derision, celebrated in the history of the world, divided among

[1] p. 305.
[2] p. 308.

ourselves . . . strong enough to harm but too weak to save
ourselves, insensible to the honor of our name, indifferent
toward our head, mistrustful toward one another, . . . a great
and at the same time a despised people which has the possibility
of happiness, but is in fact in a very deplorable state.[1]

The word *Nationalgeist* which Moser seems to have been
the first to use soon passed into common usage. It soon
appeared in the writings of Herder, Schiller, Wieland, Justus
Möser, Merck and Nicolai. The treatise itself was widely
discussed and the comments upon it were both favorable and
unfavorable. As early as 1767 Johann Heinrich Eberhard
wrote, " No writings have been so widely known as those
which were issued on the subject of the *Nationalgeist* ".[2]

But after publishing anonymously in 1766 the treatise
Was ist recht kaiserlich und was ist nicht recht kaiserlich?
and the *Patriotische Briefe* in the following year, Moser's
enthusiasm seems to have cooled. Although he did not cease
working for a strong empire after 1767, he seems to have
realized the futility of his efforts. Even Moser, the most
zealous patriot of the empire during his age, began to feel,
it seems, that the cause of the empire was beyond redemp-
tion. During his last years, from 1784 to the time of his
death in 1798, he devoted himself to the task of exciting a
feeling of spiritual unity. His message to the German
people might be summed up in his own words, " Woe to
him who is not a patriot (that is, one who works for the
common good).[3] He who loves his fatherland and its form
of government will either root out the weeds which rob the
fertile soil of its strength or tell others so that everyone
might aid in extirpating them.[4] A German patriot must

---

[1] *Von dem deutschen Nationalgeist* (Frankfort, 1766), pp. 5-6.

[2] Cited in Renner, *op. cit.*, p. 44.

[3] Moser, *Beherzigungen* (Frankfort, 1761), p. 247.

[4] Moser, *Mannigfaltigkeiten* (Zürich, 1796), vol. ii, p. 23.

never forget that he is a German, and not a Greek, a Roman or a Briton." [1]

Contemporary with Moser there was also Justus Möser (1720-1794) who stands out as a national prophet in an age of particularism and cosmopolitanism. In his *Patriotische Phantasien* he opposed the cosmopolitan philosophy of his age with its " new-fangled love of mankind at the expense of the love of fellow-citizens ".[2] By his criticism of existing conditions he endeavored to influence his countrymen to turn away from excessive admiration of foreign culture, especially French, and to develop those characteristics and institutions most typically German. Time and again he endeavored to interest the German people in their native language, their national history and their national literature, their folk ways and folk customs.[3] In the essay *Es ist allezeit sicherer Original als Copey zu sein* [4] he ridiculed the imitation of the French and told his countrymen that they could expect recognition from other nationalities only if they would develop their peculiar gifts. He also idealized the unity and power of the German people in the Middle Ages and extolled the beauties of the German literature of the past.[5] In 1768 Möser published his *Osnabrückische Geschichte* which made such an impression on Herder that he styled Möser " the author of the first German history with a German head and heart ".[6] The introduction—which Herder published separately in his *Deutsche Art und Kunst*—is

---

[1] *Beherzigungen*, p. 268.

[2] Möser, *Sämmtliche Werke*, edited by Friedrich Nicolai (Berlin, 1798), vol. ii, p. 164.

[3] See *Werke*, vol. i, pp. 18, 126, 317; vol. ii, pp. 76, 139, 250; vol. iv, pp. 13, 153; vol. v, p. 145.

[4] *Ibid.*, vol. ii, p. 224 *et seq.*

[5] *Ibid.*, vol. i, pp. 257, 317; vol. ii, p. 250.

[6] v, 347.

by many regarded as the introduction to nationalist German history.[1]

Möser generally deplored the lack of national interest among the German people. In the indifference of the Germans about one another he saw a prime cause of the weakness of the Germany of his time. " One neighbor ", he wrote, " concerns himself about the affairs of the other only in so far as his curiosity demands ".[2] Again, " Every sea-port acts only according to its own policy and the welfare of the empire which is identical with that of every part is hardly known by name ".[3] As a beginning toward economic unity in the empire Möser worked for the establishment of an imperial tariff system. The industry and commerce of Germany, he believed, were sadly in need of protection.

At the present time [he wrote] there is no empire in the world which does not have a certain system of this kind to regulate or free exports or imports according to the internal requirements of the state. Germany alone is an open empire which through trade is plundered by all its neighbors, and in which the interests of all of its sea-ports conflict most obviously with the interests of the interior of the country. No single state can make great changes in this matter by itself; it would merely turn over to a neighbor who is lying in wait the trade which up to that time passed along its highways.[4]

When Frederick II launched his attack against German literature in 1780 in his *Lettre de la littérature allemande,* Möser rose in defence of German literature in his *Schreiben über die deutsche Sprache und Litteratur.* Möser did not

---

[1] See Mollenhauer, K., *Justus Mösers Anteil an der Wiederbelebung des deutschen Geistes* (Braunschweig, 1896), p. 9.

[2] *Werke,* vol. iii; p. 68. See also vol. ii, p. 323.

[3] *Ibid.,* vol. i, p. 18.

[4] *Ibid.,* vol. ii, pp. 323-24; vol. i, p. 257.

deny that many of the statements which Frederick made
were true, but added, in effect, that constructive work instead of destructive criticism would do much to improve the
conditions which existed.

The real reason [Möser wrote] why Germany declined after the
age of the *Minnesänger* or has remained behind so long in the
cultivation of its language and fine arts seems to me to lie
principally in the fact that we have ever been educated by Latin
savants who despised our native fruits or preferred Italian or
French fruits of mediocre quality to perfecting the German
manners and arts.[1]   Methinks we must draw more on ourselves
and from our country than we have hitherto done and make use
of the art of our neighbors only in so far as it will serve to
improve our peculiar products. . . . We must, like Rousseau,
who permitted all rules and laws of his time to stand or fall,
draw upon ourselves and express only our sensations.[2]

We can hardly expect, he said in substance, to equal the
Italians in feeling, the Spaniards in the depiction of lofty,
glowing love, the English in the expression of their enthusiasm for freedom; and yet our climate has its good native
plants which we can and must cultivate and raise. If we
adhere to cultivating them, they must necessarily " become
great and beautiful after their own manner ".[3] By the year
1780 when Möser wrote these sentiments Herder had already reiterated them time and again. The foregoing statements of Möser contain not only the spirit and the ideas of
Herder, but in some instances also his phraseology.[4]

About the time of the Seven Years' War a group of men

[1] *Ueber die deutsche Sprache und Litteratur*, edited by Schüddekopf
(Berlin, 1902), p. 10.

[2] *Ibid.*, p. 18.

[3] *Ibid.*, p. 8.

[4] See, for example, Herder's *Werke*, vol. v, p. 159; i, 365; iv, 388;
xiv, 8, 152, 415.

who were to be instrumental in stimulating the national mind
appeared on the scene. Prominent in this group were the
names of Klopstock, Lessing and Herder. Klopstock
sounded a Teutonic note in his various odes.[1] Lessing
cleared the way for a native literature by undermining the
influence of French rules which were authoritative in literary
matters. His dramas paved the way for a national German
stage. In *Minna von Barnhelm* he gave to the German
people a play whose scenes are laid on German soil and in
which most of the characters are genuinely German. After
the failure of the Hamburg *Nationaltheater* Lessing wrote
in the last article of his *Dramaturgie* (1768) that it was in
vain to try to establish a national theatre

while we Germans are not a nationality. I do not speak of the
political constitution, but solely of the spiritual character. One
might almost say that it consists in not wishing to have a character of our own. We are still the sworn imitators of everything foreign, especially still the humble admirers of the never-
enough-admired French; everything that comes to us from
beyond the Rhine is beautiful, charming, lovely, divine.[2]

But Klopstock and Lessing, also Logau, Leibniz, the edi-
tors of the *Moralische Wochenschriften,* Moser and Möser,
were but the forerunners who helped to clear the field of
dense growths so that Herder could sow upon it the seeds
of a national culture. Spasmodically these forerunners had,
to a greater or lesser degree, opposed foreign influence and
advocated the development of a national culture. A national
culture built upon a national foundation, however, was for
them merely a matter of desire. The chief importance of
Herder lies neither in the fact that he remonstrated against
the foreign influences of his time nor in the additional fact

---

[1] See *infra*, p. 229-31.

[2] *Sämmtliche Schriften*, Lachmann-Muncker ed., vol. x, p. 213.

that he urged the German people to develop a national culture, even though both facts are important. Herder's importance lies above all in the fact that he tried to give the
German people an intelligent reason as to why the development of a national culture upon a native foundation was
not only desirable, but necessary. He not only urged the
German people to shatter the foreign idols which they were
worshipping; he also told them why they must do so.
Again, he did not stop at telling his countrymen to develop
a national culture on German foundations, but he went on
to tell them why they must do this if they wished to be a
vital force in civilization at large. In short, it can be said
that Herder formulated, in its broader outlines, a philosophy
of nationalism.

CHAPTER II

BIOGRAPHICAL NOTES

JOHANN GOTTFRIED HERDER was born in Mohrungen, a little town in East Prussia of about two thousand inhabitants.[1] This little town, surrounded by forests, lakes and marshes, had been founded by a group of German colonists who settled there under the protection of a castle which the Teutonic Knights had previously erected. In Herder's day only the ruins of the castle remained and they, the scene of many of the day-dreams of his youth, seem to have awakened in him an interest in the past.[2] The boy who was later to become the champion of the people and an ardent lover of popular literature, was in a more literal sense than the other classical writers, a child of the people. His father, a weaver by trade, was the sexton of the parish church and teacher of a primary school for girls; and his mother, a quiet industrious woman who loved her children with a devotion which Johann Gottfried did not forget, was the daughter of a blacksmith.

Both parents were ardent Lutheran Christians with a

[1] The best account of Herder's life is Haym, R., *Herder nach seinem Leben und seinen Werken*, 2 vols. (Berlin, 1877-85). For a shorter account see Kühnemann, E., *Herder*, 3rd ed. (Munich, 1927). The only biography in English, so far as the writer's knowledge goes, is Nevinson, H. W., *A Sketch of Herder and His Times* (London, 1884). This last account, however, is antiquated and does not do full justice to Herder's importance.

[2] *Herders Lebensbild*, edited by H. Düntzer, 3 vols. (Erlangen, 1846), vol. i, pt. i, p. 179. Will henceforth be cited as LB.

strong bent toward pietism, and their home was a sanctuary
of the Lutheran faith. Hymns were sung at the close of
each day and the daily chapter from the Bible was read
aloud. Also Johann Arndt's *Wahres Christentum,* a pietistic book of devotion, was read and studied assiduously. It
was on the blank leaves of this book that the elder Herder
inscribed the birth of Johann Gottfried on the twenty-fifth
day of August, 1744.[1] Even the choice of the name shows
the religious bent of the parents. " When my father was
pleased with me ", the son wrote long afterwards, " his face
would lighten up, and he would lay his hand gently upon my
head, calling me ' God's peace ' [*Gottesfriede*]. This was
my greatest, sweetest reward ".[2] In a poem probably written during his stay in Königsberg [3] Herder stated that his
mother had taught him " to pray, to feel and to think ".[4]
Furthermore, C. R. Williamovius, the village pastor, from
whom Herder received religious instruction also manifested
a distinct inclination toward pietism.[5] The atmosphere,
then , of Herder's youth was surcharged with pietism, a fact
which may account in part for the hostility which he exhibited toward the Enlightenment, especially in his early writings. To this period of his life also may be traced the development of his emotional nature which in later life so profoundly influenced his judgment.

Very early in life Johann Gottfried manifested a serious
turn of mind. At an age when most children seek the com-

---

[1] LB, vol. i, pt. i, p. 4.

[2] *Erinnerungen aus dem Leben Johann Gottfried von Herders,* written
and collected by his wife, Caroline Herder, and edited by J. G. Müller,
2 vols. (Tübingen, 1820), vol. i, p. 6. Will henceforth be cited as
Erinnerungen.

[3] See Haym, *Herder,* vol. i, p. 5.

[4] LB, vol. i, pt. i, p. 237.

[5] See Haym, *op. cit.,* vol. i, p. 10.

panionship of others in play, young Herder preferred to sit alone. In fact, the entire environment of his youth was serious. Even the school which Herder attended was conducted by a gloomy, morose, pedantic old man by the name of Grimm who seemed to know only that faculty of the human soul called memory. Extremely conscientious, this unpleasant-appearing bachelor exercised his calling in a manner remindful of his name. With his rod, which was seldom at rest, he enforced discipline, and few were the pupils to whom the rod was not applied. Herder, it seems, was one of the few, but the strict discipline both at school and at home had the effect upon the boy of making him shy and reserved. A schoolmate later wrote: " Herder's moods bordered on melancholy and sadness, and it could not be otherwise under the restraint and severity which he endured at school ".[1] Some of the angularity of the adult Herder is probably due to the influence of this period, for in mature life he often found it difficult to retain the affection of men who had been attracted to him in the first instance by his writings.

Although Grimm played the part of a tyrant in the schoolroom, he nevertheless laid the foundation for Herder's literary knowledge. What his method lacked in spirit was in a sense compensated by a thoroughness which left little to be desired. Young Herder found such favor in his eyes that the schoolmaster instructed him after school hours in Greek and also in Hebrew.[2] He was also one of those to whom the austere master was at times so indulgent that he permitted them to accompany him on his walks in search of cowslips and speedwell from which he brewed a tea. As a mark of special distinction he would now and then give

[1] LB, vol. i, pt. i, p. 104.
[2] *Ibid.*, vol. i, pt. i, p. 143.

one or the other a cup of this tea sweetened with a bit of sugar, a distinction which Herder was one of the few to enjoy.[1] But the relationship between young Herder and old Grimm was always that of pupil and teacher. It was not a friendship of the Socratic type in which there is a kinship of souls.

At a very early age Herder also evinced that unquenchable love of knowledge which remained with him until the end. His desire for books of all kinds was insatiable. Hardly a book in the village escaped him. Since it was financially impossible for him to buy books, he would modestly request the loan of a book whenever he saw one. With a book as his companion he would saunter through the woods after school hours sitting down in some quiet place to read and to ponder. It was on these walks that he also cultivated that deep love of nature which never left him and to which he gave expression in his writings. Next to the Bible the writings of Homer interested him most. Many years later, in a letter to Caroline Flachsland, his future wife, he related how as a boy he could not refrain from tears when he read for the first time the comparison in Homer of the generations of men vanishing like the leaves of the spring.[2]

Because his parents were too poor to support him, Herder at the age of sixteen was taken into the home of Trescho, a prolific writer on theological subjects and at that time pastor of the village church, who in return for secretarial and personal services grudgingly gave him food and lodging. This village pastor, so engrossed in himself that he saw little promise in others, prevented Herder from entertaining any bright hopes of a future. So unsympathetic was Trescho to the poetical inclinations of the youth that he attempted to dissuade young Herder from further study and

[1] *Ibid.*, vol. i, pt. i, p. 54.

[2] *Erinnerungen*, vol. i, p. 12.

advised the parents to have him learn a trade. Not even after Kanter, the publisher at Königsberg, had lavishly praised the ode *An Cyrus* [1] which Herder had surreptitiously placed with one of Trescho's manuscripts did the latter experience a change of heart, but he still continued to dissuade Herder from adopting a literary career. The impressionable youth suffered so acutely from the humiliations to which his master subjected him that as late as 1787 he used the following bitter terms in a letter to Trescho, " The first pictures of my youth were almost all melancholy, and many impressions of the slavery, when I think back to it, I would fain redeem at the price of precious drops of blood ".[2]

The great advantage which Herder derived, however, from his stay in the house of the village pastor was that he had access to Trescho's library, a library seemingly of considerable size. He could now indulge to his heart's content his love of knowledge which extended to all fields of learning. Thus through the use of Trescho's library Herder early acquired a wide reading knowledge. " Here ", his wife wrote in her *Errinnerungen,* " he learned to know for the first time his immortal Kleist, several old German writers, and his countryman Simon Dach ".[3] In the library of Trescho he also found, it seems, the songs of Gleim, writings of Gellert and Uz, some of the odes of Klopstock and some of the earliest writings of Lessing.[4] In a school address of later years he stated that this acquaintance with the best German authors during his early life had aroused in him a national feeling.[5]

[1] xxix, 3.
[2] LB, vol. i, pt. i, p. 87.
[3] vol. i, p. 20.
[4] i, 336; xxix, 280.
[5] xxx, 222.

Despite his diligent application to his studies, Herder's hopes for a literary carreer seemed doomed until an unexpected incident gave him the coveted opportunity. During the winter of 1761-1762 a Russian regiment which was returning to Russia established its quarters at Mohrungen. Divining the youth's ability, the surgeon of the regiment offered to take him to Königsberg and cure him of the lachrymal fistula from which he was already suffering and then to furnish him with the necessary means for studying surgery. In return Herder was to translate into Latin a medical treatise which the surgeon had written. Young Herder accepted the offer without hesitation and soon accompanied his benefactor to Königsberg. But the hyper-sensitive nervous system of Herder prevented him from becoming a surgeon, for when the army surgeon took him to view an anatomical dissection he, like Mazzini at a later time,[1] fainted. It was clear to him that he could never be a surgeon and so, after translating the medical treatise, Herder made known to his benefactor his decision to discontinue the medical studies.[2]

Before coming to Königsberg young Gottfried had already expressed the desire to study theology, but the insufficient means of his parents and his eye trouble put seemingly insuperable obstacles in his path. Despite both handicaps, however, he now decided to study theology and after a successful examination was matriculated in the University of Königsberg. Almost entirely without funds, he succeeded in meeting the most necessary expenses by working as a clerk in the bookshop of Kanter who had previously published the ode which he had secretly sent with Trescho's manuscripts. During his employment as a clerk at the bookseller's, Herder did not neglect to make use of the op-

[1] See King, B., *Life of Mazzini* (New York, 1911), p. 3.
[2] LB, vol. i, pt. i, pp. 28, 48, 110; *Erinnerungen*, vol. i, p. 26 *et seq.*

portunity to read many of the books which he found there, and in the bookshop he also met the teachers of the university who were in the habit of meeting there for friendly discussions in which Herder also took part. It was there that he first met Kant. By working as a clerk, and by giving private instructions, he managed to subsist through the first arduous winter. In the spring he was able to obtain a position as instructor in the *Collegium Friedericianum*, the town college, and henceforth his prospects appeared much brighter.[1]

While Herder was a student at Königsberg two men especially exercised a profound influence on him, and the first of these was Kant. Although his own intuitive and imaginative mind had little in common with the coldly rationalistic intellect of Kant, Herder entered into a warm friendship with him. Because there was no fundamental sympathy between the two, the friendship cooled in later years, but as a student at Königsberg, and for many years after, Herder was an enthusiastic admirer of Kant. During the years 1762-1764 Herder attended all of Kant's lectures on physical geography, mathematics, logic, philosophy, ethics and metaphysics. The wide range of his instructor's knowledge and the boldness with which he pursued his studies fascinated the young student of theology. In writing to Hamann at a later time Herder stated that Kant alone of all his instructors had not been a pedant.[2] Kant, in turn, who at that time had not yet written his epochal *Kritik,* fostered in the young man an interest in history and philosophy. Under Kant's guidance Herder read the works of Leibniz, Newton, Locke, Shaftsbury, Hume and Rousseau. Herder probably also received his first incentive for the study of natural science from Kant's lectures on physical

[1] LB, vol. i, pt. i, p. 155 *et seq.*
[2] LB, vol. i, pt. ii, p. 178.

geography. In her *Erinnerungen* Caroline Herder stated that her husband enjoyed most of all Kant's lectures on physical geography. This may account for much of Herder's later interest in physical environment which he considered the chief factor in the development of national peculiarities. On one occasion he was so moved by one of Kant's lectures that he immediately went to his room and put his mentor's ideas into verse. Kant, to whom Herder presented the verses on the following morning, read them before the class with lavish praise.[1] On another occasion Kant said, after reading a poem by Herder which had appeared in the *Königsberger Zeitung,* " When this boiling genius has ceased fermenting, he will be a very useful man by his talents ".[2] Before many years passed Kant himself saw this prophecy fulfilled. As an expression of the high esteem in which Herder held Kant we have that much-cited testimonial in the *Humanitätsbriefe,* written many years after Herder left Königsberg:

I once enjoyed the good fortune of knowing a philosopher who was my teacher. He had the joyous cheerfulness of youth at that happy time, and this cheerfulness, I believe, he retained even in his old age. His open forehead, created expressly for thought, was the seat of imperturbable serenity and happiness; his speech, redundant with ideas, flowed from his lips; he always had some humorous trait, some witty sally at his disposal, and his teaching was the source of the most instructive intercourse for me . . . . He would constantly bring us back to the simple unaffected study of nature and the moral worth of man. . . . He gave me confidence and obliged me to think for myself.[3]

[1] vol. i, p. 62.
[2] LB, vol. i, pt. i, p. 137.
[3] xvii, 404.

He also celebrated Kant in the following lines:

" When there where nothing is thought—nothing felt,
I yet bore fetters, gnawed by dust, and sweat, and tears,

> I sighed—for how can a slave sing!
> And Apollo, the god, came.
> Away with the chains! My terrestrial glance
> Was uplifted—he gave me Kant." [1]

Even more fruitful was Herder's intercourse with the pietist and mystic, Johann Georg Hamann, (1730-1788) who because of his oracular utterances was called the Magus of the North. Although today his name is scarcely known except to specialists in philosophy or literature, he was widely known in his day.[2] Hamann's interests were those of the theologian, the linguist, the historian and the writer. From Herder's student days in Königsberg until Hamann's death more than twenty years later the ardent friendship of these two men, so dissimilar in age, was seldom marred by misunderstandings and never seriously endangered. Caroline Herder wrote concerning this friendship:

In him he [Herder] found what he sought and needed — a sympathetic, loving, ardent heart for all that was great and good, a spiritual religiosity, the strictest moral principles, and a lofty, consecrated genius both in mind and in spirit. As such he cherished his Hamann, and the most complete sympathy united them for time and eternity. . . . When he received a letter from Hamann it was for him a day of joy; then he could not remain indoors, but had to go out in the open, for his whole soul was moved. . . . Tears of joy filled Herder's eyes ".[3]

[1] LB, vol. i, pt. i, p. 187.

[2] For a statement concerning Hamann's influence see Goethe's *Werke,* Cotta ed., vol. xxiv, p. 81.

[3] *Erinnerungen,* vol. i, p. 65.

To Hamann Herder was indebted for many of his literary interests. Together they sought the original and the spontaneous, deploring everything which to them seemed artificial. By introducing him to such writings as Ossian's poems and Percy's *Reliques,* Hamann, who had a passion for the primeval, opened the way to Herder for the study of folk poetry and early literature. Through Hamann, under whose guidance he learned English, Herder was first led to study English literature, especially Shakespeare. Furthermore, Hamann infused into Herder, whose pietistic background made him an apt pupil, a spirit of hostility to the Enlightenment. Much of Herder's early hostility toward the Enlightenment can undoubtedly be traced to the influence of Hamann who, asserting that reason was insufficient for a comprehension of the deeper truths, was ever ready to defend the emotions against reason. Thus a *Weltanschauung* toward which Herder was temperamentally inclined was confirmed in him by these two years of companionship with Hamann.[1]

Through his association with both Kant and Hamann Herder came under the influence of Rousseau. Through the works of Rousseau Herder became imbued with a love of the primitive, the natural, the original. From Rousseau he borrowed the idea of the artificiality of the culture of his age, and thereafter endeavored to bring his generation back to a life founded on the laws of nature. Rousseau's nature gospel was, in a sense, to become the foundation of Herder's idea of nationality. Rousseau's influence upon Herder was so great that the latter is by some called " the German Rousseau " which is, of course, a misnomer.[2] Yet Herder

---

[1] See Unger, R., *Hamann und die Aufklärung*, 2 vols. (Jena, 1911), *passim.*

[2] See Bartels, A., *Geschichte der deutschen Literatur* (Leipzig, 1924), vol. i, p. 448; Japp, A. H., *German Life and Literature* (London, 1880), p 243.

was so enthusiastic over Rousseau that he styled him " a colossus among the writers ",[1] and to him Herder also addressed one of his first poems :

> " I will seek my own self,
> That I might find myself,
> And then never lose myself,
> ....
> Come, me my guide, O Rousseau! " [2]

In 1764 upon the recommendation of Hamann, Herder, then only twenty years of age, was offered the position as teacher of the cathedral school in Riga, a city in Livonia which at that time was under Russian rule, and immediately accepted it. To his duties as teacher he added occasional ministerial duties and after passing a theological examination before the ministry of Riga was appointed assistant-pastor of the cathedral. The years Herder spent in Riga, where much of the spirit of the old Hanseatic League still lingered, seem to have been the most carefree of his life.[3] Stimulated by the thoughts of Lessing and Winckelmann, yet writing in an original vein, he produced his *Fragmente über die deutsche Literatur* and his *Kritische Wälder,* in both of which he launched his vigorous attacks on the traditional imitation of other nationalities by the German people. Minor works of this period are the *Torso über Abbt* and *Haben wir noch jetzt das Publikum und Vaterland der Alten?* During this time he also pursued with intense eagerness studies in theology, philosophy and natural history. All in all, it was a profitable and happy period in Herder's life.

[1] x, 307.

[2] LB, vol. i, pt. i, p. 252.

[3] *Erinnerungen*, vol. i, p. 90 *et seq.*. LB, vol. i, pt. i, p. 158; pt. ii, p. 37.

Noteworthy in the Königsberg and Riga period of his life is a marked antipathy to Prussian bureaucracy and militarism. Although he was born in East Prussia, Herder could hardly at any time of his life be called a Prussian patriot. The example of his father whom Herder styled " a patriot for two generations " [1] and that of Hamann who was an ardent Prussian patriot, seem to have had little, if any influence on Herder in arousing a feeling of Prussian patriotism. In 1769 Hamann wrote to Herder: " You consider it an honor to be a German, but to be a Prussian, which would be much better, you are ashamed ".[2] Herder was repelled by the despotism of the Prussian monarch,[3] and his inherent love of freedom, his delicate physical condition and the impressions which the Seven Years' War had made upon his sensitive nature rendered him an avowed enemy of militarism. As the amanuensis of Trescho he had already sung the praises of the Russian monarch, Peter III, for having bestowed peace upon a war-ridden nation.[4] Moreover, he always had a great dread of military service and even went so far as to compare the red collars of Frederick's warriors with the iron rings of the galley slaves.[5] " How this military discipline ", he wrote from Königsberg, " paralyzes the poor folk in Prussia with fear and abject slavery. They hardly venture to reflect or dare think anything of themselves ".[6] While still in Mohrungen he was already enrolled in the military list of the district and thereafter lived in perpetual dread lest

[1] xxix, 281; LB, vol. i, pt. i, p. 238.

[2] LB, vol. i, pt. ii, p. 423.

[3] See, for example, i, 26; v, 547 *et seq.*

[4] In the ode *An Cyrus*, xxix, 3.

[5] xviii, 216; *Erinnerungen*, vol. i, p. 24.

[6] *Erinnerungen*, vol. i, p. 24. See also *Werke*, iv, 362; xxix, 321.

he be obliged to abandon his studies to become a recruit.[1]
Shortly before his departure for Riga an accident occurred
which completed his estrangement from Prussia. In order
to receive permission to leave Prussia, Herder had to promise on oath to return in the event that the Prussian army had
need of him. This call to military service, suspended over
him like the sword of Damocles, caused Herder to live in
constant dread of being forced to return to Prussia and to
the barracks.[2] When he left Prussia for Riga it was with
a bitter farewell, for, as he said later, he felt so free and
happy after leaving Prussian territory that he was " ready
to kiss the ground for joy ".[3] So indelible were the impressions of these years that he was never quite able to conceal
his indignation over the military system of Prussia and even
in later years felt little sympathy for that state.

This aversion to militarism and despotism was also the
basis of Herder's hostility to Frederick II whom he regarded
as the incarnation of both. Although his dislike of the
Prussian king was at first expressed in vague terms,
Herder later became openly hostile to him.[4] He did not
hesitate to express his indignation at the despotic methods
of Frederick. " The states of the king of Prussia ", he
wrote, " will not be happy until they are dissolved in the
common fraternization ".[5] He believed also that Frederick
was putting obstacles in the way of German cultural unity.
" What has his Academy achieved? " he asked. " Have his
Frenchmen brought Germany and his provinces as much

[1] *Ibid.*, p. 23.

[2] *Ibid.*, p. 68.

[3] *Ibid.*, p. 112.

[4] See ii, 290; iv, 469 *et seq.*; xxix, 5 *et seq.*, 118; viii, 2; *Aus Herders Nachlass*, vol. ii, p. 123; *Herders Briefe an Hamann*, edited by O. Hoff-mann (Berlin, 1889), p. 113.

[5] iv, 405.

prestige as is generally believed? No, his Voltaires have despised the Germans without knowing them. His Academy has also contributed to the decline of philosophy. His Maupertuis, Premontvals, Formeis, d'Argens,—what kind of philosophers were they? What kind of writings did they honor with a prize? They did not understand Leibniz and Wolff." [1]   Much later, however, after the death of Frederick, Herder's attitude toward the great monarch underwent a change. Henceforth the king is mentioned with respect. "When he died", Herder wrote, "it seemed as if a great genius had left the earth; friends and enemies of his glory were moved. It seemed as if his earthly form might also have been immortal ".[2]

Of Herder's happiness in Riga mention has already been made. To him the city was a revelation. Accustomed as he had been to the military constitution, bureaucratic organization and lack of personal freedom which had characterized life in East Prussia, he was greatly attracted to, and stimulated by, the spirit of Russian patriotism which prevailed in Riga, by the general participation in public affairs and by the freedom of speech, thought and action which obtained.[3] The young Prussian who had not known the feeling of local patriotism as long as he was under the rule of Frederick II soon became an enthusiastic patriot. Yet this Russian patriotism did not prevent him from being, at the same time, a German patriot, for he was a Russian patriot only in the sense that he preferred the atmosphere of freedom in Riga to that of militarism in Prussia.[4] The

---

[1] *Ibid.*

[2] xvii, 28. See also ix, 369; xvi, 32; xvii, 29; xviii, 525, 557; xx, 332; xxiv, 260; *Herders Briefe an Hamann*, pp. 167, 174.

[3] *Erinnerungen*, vol. i, p. 91.

[4] See *Briefe an Hamann*, p. 33.

spiritual relationship between the Germans of the former
Hansa town and the mother country still existed at that time.
At heart Riga was still a German town, the majority of the
population was German and the language most commonly
used was German.[1] It was because of the German spirit
that reigned in Riga that Herder felt so much at home. At
no time does his German patriotism seem to have been in
jeopardy. In the speech, *Haben wir noch jetzt das Publikum und Vaterland der Alten?*, Herder gave evidence of
his German patriotism by praising the German tongue and
German patriotism and by deprecating the low estate of
German art and literature.[2]

Gradually, however, Herder's ardor for Riga cooled, and
he no longer felt at ease in the Livonian city. His discontented nature began to assert itself and he discovered, as
he thought, that but a shadow of the former Hanseatic spirit
remained in Riga. From this time until his departure from
Riga his correspondence is an unbroken series of complaints.
In a letter to Schaffner he wrote:

My present almost melancholy situation makes everything
difficult and also makes me unfit for everything. Everything
here bores me, the place in which I live, my profession, my
labors and the people with whom I am obliged to associate, and
anything is easier to explain than the fact that I, so to speak,
chained myself to Riga through my pastoral calling. I long
for nothing but a change, and in this discontent I am virtually
devouring myself.[3]

That impatience which throughout life moved him to go

---

[1] See Krohnert, O., *Herder als Politiker und deutscher Patriot*
(Gumbinnen, 1905), p. 6.

[2] i, 13 *et seq.*

[3] LB, vol. i, pt. ii, pp. 355-356. See also Hamann's *Schriften* (Berlin,
1822), vol. iii, p. 361; *Briefe an Hamann*, p. 57.

from one idea to another and from one place to another
showed itself when he wrote to Nicolai:

Never, never would Lessing have been the man that he is if he
had been confined in the close atmosphere of a little town or,
which is worse, in a study. . . . I envy Lessing in more than
one respect. He is a man of the world who rushes from one
art to another and from one situation to another and always
with his whole youthful soul which never grows old. Such a
man can enlighten Germany.[1]

At last he decided he could no longer suffer the boredom
he experienced and made preparations to leave Riga.

Moved by an urgent desire to see more of the world before
settling down to the work of his life he resigned his position
and took passage on a ship bound for France. Herder's
Reisejournal which Haym has styled "the most important
document of Herder's mind"[2] affords us an unusual insight
into Herder and shows that this voyage of almost two
months proved to be an intellectual crisis for him. In it
are plainly visible the germs of many ideas on history, literature and theology which were to be so influential in
molding the thought of the German people. "What a
vast sphere of reflection", he wrote "is opened by a ship
floating betwixt sky and ocean. Everything here lends to
the thought wings and movement and gives it a wide horizon.
. . . On the earth one is bound to a small immovable spot
and hemmed in by the narrow circle of a situation. . . . But
let one quit it suddenly, and what a different aspect presents
itself!"[3] Moreover, the importance of this voyage for the
formation of his ideas on nationality can hardly be exaggerated. During the voyage he developed in his mind the

[1] LB, vol. i, pt. ii, p. 406.
[2] *Herder*, vol. i, p. 317.
[3] iv, 348.

relationship between culture and environment.[1]   It was also during this voyage that he conceived the plan of *Auch eine Philosophie der Geschichte der Menschheit.*[2]

On the sixteenth of July, 1769, Herder arrived at Nantes where he had planned to reside a few months in order to improve his knowledge of the French language and then to spend some time in Paris which at that time was regarded as the social and intellectual center of Europe.   But Herder did not remain in France as long as he had at first intended. His high opinion of everything that was French changed soon after he came into direct contact with the French and with French culture.   He discovered, as he thought, that under the magnificence and pomp of French culture and life there was an empty frivolity.   Hence his contact with the culture of France served but to intensify his German patriotism, and henceforth his thoughts and feelings were decidedly anti-French.[3]

While Herder was in Paris he received an offer to become the private tutor of the young prince of Holstein-Eutin at a good salary.   According to the terms agreed upon Herder was to accompany the prince on his travels for three years and at the expiration of this term was to receive a professorship at Kiel.   Instead, therefore, of continuing his journey as he had originally planned Herder started toward Kiel where he was to meet the young prince.   On the way he visited Brussels, Antwerp, the Hague and Amsterdam.   Before reaching Kiel he also met Lessing at Hamburg, but no very intimate friendship resulted from the meeting.[4]

Herder's association with the prince, however, was of but

[1] See iv, 357, *et seq.*

[2] *Ibid.*, 345 *et seq.*

[3] *Erinnerungen*, vol. i, p. 25; LB, vol. ii, p. 39; Haym, *Herder*, vol. i, pp. 339, 414.

[4] *Erinnerungen*, vol. i, p. 143.

short duration. Graciously received by the duke and the duchess, the parents of the prince whom he was to assist in his studies, Herder soon found his ideals at variance with those of the manager of the party, a certain Herr von Kappelman. The first few months were spent at the court of the duke and the duchess and then the party set out on the travels on which Herder was to accompany the prince. But Herder remained with the party only until it reached Strassburg. Although he and the young prince had grown fond of each other, Herder found his association with the manager of the party so disagreeable that he requested his release which was reluctantly granted by the duke. The journey from Kiel to Strassburg was to prove eventful in Herder's life, for it was at Darmstadt where the party stopped on its way that Herder first met Caroline Flachsland, his future wife.

In Strassburg Herder took advantage of the opportunity to consult the noted occulist Lobstein regarding his eye affliction. The lachrymal duct of his right eye was defective and upon the promise of Lobstein to make an artificial passage Herder submitted to a series of operations. For six months he remained in close confinement bearing the intense pain of the repeated operations without complaint, only to be told in the end that the treatment had been ineffectual and that the malady could not be relieved. The operations had but aggravated the condition and, in addition, Herder's face was disfigured for life by a scar.[2]

Intellectually, however, the stay in Strassburg was profitable to Herder. Besides sketching the outlines of two of his later works, he made the personal acquaintance of Goethe, Jung Stilling and Lenz. During the winter of 1770-71, much of which Herder was obliged to spend in his room,

---

[1] *Ibid.*, p. 145 *et seq.*

[2] *Ibid.*, pp. 157, 169 *et seq.*

Goethe often kept him company. During the long winter evenings they conversed, read aloud and exchanged thoughts. Herder revealed to Goethe the beauties of Shakespeare, Homer and Ossian, and together they read and re-read Percy's *Reliques of Ancient Poetry, The Vicar of Wakefield* and *Tristram Shandy*.[1] Through Herder Goethe became acquainted also with the writings of Justus Möser who like Herder was an influence in arousing Goethe's interest in the German middle ages.[2] Herder and his circle also awakened in Goethe an interest in Gothic architecture which Goethe had up to that time regarded as barbarian.[3] The latter gave expression to this interest in the essay entitled *Von deutscher Baukunst* which Herder later included in *Von deutscher Art and Kunst*. Above all, Herder so impressed Goethe with the idea of being true to oneself and to one's nationality that the latter turned away from French to German literature.[4]

Goethe, for his part, recognized the benefits which he derived from his intercourse with Herder and freely acknowledged his indebtedness. In his autobiography he wrote:

The most important event which for me was to have the weightiest consequences was my acquaintance with Herder and the intimate association which followed. . . . There was not a day which was not instructive for me in the most fruitful way. I learned to see poetry from an entirely different angle than I had known it.

Goethe learned " that the poetic art is a world, a national gift,

---

[1] Goethe's *Werke*, Cotta ed., vol. xxiii, p. 254; vol. xxiv, p. 57 *et seq.*

[2] *Ibid.*, vol. xxiv, p. 179.

[3] *Ibid.*, p. 73.

[4] *Ibid.*, vol. xxiii, p. 239; vol. xxiv, p. 73 *et seq.* See also Fischer, Kuno, "Goethes Faust", in *Deutsche Rundschau*, vol. xii (1877), p. 83 *et seq.*

not the private inheritance of a few cultured individuals ".[1]
Later he said, " He [Herder] had rent the curtain which
concealed from me the poverty of German literature; he had
destroyed with cruelty many of my prejudices; in the heaven
of the fatherland there remained but few important stars ".[2]

Although Goethe was intense in his admiration of his
mentor, Herder, on the other hand, does not seem to have
appreciated the greatness of Goethe. Even several years
later when Goethe had already published his *Götz von Berlichingen* and his *Werther* and had become famous as the
editor of the *Frankfurter gelehrte Anzeigen* Herder said of
him, " Goethe is really a very good fellow, except that he is
rather giddy and fickle, for which I constantly reproved him.
He was at times the only person who visited me during my
confinement in Strassburg and whom I was glad to see. I
believe, too, without boasting, that I gave him impressions
which are likely to influence his life ".[3] But shortly after his
arrival in Weimar (1776) he wrote to Lavater, " I found
Goethe much better, profounder and nobler that I had
thought him to be ".[4] In the same year he wrote to Zimmermann, " Goethe is swimming down to eternity on the
golden waves of the century ".[5]

In the spring of 1771 Herder accepted the invitation of
Count Wilhelm of Schaumburg-Lippe to become court
preacher of that little principality. Upon arriving at Bückeburg, the capital of the state, he was so displeased with the
general condition of affairs that he was ready to leave.
There was little sympathy between the count and Herder.
The former was anything but pleased with the piety of his

[1] *Ibid.*, vol. xxiii, pp. 225-33.
[2] *Ibid.*, vol. xxiv, p. 5.
[3] *Erinnerungen*, vol. i, p. 218.
[4] Cited from an unpublished letter by Haym, *Herder*, vol. ii, p. 4.
[5] Cited in Nevinson, *A Sketch of Herder and His Times*, p. 234.

court preacher and the latter was repelled by the cold rationalism and the military bearing of his master. In August, 1772, Herder wrote to Gleim, " I am here in all respects dead while living, Lazarus in the grave, Prometheus at the cliff, Theseus on the fateful rock ".[1] But in time his loneliness was dispelled by a friendship which sprang up between him and the countess, and gradually also his relations with the count improved. He also found much pleasure in rides and walks in Teutoburg Forest which filled him with patriotic enthusiasm. In one of his letters to his future wife he wrote:

I am now in the country, in the most beautiful, the most rugged, the most German, the most romantic region of the world. The very same field on which Hermann fought and Varus was defeated; still an awful, rugged, romantic valley surrounded by singular mountains. However much of the German valor and of the Klopstockian ideal of morality and greatness may be lost, the soul is nevertheless disposed by the daring singular demeanor of this Germany to believe that there is a beautiful, rugged German nature.[2]

In the spring of 1773 Herder's marriage with Caroline Flachsland which he had postponed so frequently finally took place. It was a happy union indeed. So eminently suited were they to each other that Caroline could truthfully write, " A more perfect understanding, a more intimate relation between two souls there cannot be ".[3] Herder, in turn, wrote to Friedrich Jacobi that his Caroline was " the support, the comfort, the happiness of his life ".[4] The passing of time affected no change in this relationship of Herder and

---

[1] *Von und an Herder*, vol. i, p. 25.

[2] *Erinnerungen*, vol. i, p. 221.

[3] *Ibid.*, p. 152.

[4] *Aus Herders Nachlass*, 3 vols. (Frankfurt, 1856-57), vol. ii, p. 249.

his wife.   In 1796 Gleim wrote, " Without Caroline Herder
there would be no Johann Gottfried Herder ".[1]   With
Caroline at his side Herder took a new interest in life and
for a time the complaints disappear from his correspondence.
" All his ambitions to realize his spiritual aspirations ", his
wife wrote, " were revived, and he immediately applied himself to his tasks ".[2]   In 1771 he had carried off the first prize
in a contest sponsored by the Berlin Academy with his essay,
Ueber den Ursprung der Sprache.   Devoting himself to his
work with renewed ardor, he finished the treatise, *Ueber die
Ursachen des gesunkenen Geschmacks bei den verschiedenen
Völkern* and in 1775 was against rewarded the prize by the
same academy.   Other works of the Bückeburg period are
*Aelteste Urkunde des Menschengeschlechts, Provinzialblät-
ter, Auch eine Philosophie der Geschichte der Menschheit.*
It was probably the most productive period of his life.

Despite his happy married life and the many writings he
produced, Herder soon became disgruntled.   He was never
able to adapt himself to his environment.   His discontent
was so chronic throughout life that one might almost say that
he would have ceased to be Herder if he had stopped com-
plaining.   Although in 1775 he was promoted to be superintendent of the clergy of Bückeburg, Herder was still dissatis-
fied.   In the death of the countess a short time later the last
tie which held him in Bückeburg was cut, and Herder looked
forward eagerly to the time when he could leave.

In 1766 he was offered a chair of theology in the University of Göttingen, a position which he had long desired,
and he was also to be the university pastor.   Rumor had it,
however, that some of Herder's views were not quite ortho-
dox.   To dispel all doubts concerning his orthodoxy he was
requested by the Hanoverian ministry to submit to an ex-

---

[1] *Von und an Herder*, vol. i, p. 199.

[2] *Erinnerungen*, vol. i, p. 238.

amination before the theological faculty of Göttingen.
Herder became quite indignant at this request, the fulfillment of which he considered beneath his dignity. " The
times are past ", he wrote, " when pilgrimages were made to
Rome to establish one's orthodoxy, and even if they did exist, Göttingen is not Rome.[1] Nevertheless, the negotiations
continued by letter for some time afterward. Just as the
issue was about to be settled by a compromise Herder received a letter from Goethe asking him if he would accept
the position of superintendent of the ecclesiastical depart-
ment of Weimar. Goethe who wished to have his old friend
near him had prevailed upon the Duke of Weimar to offer
the position to Herder. With little hesitation Herder answered in the affirmative, and soon left Bückeburg with his
family for Weimar where he was to spend the rest of his life.

At Weimar, which through the efforts of the Duchess
Amalia and her son Karl August had become the intellectual
center of Germany, Herder's reception was most cordial.
On the fifteenth of October, 1776, he was duly installed in
his new office and for a time things went comparatively well.
Karl August and Goethe who had feared that he might incur
the hostility of the pleasure-loving grandees with his preaching were pleased at the mild tone of Herder's discourses.
Wieland wrote to Friedrich Jacobi:

The citizens of Weimar were prejudiced against him. Nevertheless he made a great impression by his first sermon and, to
use a current phrase, won their hearts. He preached as no
one had preached before, so sincerely, so simply, so compre-
hensibly, and yet everything so profoundly thought out, so
clearly felt, so solid in content.[2]

[1] *Ibid.*, p. 319.
[2] Friedrich Jacobi's *Auserlesener Briefwechsel* (Leipzig, 1825), vol. i,
pp. 254-55.

The presence of such men as Goethe, Wieland, Gleim, Knebel, Dahlmann, Dalberg, Einsiedel and others gave him the opportunity to enjoy the choicest intellectual friendships. Festivals, plays, concerts, entertainments and social gatherings offered Herder pleasant diversion from his professional duties. At some of these gatherings readings from the works of Shakespeare, Lessing, Goethe, Wieland, Herder or some other author, and discussions on art, literature or current events, occupied the time. Furthermore, his friends, especially Goethe, did all in their power to make life pleasant for Herder and his family.[1]

But even here Herder's discontented disposition soon gained the upper hand and the evening of his life was destined to be more troubled than the noon-time had been. During the many years that he lived in Weimar he did not succeed in ridding himself of the feeling of being a stranger. On the contrary, the feeling was aggravated with the passing of time. Painfully sensitive to the opinion of others, he interpreted everything which resembled objection or contradiction as a personal slight. The tragedy of Herder's life, therefore, lay not so much in the circumstances by which he was surrounded as in Herder himself. At times he realized this. " Nothing drives and oppresses me here but my inner man, but he oppresses me very much and makes me opposed to other human beings ", he wrote to Heyne in 1782 and in a letter to Caroline he said, " I have too little reason and too much idiosyncrasy." [2]   But lest we judge him too severely, it might be well to remember that during the Weimar period of his life he was frequently indisposed because of physical maladies which may have been responsible in large part for his chronic discontent.

[1] *Erinnerungen,* vol. ii, p. 5 *et seq.*

[2] *Von und an Herder,* vol. i, p. 194; *Erinnerungen,* vol. ii, p. 37; Lehmann, R., *Die deutschen Klassiker: Herder, Schiller, Goethe* (Leipzig, 1921), p. 23.

Before many months passed the duties of his profession became a perpetual source of irritation to him. The worldly tone of the court and the loose living of the nobility wounded his austere moral sense, and both the grandees and the people, he felt, were apathetic toward matters of religion. According to Caroline, many of the citizens of Weimar regarded moral training as being unnatural and therefore ridiculed it and claimed against it.[1] The unspiritual orthodoxy of his ecclesiastical brethren in the consistory, who met his every attempt at reform with the most determined opposition, was also a thorn in his flesh. They regarded Herder as a dangerous innovator and therefore opposed his ideas as being impracticable and visionary. Their continued thwarting of his plans was another cause of his disquietude. In addition, his salary was not sufficiently large to meet the expenses of his household. His large family, for he had eight children, brought pecuniary cares which further galled him. He was a most unhappy man.[2]

As time passed he also lost the friendship of some of his oldest friends. Although Goethe constantly assisted Herder in whatever way he could, the friendship of these two men gradually lost its ardor. On the one hand Goethe complained about Herder's irritable moods,[3] and on the other Herder's sense of morality was shocked by the relations of Goethe with Frau vom Stein. The arrival of Schiller also widened the slowly forming breach. Herder's ministerial airs offended Schiller, and the latter's rationalism was repulsive to Herder. Hence it was natural that the more intimate Goethe became with Schiller, the more Herder and Goethe became estranged. Despite the entreaties of his

---

[1] *Erinnerungen*, vol. ii, p. 13.

[2] See *ibid.*, p. 14 *et seq.*

[3] Goethe's *Werke*, Cotta ed., vol. xxiv, pp. 83, 211.

friends Herder also declared war on Kant because the latter had criticised his works. Stung to the quick by this criticism, Herder attacked his former teacher with virulence in the two treatises, *Kalligone* and *Metakritik*. At Herder's arrival in Weimar, Wieland had received him with great cordiality and had taken an ardent fancy to him.[1] Soon, however, he was repelled by what he termed Herder's haughtiness. In writing to Merck, Wieland said of Herder, " I cannot for the death of me endure it when a person feels his own worth so strongly, and when a strong man eternally finds pleasure in tantalizing and mocking others, then I should like to have a dozen Pyrenees between me and him ".[2]

Despite the difficulties and complaints Herder continued to write. During the hours he was able to snatch from his professional work he displayed prodigious activity. Almost every year saw the production of new writings, and important contributions continued to appear even up to the time of his death. Not only *Ideen zur Philosophie der Geschichte der Menschheit,* but also his *Stimmen der Völker in Liedern, Gespräche über Gott, Geist der ebräischen Poesie, Briefe das Studium der Theologie betreffend, Adrastea,* his version of *The Cid* and other works have come to us from the Weimar period. In 1776 he received the prize from the Bavarian Academy for his essay, *Ueber die Würkung der Dichtkunst auf die Sitten der Völker.* Two years later, in 1778, the Berlin Academy awarded him the prize, his third one from that academy, for the essay, *Vom Einfluss der Regierungen auf die Wissenschaften.* Again in 1781 he received his second prize from the Bavarian Academy for the essay, *Ueber den Einfluss der schönen in die höheren Wissenschaften.*

---

[1] See Wieland's letter to Jacobi in Jacobi's *Auserlesener Briefwechsel,* vol. i, p. 254-55; also *Von und an Herder,* vol. i, p. 50.

[2] Haym, *Herder,* vol. ii, p. 40.

In 1788 he received from an anonymous donor a gift of two thousand Rhenish florins and, after paying some of his most urgent debts, used the remainder to satisfy the long-cherished desire of seeing Italy. Since Herder's mind had lost much of its youth and elasticity, his journey was not so profitable as that of Goethe had been; nevertheless, it was an important event in his life.

For me [he wrote] Italy was the greatest school of training. Everyone who is cultured or striving to be so, and who is equipped with the necessary knowledge of the history, the literature and the language of the country, will find there a liberal education, and will learn to adjust his judgments according to lofty standards.[1]

On the journey his salient interest was in nature, and he felt that he had learned many secrets of the history of mankind. And yet, although his health was much improved and although, in his own words, he was in all respects benefitted by the journey, he was anxious and impatient to return to his family circle and to his beloved Germany.[2]

After declining a new call to the University of Göttingen shortly after his return to Weimar in the summer of 1789, Herder resigned himself to the thought that Weimar would be his home for the remainder of his earthly existence. Raised to the dignity of vice-president of the Consistory in 1789, he was freed from material want by the increase in salary, and the burden of his clerical duties was also made lighter. Noteworthy also in the last period of his life is the fact that in 1801 the title of nobility was bestowed upon him by the Elector of Bavaria. Herder with his democratic tendencies had no desire for the title and accepted it only because it gave his son the right to retain an estate in Bavaria

[1] *Erinnerungen,* vol. ii, p. 25.
[2] *Ibid.,* p. 28 *et seq.*

which otherwise, according to custom, he would have been forced to sell if a nobleman had desired to buy it.[1]

Even though in later years he lost the friendship of some of his older friends, Herder retained his influence over the younger generation to the end.   An event which brought unusual cheer and happiness into the last years of his life was the arrival in 1790 of Jean Paul Richter.   Herder felt that Jean Paul was a special gift of Providence at a time when his own life was most harassed.   In a letter to Friedrich Jacobi in 1798 he wrote,

In Richter, Heaven has given me a treasure which I have neither merited nor even expected. Every new meeting with him reveals to me a new and larger chest filled with those things which the three wise men brought. In him dwell the three and the star is ever over him. I cannot but say of him that he is all heart and spirit; a harmonius tone on the great golden harp of humanity in which there are so many broken strings and so many discordant tones.[2]

Another of the younger generation who became a warm admirer of Herder was Georg Müller, the younger brother of Johannes von Müller, the historian of Switzerland.   His enthusiasm excited by the reading of Herder's writings, young Müller journeyed to Weimar on foot and begged to be received into the Herder home.   Herder received him most cordially and took him in as one of the family. Müller remained with the Herder family several years, and later in his little volume entitled *Im Herderschen Hause* painted a picture of the family life in the Herder home. After the decease of Herder, Müller gave evidence of the high esteem in which he held his master by supervising the

---

[1] See *Von und an Herder*, vol. i, p. 293.

[2] Jacobi's *Auserlesener Briefwechsel*, vol. ii, p. 266.

publication of a part of Herder's writings.[1] Thus Herder retained the ability to stimulate and to provoke to the end.

The evening of his life Herder devoted to his clerical and literary work. During the last few years the old affliction of his eyes became so severe that it impaired the free use of books and pen, but to the end of his days he retained his interest in new ideas and new studies. He had just finished *Der Cid* and was working on his *Adrastea* when in 1803 a long illness attacked him. In the midst of it Herder exclaimed, " Oh, if some great and new idea would only come to me, some idea which would seize hold of and rejoice my whole soul, I should soon be well again ".[2] But the idea did not come, and broken in mind as well as in body, Herder passed away on the eighteenth of December of the same year. On the twenty-first his remains were laid to rest in the church in which he had so often preached. A congregation of about four thousand, including literary friends from neighboring cities, assembled to pay their respects and to participate in the obsequies. Upon the plain slab which covers his tomb Karl August had inscribed the words, " Light, Love, Life ".

Few writers have been so prolific and at the same time so multiform in their writings. From the time his first work appeared until a few days before his death his literary activity was unceasing. His works, collected in thirty-two volumes exclusive of his correspondence, appeared in such diversified forms as poems, essays, epistles, treatises, book-reviews, dramas, sermons and addresses. Included in the subjects upon which he wrote are science, philosophy, eccle-

[1] See Baumgarten, H., "Herder und Georg Müller', in *Preussische Jahrbücher*, vol. xxix (1872), p. 32 *et seq.*

[2] *Erinnerungen*, vol. ii, p. 330. See also Deetjen, W., "Aus Herders letztem Lebensjahre: Ungedruckte Briefe", in *Jahrbuch der Goethe-Gesellschaft*, vol. xiv (1928), pp. 117-29.

siastical and secular history, art, poetry, religion, criticism, ethnology, esthetic theory, education, literature and language. In the *Ideen* he calls upon geology, anthropology, botany, psychology, philology, zoology and economics to aid him in discussing such questions as the origin of the earth and the stars, the development of the mineral, vegetable and animal kingdoms, and the rise of man from barbarism to civilization. Lavater wrote to Herder, "Your preponderating erudition, your genius which devours me, would appear terrible to me if you were not flesh of my flesh and bone of my bone ".[1]

But varied and numerous as his writings are, not one of them can be styled a finished masterpiece either in thought or in form. The range of subject on which he wrote was so wide that it entailed the sacrifice of depth and thoroughness. His restless mind could not for any length of time concentrate upon one idea, or, as Madame de Staël expressed it, " We find in Herder that noble negligence of genius, ever impatient to acquire new ideas ".[2] The irresistible impulse to discover new ideas and to blaze new trails of thought robbed him of the necessary patience to exhaust a subject thoroughly. So quickly did he tire of a subject or undertaking that all of his works have remained fragments. His works have the appearance of rough-hewn statues which show the outlines of the intended masterpiece, but still lack the finishing strokes. Even his *Ideen zur Philosophie der Geschichte der Menschheit,* his chief work, was never completed.

But although Herder's works are fragments and often lack depth, they are pregnant with ideas, and have a stimulating and suggestive quality which can be found in the writings of few authors. Herder himself said, " A man of good

[1] *Aus Herders Nachlass,* vol. ii, p. 27.

[2] *Germany,* trans. by O. W. Wight (New York, 1861), vol. ii, p. 87.

heart will feel more pleasure from what he excites than from what he says ".[1]   As the originator of new ideas and as a sower of seeds which took root and grew in the minds of others Herder occupies a place distinctly his own.   In the words of a German writer, " Herder was perhaps richer in ideas than any other German writer." [2]   This wealth he gave to the German people in his writings.   So great was the effect of his ideas upon his time and generation, and also upon future times and generations, that one feels justified in saying that he was one of the great incentive powers of history.   Therein lies his claim to greatness.   Few, if any, of the writers of Germany did more to stimulate the national mind, and one of the great ideas which he launched, and which was to become the central idea in the nineteenth-century gospel of nationalism, was his conception of nationality.

[1] xiii, 6.
[2] Lindau, H., " Herder ", in *Nord und Süd,* vol. cvii (1903), p. 292.

CHAPTER III

HERDER'S CONCEPTION OF NATIONALITY

WHEN Herder considered the relation of individuals, nationalities and states, he had no intention of solving sociological and geographical problems. His chief aim was to understand the purpose and the destiny of man as an inhabitant of this earth.[1] After surveying the history of peoples and nations, he concluded that, confused and incalculable as the history of man might seem, it has a definite purpose, and that purpose is the development of humanity. "In all states, in all societies", he wrote, "man has had nothing in view, and could aim at nothing else, but humanity, whatever may have been the ideas he formed of it".[2] This idea, that the "end of human nature is humanity", Herder made the central idea of his whole philosophy of history, and as such it penetrated and pervaded all his thinking. To make the development of this humanity clear, however poorly he may have succeeded, was the great aim of his life.[3]

Just what idea or, better, ideas Herder wished to convey with the word humanity, it is difficult, if not impossible, to establish with certainty. He constantly accentuated the word humanity, but became very vague when he tried to define it. Humanity to him seems to have been too much a matter of feeling to admit of the laying-bare of its bone and

[1] xiii, 7.

[2] xiv, 208. See also xiii, 167, 355; xiv, 230; xvii, 407; xviii, 529.

[3] xiii, 350; xii, 161; xiv, 207.

tissue by the scalpel of reason.[1] It was the hybrid offspring of the eighteenth-century idea of universal culture
and the new spirit of romanticism. In so far as it can be
defined it is the sum of the virtues and talents which are
peculiar to man; in other words, it is the divine in man.[2]
Exactly what the divine in man is Herder did not tell us.
To him man was the crown of creation and sharply separated from all other species. He was a human being,
" nothing more, but also nothing less than this name indi-
cates ".[3] In contradistinction to Lord Monboddo and
Rousseau who did not hesitate to include the orang-outang
in the species of man [4] Herder specifically excluded the ape.[5]
Hence, since man is the crown of creation and the genus of
man is strictly circumscribed, he must not seek the purpose
of life outside of himself. " Let man be man ", Herder
said. " Let him develop his condition to the best of his
knowledge ".[6] The purpose of man's existence, then, must
simply be the harmonious development of the highest and
best in man; he must become whatever he is capable of becoming in a higher sense. He must develop his finer senses,
his instincts and his reason; he must promote the development of language, art, literature and religion, and foster liberty, health and happiness. " The most genuine humanity ", Herder wrote, " is contained in the few discourses of
His [Jesus] that are preserved; humanity He showed in His

[1] See xiii, 154; xvii, 407.

[2] xiii, 350; xiv, 230.

[3] xvii, 54.

[4] xv, 179 et seq. See also Grundmann, J., Die geographischen und
völkerkundlichen Quellen und Anschauungen in Herders Ideen zur
Geschichte der Menschheit (Berlin, 1900), p. 9; Günther, F., Die Wissenschaft vom Menschen (Gotha, 1906), p. 33.

[5] xiii, 255, 257; xv, 185.

[6] xiv, 209.

life and confirmed by His death; and the favorite name by which he chose to distinguish himself was that of the Son of Man ".[1] He also wrote, " Religion is the highest humanity ".[2] Humanity, then, is Herder's last word in history and also his last word in religion.

The unit in the development of humanity, however, is not the individual, but the group. The individual by himself cannot achieve the fullest development and the most complete expression of his virtues and talents; he can do this only as an integral part of a group.[3] The group as such is the vehicle of humanity. Moreover, the group which is the chief factor in the development of humanity is a group of a specific type; it is the national group or nationality. A religious sect, for example, does not measure up to the standard set by Herder.[4] Only a nationality can serve as a pillar to support the structure of humanity. In the perfection of the national type Herder saw the way to the perfection of both the individual and of humanity at large. " In a certain sense ", Herder wrote, " every human perfection is national ".[5] But the development of the national individuality is also an end in itself, for " every nationality bears in itself the standard of its perfection, totally independent of all comparison with that of others ",[6] or, as he expressed it in *Auch eine Philosophie,* " Each nationality contains its center of happiness within itself, as a bullet the center of gravity ".[7]

[1] xiv, 290. In the original there is a word play of the words *Menschheit* (humanity) and *Menschensohn* (son of man).

[2] xiii, 161.

[3] i, 366; viii, 194; xi, 1, 238; xiii, 159, 343, 346; xiv, 83, 84, 227.

[4] xiv, 311.

[5] v, 505. See also v, 425.

[6] xiv, 227.

[7] v, 509. See also v, 502; ix, 350-52.

In his philosophy of history Herder regarded each nationality as an organic unit and each branch of culture as an organic part of the larger unit. In the *Ideen* he spoke of a nationality as a " national plant " and again as a " national animal ",[1] and in the treatise *Von der Aehnlichkeit der mittleren englischen und deutschen Dichtkunst* he used the phrase, " physiology of the whole national group ".[2] To the national group he also ascribed growth, maturity and decay, the fundamental characteristics of everything organic.[3] We already find this idea in the *Fragmente,* his first important work. Every nationality, he stated, is subject to the same law of change " from the bad to the good, from the good to the better and best, from the best to the less good, from the less good to the bad. . . . So it is with art and science; they grow, produce buds, bloom and wither. So it is with language also ".[4] In the *Ideen,* his most important work, the history of mankind is pictured as a series of national organisms, each one " growing like a tree on its stem ".[5] After a period of growth each national organism matures, make its contribution to the general scheme of things and then sinks into senility, making way for others which pass through the same cycle.

In each national organism there is inherent a creative and regulative power, the national soul.[6] Although Herder in-

---

[1] xiv, 8; xiii, 384.

[2] ix, 523.

[3] i, 137 *et seq.*; v, 504.

[4] i, 151.

[5] xiv, 31.

[6] Herder used various terms to express this unity of action in the national group; *Nationalgeist,* i, 263; iii, 30; viii, 392; xxv, 10—*Seele des Volks,* v, 185—*Geist der Nation,* ii, 160—*Genius des Volks,* ii, 160; ix, 328, 379; xiii, 306, 364—*Geist des Volks,* v, 217; xiv, 384. " In the ancient languages ", Herder wrote, " spirit or soul is the term used to designate an invisible force ". xvii, 80.

sisted upon the autonomy of the human soul, he conceived of it from the first as an integral part of a larger unit, the national soul. " The full cooperation of active powers ", Herder wrote, " in their most determinative individuality, govern all events among mankind ".[1]   This national soul or genetic power " is the mother of all culture upon the earth ", and, conversely, all culture is but the expression of the national soul.[2]   In other words, this soul is the national counterpart of the monad which, according to Leibniz, was to be regarded as the controlling element in individual persons. Like Ranke at a later time, Herder saw in this harmony of spiritual powers the secret of history.[3]   It is to him " singular, wonderful, inexplicable, ineradicable, and as old as the nationality ", and it works instinctively and intuitively.[4] Although he was at a loss to define it, Herder did not harbor doubts as to its existence.   " There is ", he wrote, " a living organic force—I know not whence its origin, nor what is its essence; but that it exists, that it is a living force, that it fashions organic units from the chaos of homogeneous matter, that I see, that is indisputable ".[5]   He also had a theory concerning its origin.   " Since the individual ", he stated, " can not well exist by himself, a higher maximum of coöperating powers forms itself with every society.   In wild confusion they oppose each other until, according to infallible laws of nature, the adverse principles limit each other and a kind of equilibrium and harmony of movement is established ".[6]

[1] xiv, 84.

[2] iii, 29; xiii, 273.

[3] Ranke, L. von, *Sämmtliche Werke*, vol. xxiv (Leipzig, 1876), p. 39.

[4] xiv, 38; iv, 436.

[5] iii, 269.

[6] xiv, 227.   See also xvii, 121.

Having a body and a soul, so to speak, the group becomes a single being, an individuality, a personality. This being expresses itself in all the phenomena of its history, in language, in literature, in religion, in custom, in art, in science, in law, and the sum of these expressions is the culture of a nationality. Each nationality in exercising its powers functions as a unit—it is a " genetic individual " [1]—and whatever it produces is a collective work, the result of a union of all faculties and forces. Culture, then, is a product of the group mind, and not of the mind of the individual. A national language, for example, is not the invention of individual men who coined the words; it is the expression of the collective experience of the group.[2] The poet does not sit down and laboriously manufacture poetry; he writes when the national soul moves him and he writes what it inspires.[3] The individual prophets, writers, artists or poets are but the means employed by the national soul to give expression to a national religion, a national language or a national literature. They are those of the national group who are most responsive to the stimuli sent out by the national mind. The nationality speaks through them; they are, as it were, the mouth of the group.[4]

But cultures, like persons, differ widely; no two are identical. Each nationality has something peculiarly characteristic about it which to Herder was " inexpressible ".[5] This gives a peculiar stamp to its character which in turn is impressed upon all the phenomena of its history, upon its science, its art, its language, its literature, its religion and upon

[1] xvii, 285.

[2] See xi, 225; xvii, 59; xviii, 346; xxx, 8.

[3] i, 362; ii, 60, 160; ix, 318; xi, 175 *et seq.*; xviii, 136.

[4] See ii, 265; xii, 123; xiv, 38, 425.

[5] v, 502.

all the other manifestations of the group. " Every nationality ", Herder observed, " is one people, having its own national culture as well as its language ".[1] It " blooms like a
tree upon its own roots " and " on the different stems fruits
grow according to the climate and care ".[2] True to its own
character each nationality is a little world in itself and " contains its center of happiness within itself ".[3] It preserves its
unity despite the unceasing change which is ever taking place
in the various phases of its activity. In the *Ideen* [4] Herder
represented the history of mankind as a succession of national organisms, each revolving about its own center, each
having its own national character, its own language, literature, art, religion and society. All nationalities, however,
have this in common that there is inherent in each the tendency to express itself to the fullest extent of its possibilities.
These possibilities can never be exhausted, for new possibilities are continually unfolded according to time and circumstance.

But how did these different cultures or cultural organisms
originate? Why has each nationality a peculiar culture?
The different cultures are not to be explained by the poly-
genous theory, for, according to Herder, all men originated
in one and the same race. " Notwithstanding the varieties
of the human form ", he wrote, " there is but one and the
same species of man throughout the whole earth ".[5] " The
new Zealand cannibal and a Fenelon, a Newton and that
wretched Pesheray are all creatures of one and the same
species ".[6] He also styled the nationalities " branches from

---

[1] xiii, 258.   See also xxiii, 551; xxvii, 171.
[2] xxiv, 48.
[3] v, 509.
[4] vols. xiii and xiv.
[5] xiii, 252.
[6] xiii, 147.   See also iv, 253; v, 134.

one stem " and " plants from one primitive nursery ".[1] Research into the languages, customs, inventions and traditions, he was convinced, was establishing ever more firmly the idea that all mankind originated in one species.[2] He was opposed to all attempts to divide mankind into races. " Some for instance ", he wrote, " have ventured to apply the term races to four or five divisions which originally were made according to countries or even according to complexions, but I see no reason for this appellation. Race denotes a difference of origin ".[3] Not a difference of origin, but a number of environmental forces and influences are responsible for the different cultures. A thousand different forces are at work in each instance and by these the national soul is influenced and conditioned.[4] And since the number, variety and effect of the forces are different in each instance, no two cultures are identical. Herder did not try to enumerate the different factors; his chief aim seems to have been to establish the peculiarity and individuality of each national cultural organism.[5] Yet at different times he mentioned some of the most potent factors.

1. The chief differentiating factor in the development of cultural organisms is the physical environment. Again and again, almost to weariness, Herder stressed the effect of the climate.[6] For example, he wrote:

[1] xiii, 405.

[2] v, 447.

[3] xiii, 257; v, 504.

[4] v, 539.

[5] xiii, 268, 273.

[6] See, for example, xiii, 190, 216, 226, 272; xiv, 29, 257, 424. In this connection Herder used the word climate synonymously with physical environment in the wider sense. See, for example, xiii, 269, 284; iv, 263 *et seq.*

Man is no independent substance, but is connected with all the elements of nature; he lives by inspiration of the air and derives food and drink from the most unlike productions of the earth; he employs fire, absorbs light and contaminates the air he breathes; awake or asleep, at rest or in motion, he contributes to the change of the universe; shall not he also be changed by it?[1] As every region of the earth has its peculiar species of animals which cannot live elsewhere, and consequently must have been born in it, why should it not have its own kind of men? Are not the varieties of national features, manners and character, and particularly the great differences in language proof of this?[2]

Concerning the members of a national group he stated that the

constitution of their body, their way of life, and the pleasures and occupations to which they have been accustomed from their infancy, and the whole circle of their ideas are climatic. Deprive them of their country and you deprive them of everything.[3] Had the power which constructed our earth given its mountains and seas a different form; had that great destiny which established the boundaries of nationalities caused them to originate elsewhere than from the Asiatic mountains; had the eastern part of Asia possessed an earlier commerce and a Mediterranean Sea which its present situation has denied; the whole current of culture would have been altered.[4] For on the whole earth nature has effected more permanent differences by mountains than by any other means. Here nature sitting upon her eternal throne sends out rivers and storms, and distributes the inclinations and often the destiny of nationalities in the same manner as the climate.[5] Nature incited man to the

[1] xiii, 253.
[2] xiii, 399.
[3] xiii, 261-62.
[4] xiv, 92.
[5] v, 527.

acquisition of knowledge and science; so that even these gifts are as much local productions, as any others upon earth.[1]

Herder also gave examples of the influence of the physical environment upon specific nationalities. " The Arab of the desert ", he wrote, " belongs to it, as much as his noble horse and his patient indefatigable camel ". His simple clothing, his maxims of life, his manners and his character are in unison " with his own region; and after a lapse of thousands of years, his tent still preserves the wisdom of his forefathers ".[2] Again, " the various skill in the arts for which Babylon was particularly famed are perfectly consistent with the spirit of the country and the national character of the inhabitants." [3] He discussed also the effect of the cold upon the mind and body of the Greenlander, the influence of the warmer climate upon the Hindu and the change which came over the Phoenicians after they settled upon the shores of the Mediterranean. " In this manner ", he wrote, " I might continue and exhibit climatic pictures of several nationalities, inhabiting the most different regions from Kamchatka to Tierra del Fuego, but why should I give these brief sketches since every traveller who saw with accuracy or felt as a man gave the shade of climate to every little stroke of his delineations ".[4]

2. Education is another factor which makes for peculiarity. " Men ", Herder wrote, " are formed only by education, instruction and permanent example ".[5] " The mode of education pursued by the Chinese conspired with their national character to render them just what they are and noth-

---

[1] xiv, 47. See also xiii, 37 *et seq.*; xiv, 32.
[2] xiii, 259.
[3] xiv, 44.
[4] xiii, 261.
[5] xiv, 34.

ing more ".[1]   The Hebrews " were a people spoiled in their
education, because they never arrived at a maturity of political culture on their own soil, and consequently not to any
true sentiment of liberty and honor." [2]

3. Intercourse or non-intercourse with other national
groups is also a factor in the development of national characteristics.   Herder styled this " the external circumstances
by which it is surrounded ".[3]

A secluded national group [he wrote] which lives far from the
seacoast and is separated from intercourse with other national
groups by mountains, a nationality which derived its knowledge
from a single place . . . . may acquire great peculiarity of
character and retain it long; but this continued peculiarity will
be far from giving it that useful versatility which can be gained
only by active competition with other nationalities.   Egypt and
all the countries of Asia are examples of this.[4]   It was and it
is the same with all the national groups of antiquity, Egyptians,
Chinese, Arabs, Hindus, etc.   The more secluded they lived,
nay frequently the more they were oppressed, the more their
character was confirmed; so that, if every one of these national
groups had remained in its place the earth might have been
considered as a garden where in different plots human
national plants bloomed, each in its own culture and nature.[5]
The numerous widespread Gallic peoples differed much according to place, time, circumstances and their various degrees
of civilization so that the Gaels on the coasts of Ireland or
in the highlands of Scotland could have little in common
with a Gallic or Celtiberian people who had long enjoyed the
neighborhood of more cultured national groups or towns.[6]   We

[1] xiv, 10.
[2] xiv, 67.   See also v, 439; xiv, 76.
[3] xiv, 86.
[4] xiv, 92.
[5] xiv, 84.
[6] xiv, 262.

Germans would still, like the Americans,[1] be living quietly in our woods or, rather, would still be fighting in them in a primitive manner and becoming heroes if the chain of foreign culture had not pressed so close to us and with the force of centuries had spurred us to activity. The Romans got their culture thus from Greece, the Greek obtained it from Asia and Egypt, Egypt from Asia, China perhaps from Egypt— thus the chain continues from the first link and will perhaps at some time span the earth.[2]

4. Tradition also molds the culture of each national group.

In general ideas every nationality has its particular way of seeing, founded for the most part on the mode of expression, that is to say, on tradition; and as the philosophy of the Greeks arose from poems and allegories, this gave to their abstract ideas a peculiar stamp to themselves perfectly clear.[3] The feelings and instincts of men are everywhere conformable to their organization and the circumstances in which they live; but they are everywhere swayed by custom and opinion.[4]

The special means through which individuals and generations act on one another is language. " It is generally acknowledged to be the means for transmitting human ideas, inclinations and deeds; by means of it we bequeath the treasures of former times to later generations.[5] " By means of its language a nationality is educated and formed." Even the mode of writing, Herder believed, has a great influence on the national mind. He mentioned especially the mode of writing of the Chinese which, he said, " enervates the

[1] American Indians.
[2] v, 142.
[3] xiv, 125.
[4] xiii, 319.
[5] xvi, 46.

thoughts and reduces the whole national way of thinking to arbitrary characters which are painted or drawn in the air ".[1]

5. In addition to environment, however, heredity also plays a part. As a result of the action or influence of the different forces upon the national soul a national character is developed. This generated character or sum of acquired tendencies, is in turn, passed on to the next generation, as it were, in the blood and becomes a generating influence. " The climate ", Herder is reported to have said, " never gives a nationality buoyancy and spirit; that lies in the seeds of the fathers ".[2]   " The noblest which we possess ", Herder wrote, " is not of ourselves; our fatherland with its powers, the manner in which we think, act and live, are so to speak bequeathed to us ".[3]   " Everything earthly and human is governed by time and place, as every particular national group is by its character, uninfluenced by which it can do nothing ".[4]   Even though a nationality leaves its environment, the descendants will exemplify the character of the original environment for generations.

The climate, it is true [Herder wrote] stamps on each its mark or spreads over it a slight veil, but not sufficient to destroy the original national character.[6]   The mode of thinking of the Jews, which is best known to us from their writings and actions, may serve as an example.   In the land of their fathers, and in the midst of other nationalities, they remain as they were; and even when mixed with other people they may be distinguished for some generations afterward.[5]   In India, the great market-place of commercial peoples, the Arab and the Chinese, the

[1] xiv, 14. See also xiv, 430.
[2] Bächtold, J., *Aus dem Herderschen Hause* (Berlin, 1881), p. 111.
[3] xvi, 34.
[4] xiv, 38.
[5] xiii, 258.
[6] xiv, 84.

Turk and the Persian, the Christian and the Jew, the negro and the Malay, the Japanese and the Gentoo, are clearly distinguishable; thus on the most distant shores every one bears the character of his native country and its mode of life.[1]

Herder believed that " the character of the Germans still resembles in many leading features the picture drawn by Tacitus " and that " the ancient Gaul is still discernible in his modern descendants in spite of all the changes which time has wrought ".[2]

Although human factors enter, in a sense, into the development of national groups, Herder regarded each nationality as a product of nature and its growth as regulated by the laws of nature. Rousseau's barrier between nature and culture did not exist for Herder; in fact, he found the process of the development of culture to be the antithesis of the *Contrat social*. The natural and the national were synonymous in Herder's mind. He definitely stated that " a nationality is a plant of nature ",[2] and the development of cultural nationalities is " a phase of a perpetual system of nature ".[4] In the same sense he referred to Greek culture as a " flower of nature ".[5] Rousseau implies in the *Contrat social* that legislation makes a people mutually dependent.[6] This function Herder ascribed to nature. For him nature was the great architect who planned and constructed the group.[7]

Herder's opposition to the cosmopolitanism of the eigh-

[1] xiii, 261.

[2] xiv, 262.

[3] xiii, 451.

[4] xv, 3.

[5] v, 616.

[6] Garnier edition (Paris, n. d.), p. 261.

[7] v, 527.

teenth century was based in part upon the fact that the supporters of the Enlightenment did not recognize the national lines that nature had drawn.   In *Auch eine Philosophie* he launched a bitter tirade against the idea of cosmopolitanism. He wrote derisively about the civilization which was to be uniform in all parts of the earth.   The wise men of the *Aufklärung,* he stated, do not seem to consider

that man can be modified in a thousand different ways and must be according to the structure of the earth; that there are products of the climate and circumstances, consequently national and secular virtues, flowers which grow under the heavens and thrive on almost nothing and in other places die or fade miserably; that all these can and must exist, but that under the husk, changed so variously, always the same essence of nature and happiness can be, and according to human expectations almost must be, preserved.[1]

In a spirit of bitter irony he arraigned the spirit of cosmopolitanism when he wrote:

All national characters, thank God, have become extinct!   We all love one another or, rather, no one feels the need of loving anyone else.   We associate with one another, are all completely equal—cultured, polite, very happy!   We have, it is true, no fatherland, no one for whom we live; but we are philanthropists and citizens of the world.   Most of the rulers already speak French, and soon we shall all do so.   And then—bliss!   The golden era is dawning again when all the world had one tongue and language!   There shall be on flock and one shepherd!

Mournfully he asked in conclusion, " National characters, where are you? " [2]   " The whole earth ", he wrote in another place, " has become a dunghill on which we seek grains

[1] v, 558.
[2] v, 550.

and crow! Philosophy of the century!"[1] In the *Ideen* he wrote:

The savage who loves himself, his wife and child with quiet joy and glows with limited activity for his tribe as for his own life is in my opinion a more real being than that cultivated shadow who is enraptured with the shadow of his whole species. . . . The former has room in his hut for every stranger. . . . The inundated heart of the idle cosmopolite is a home for no one.[2]

In the *Humanitätsbriefe* he wrote, "God did not permit Himself such an amalgamation; therefore he has instructed each national group after its own manner ".[3] "Where nature has separated nationalities by language, customs and character one must not attempt to change them into one unit by *artefacta* and chemical operations ".[4]

Since every nationality is a product of nature, man cannot set the limits for its development, but he can develop it within the bounds set by nature. Moreover, it is man's duty to do this. The development, however, must be in harmony with the forces that were responsible for the growth of that national group. Only the original and the spontaneous can promote the progress of the group toward humanity. Submission to artificial rules and regulations, and imitation of the ancients or of other nationalities, is therefore fatal to genuine progress, for thereby the functions of the national soul are impeded.[5] A vital and lasting culture can be built only on a foundation of the peculiar gifts and the innate abilities which nature has given the corporate individuality.

[1] v, 555.
[2] xiii, 339.
[3] xvii, 59.
[4] xviii, 206.
[5] ii, 161; v, 510.

As each monad had within itself its own formula of development and finality independent of the others, so " every nationality bears within itself the standards of its perfection, totally independent of all comparison with that of others ".[1] " The history of Alexander's successors," Herder wrote, " particularly claims out notice ", because " it furnishes melancholy examples of empires founded on foreign acquisitions as well of territory as of sciences, arts and culture ".[2] Rousseau said, in substance, cultivate your individuality, your difference from other men; cultivate your spontaneous self, and do not permit it to be cramped by conventions.[3] Herder, in turn, said in substance, cultivate your national individuality, the genius of your national group; develop your national gifts and do not permit the spontaneity of your nationality to be cramped by artificial rules and regulations or by imitation of other nationalities, past or present.[4]

As much as Herder exalted the ages in the past when the national soul was not fettered by rules and regulations, he did not, like Rousseau, see the golden age in the past.[5] He was the prophet of progress. For him the development of humanity was still in its first stages and national and universal happiness was still in the future. " Look about you ", he wrote, " most of the nationalities of the earth are still in their childhood; they will speak the language, have the customs, and set the examples of that stage of development ".[6] Hence, Herder told his age, there is much to be done before the possibilities of each nationality are exhausted. If not awakened the most valuable gifts of a na-

[1] xiv, 227.

[2] xiv, 141.

[3] See Babbitt, I., *Rousseau and Romanticism* (Boston, 1919), p. 98.

[4] v, 510; viii, 34; xvii, 25; xviii, 223; xxiii, 160-161.

[5] See iv, 364.

[6] v, 556.

tionality might lie dormant for centuries. The potential
energies of a national group must be released if it would
attain the maximum development. The idea of maximum
development and maximum happiness were in Herder's mind
closely related, if not identical. In several instances he used
the words happiness (*Glückseligkeit*) and humanity synonymously.[1] Hence the more complete the expression of the
corporate individuality, the closer the approximation to national contentment and happiness.[2]

Despite the fact, however, that Herder urged the cultivation of national characteristics, his ideal was universal.
According to Herder's philosophy of history each nationality contributes the expressions of its national type to the
development of humanity in general. The distinctive culture of a nationality represents the special contribution of
that group to civilization at large. " The multifarious variety ", he wrote, " that actually exist on our earth is astonishing; but still more astonishing is the unity that pervades
this inconceivable variety ".[3] " Thus here, too, probably
the greatest variety tends to uniformity, and all-comprehen-
sive nature will have one point in which the noblest exertions
of so many beauteous creatures unite and the flowers of all
worlds are collected into one garden ".[4] The earth, then,
according to Herder, might be regarded " as a garden where
here one human national plant " and there another "bloomed
in its proper form and nature ".[5] Each national plant has
its allotted place in this garden and also its characteristic
beauty and its peculiar fragrance. This beauty and frag-

[1] xiii, 350; xiv, 252.
[2] See, for example, v, 509.
[3] xiii, 25.
[4] xiii, 20.
[5] xiv, 84.

rance each national plant contributes to the general beauty and fragrance of the garden. Although the *fleur-de-lis* and the goldenrod, the *Kaiserblume* and the rose are different flowers, each one contributes a beauty and a fragrance not possessed by the others and all contributions blend to make the garden as a whole beautiful and fragrant. Although Herder's ideal was universal, this universal ideal did not tend to minimize national differences; on the contrary, Herder's *Weltanschauung* accentuated the national peculiarities, for the development of the national peculiarities was the *sine qua non* of the development of humanity at large.

In the idea that the development of humanity at large rests upon the development of the peculiarities and characteristics of each national group lies the fundamental difference between Herder's idea of humanity and the universal ideals of such predecessors and contemporaries as Leibniz, Rousseau and Lessing. Rousseau, as has already been stated, saw the way to the perfection and happiness of mankind in the development of the innate abilities of each individual person. The only natural society which he recognized was the family, but even that, as soon as there was no longer occasion to protect the children, ceased being a natural union and became a voluntary union.[1] Lessing built his idea of the perfectibility of the human race upon individuals. He regarded mankind as an aggregation of single human beings rather than as a number of national or racial groups.[2] Also in Schiller's mind the idea of nationality and that of humanity seem to have been incompatible.[3] In fact this attitude was characteristic of the age of the *Aufklärung*. To quote Jastrow, " Carried away by the idea of a universal love of mankind the Enlightenment of the eighteenth cen-

[1] *Contrat social*, livre i, chapitre ii.

[2] *Sämmtliche Schriften*, Lachmann-Muncker ed., vol. xiii, p. 435.

[3] Saupe, *Die Schiller-Goetheschen Xenien*, p. 117.

tury saw in the existing nationalities nothing but obstacles to pure humanity which the modern enlightened man with a cosmopolitan sense must strive to remove ".[1] In Herder's philosophy of history the determining factor was not the individual person, but the nationality. He saw no antithesis between nationality and humanity. Both found room in his mind. Moreover, be brought the idea of nationality and the humanitarian ideal into intimate relation. His philosophy of history was, so to speak, the stepping-stone between the cosmopolitanism of the eighteenth century and the nationalism of the nineteenth.

Herder did not work out his conception of nationality methodically and systematically nor did he express it in unambiguous terms. He was content with enthusiastic assertion of the idea of nationality and did not grapple with the problems involved in the idea which he posited. Like the prospector who is pressed for time, Herder picked up only the nuggets of thought that were lying on the surface, leaving the actual mining for those who were to come after. The theory is implicit rather than explicit in his works, but the principles are unmistakable. Some of Herder's statements are inaccurate, some fragmentary, some shallow, some even false; and yet, when all is said, the inspirational power of his idea of nationality was far-reaching. The incompleteness of his theory does not seem to have detracted from its influence; on the contrary, much of the stimulating influence of the idea might be ascribed to the manner in which it was expressed. Herder himself realized that his ideas were imperfect and incomplete, and asked his readers not to dismiss them with criticism on that account, but to improve them, to elaborate them and to use them as a foundation for further work.[2]

[1] *Geschichte des deutschen Einheitstraumes und seiner Erfüllung*, p. 80.
[2] xiii, 6.

His plea was not in vain, for his philosophy of culture soon aroused a wide interest, and many of the fertile suggestions which he made were later worked out and applied in special branches of knowledge. The influence of Herder's nationalist ideas on Fichte, for example, was profound. From Herder, it seems, Fichte borrowed the idea that the members of a nationality and state are joined together by inner spiritual bonds.[1] Hegel's and Friedrich Schlegel's conceptions of the national groups as individualities and of national cultures as organisms owe much to Herder.[2] The idea that the fullest development of humanity is possible only in the more temperate zones to which Hegel later gave such prominence was first suggested by Herder although he did not exhaustively formulate it.[3] Both the term and Herder's idea of the *Volksgeist* were taken over into philosophy, jurisprudence, philosophy, history and politics. The romanticists adopted the idea of the *Volksgeist* and it is also to be found in the writings of Grimm and Savigny.[4] The idea of the national soul or folk soul was applied in the different branches of learning by such men as Vischer in aesthetics, Wackernagel in poetry, Steinthal in the science of language, Roscher in political economy, and Moritz Lazarus and Wundt in psychology.[5]

[1] See Fichte's *Werke* (Leipzig, 1911), vol. ii, p. 189; Janson, F., *Fichtes Reden an die deutsche Nation* (Berlin and Leipzig, 1911), p. 51; Wundt, Max, *Fichte* (Stuttgart, 1927), pp. 86, 225.

[2] See Willmann, O., "Herders Bedeutung für das deutsche Bildungswesen", in *Hochland*, vol. i, (1903), p. 319; Dittmann, F., *Der Begriff des Volksgeistes bei Hegel* (Leipzig, 1909), p. 93 *et seq.*; Rothacker, E., *Einleitung in die Geisteswissenschaften* (Tübingen, 1920), p. 85.

[3] See xiii, 402; xiv, 32.

[4] Kluckhohn, P., *Persönlichkeit und Gemeinschaft: Studien zur Staatsauffassung der deutschen Romantik* (Halle, 1925), p. 14; Preuss, *Die Quellen des Nationalgeistes der Befreiungskriege*, p. 29.

[5] Rothacker, *op. cit.*, p. 80.

" The most important gift of Herder ", Hauffe wrote, " by means of which he influenced our spiritual development so mightily lies in his profound and fine sense for the group mind and its development in feeling, thought, actions and life ".[1]

The idea of nationality as expressed by Herder reached its fullest development in his *Ideen* which he considered the chief work of his life.[2] Everything Herder wrote is more or less intimately related to the *Ideen*. Although Herder feared the criticism of his contemporaries and abandoned the idea of completing this work, it contains the whole of his philosophy of history. The *Ideen* enjoyed a wide circulation and made a deep impression upon the time. Men like Hamann, Heyne, Friedrich Jacobi, and Georg Forster were enraptured when they read the first part of the work and anxiously awaited the continuation and completion of it.[3] In referring to the *Ideen* Goethe stated that Herder's thoughts had been borrowed so extensively by others that they rapidly became a part of the general stock of knowledge and in a short time even became commonplace. Goethe himself read the book several times and it was to him the "most congenial of gospels".[4] In a book review of Quinet's French translation of the *Ideen* in 1828 Goethe wrote concerning the original, " It had an incredible influence upon the culture of the nationality [Nation] ".[5] In 1789, before Herder had published the fourth part of his *Ideen,* Hartknoch, the publisher, wrote to Caroline Herder, " The fond-

---

[1] Hauffe, G., *Herder in seinen " Ideen zur Philosophie der Geschichte der Menschheit "* (Leipzig, 1890), p. 1.

[2] xiv, 653.

[3] See *Von und an Herder*, vol. ii, p. 197; *Aus Herders Nachlass*, vol. ii, pp. 239, 383; Grundmann, J., *op. cit.*, p. 3.

[4] *Werke*, Cotta ed., vol. xxxviii, p. 215.

[5] *Ibid.*, p. 169.

ness for scribbling and the thievery of the writers are great; they usurp Herder's ideas when he has hardly half stated them, and therefore these ideas are already old when they appear ".[1] In 1785 Gleim wrote to Herder, " All scripture such as this [*Ideen*] and the *Zerstreute Blätter*—who can gainsay it—is inspired of God. I also heard this opinion voiced unanimously on my long journey from Pyrmont to Hanover, Bremen, Oldenburg, Hamburg and back by way of Lüneburg, Celle and Brunswick ".[2] A few weeks later he wrote, " I have hitherto lived and had my being in the *Ideen* ".[3] Again, " May Heaven grant that I live to see the last part of these glorious and clear *Ideen* ".[4] Lehmann, one of the modern German writers, says:

This work also was not completed, but remained a fragment; nevertheless it is the complete expression of a new view embracing the whole nature of mankind which has been of infinite fertility for the development of German intellectual life. It was also the womb of historical science and the historically orientated philology of the nineteenth century.[5]

In a letter of the ninth of August, 1830, Macaulay wrote to Napier, " The appearance of this book is really an era in the intellectual history of modern Europe ".[6]

Since the development of national characteristics appeared so necessary for the development of humanity in general, it was a matter of great importance to Herder that more be known concerning them. The knowledge of the cultural

[1] *Von und an Herder*, vol. ii, p. 106.

[2] *Ibid.*, vol. i, p. 113.

[3] *Ibid.*, p. 114.

[4] *Ibid.*, p. 146.

[5] *Die deutschen Klassiker*, p. 23.

[6] Trevelyan, G., *The Life and Letters of Lord Macaulay* (New York 1877), vol. i, p. 195.

development of the different national groups, he thought, was too important to be based on guesswork, and was worthy of accurate delineation. He saw, however, that before the information concerning national peculiarities could be made authentic, it was necessary to develop archeology, anthropology, mythology and philology to greater accuracy and authenticity. He therefore modestly but earnestly urged the importance of scholarly research which would increase the fund of human knowledge concerning national languages, national literatures, national traditions, in short national cultures generally.

One of the best means to obtain a better knowledge of national characteristics, Herder observed, was by a philosophical comparison of languages.[1] Language was to him the outstanding mark of nationality. It developed simultaneously with thought and was therefore inextricably interwoven with it.[2] Hence he urged his contemporaries to study the language of a nationality if they would know something about its thought-life.

A philosophical comparison of languages [he wrote] should form the best essay on the history and diversified character of the human heart and understanding; for every language bears the stamp of the mind and character of a national group. Not only do the organs of speech vary with regions, not only are there certain sounds and letters peculiar to almost every nationality, but the giving of names, even in denoting audible things, nay in the immediate expression of the passions, in interjections, varies over the earth. With respect to visible things and subjects of cool reflection, this variation is still greater; and in allegorical expressions, in figures of speech, it is almost infinite. The genius of a nationality is nowhere more displayed than in the physiognomy of its speech. Why can I yet quote

[1] v, 116.
[2] ii, 16-23.

no work that has even in a slight degree fulfilled the wish of
Bacon, Leibniz, Sulzer and others for a general physiognomy
of nationalities from their languages?[1] If Büttner, the ablest
philologist of them all who have studied the history of ancient
and modern nationalities, would impart to us the treasures his
modesty conceals, and trace, as he undoubtedly could, a series
of national groups to their parental stock, of which they themselves are ignorant, he would confer no small benefit on mankind.[2] The useful endeavors that have been made toward collecting and rendering public the languages and work of Asia
are preparatory steps to the erection of an edifice the first
foundation stone of which I should be glad to see laid.[3]

To Herder credit in great measure is due for the founding of the comparative study of languages. When in his
Ursprung der Sprache he attacked the supposition that language had been given to man by divine communication [4] and
when he in place of this supposition established the natural
development of language, scholars set out to discover how
language really developed, and the rise of the science of philology was a direct result. One might, therefore, say without exaggeration that it was in part due to the stimulus
which Herder gave to the comparative study of languages
that the Schlegels, Wilhelm von Humboldt, Jakob Grimm,
Friedrich Bopp and others who followed them established
comparative philology as a science.[5] Herder's influence on
Wilhelm von Humboldt, whom Steinthal regarded as the

[1] xiii, 363. Italics are Herder's.

[2] xiii, 406.

[3] xiv, 33.

[4] The idea of the divine origin of language had been defended by
Süssmilch in the treatise *Beweis, dass der Ursprung der menschlichen
Sprache göttlich sei* (Berlin, 1766).

[5] See Schmidt, G., *Herder und August Wilhelm Schlegel* (Berlin,
1917), p. 27 *et seq.*; Vaughan, C., *The Romantic Revolt* (Edinburgh
and London, 1907), pp. 292-95.

founder of the science of language,[1] was, to put it mildly, considerable. Humboldt's conception of language is in essence that of Herder. In the words of Haym, Humboldt " stood on Herder's shoulders " and " repeated Herder's fundamental ideas ".[2] He took the ideas which Herder had posited and clarified and expanded them.[3] " Herder, not Humboldt ", writes Sturm, " first took the path in which the later philosophy of language was further developed. Hence we might in this respect recognize him as the real father of the modern philosophy of language ".[4]

The study of the various national literatures also, Herder thought, would contribute much toward increasing the knowledge of national characteristics. In the essay *Ueber die Aehnlichkeit der mittleren englischen und deutschen Dichtkunst* he suggested that some capable and worthy individual write a history of civilization based on the various national literatures.[5] By publishing his collection of *Volkslieder,* which comprised folk songs of many nationalities, Herder helped to prepare the way for the study of comparative literature. Furthermore, he urged that the fables and myths of the different nationalities be collected as a foundation for the study of comparative literature.[6]

Individual and group characteristics, Herder told his generation, might also be set forth more accurately by the study

[1] Steinthal, W., *Der Ursprung der Sprache*, 4th ed. (Berlin, 1888), p. 10.

[2] *Herder*, vol. i, p. 408.

[3] See for example Humboldt, W. v., " Ueber das vergleichende Sprachstudium ", in *Werke*, vol. iv (Berlin, 1905), pp. 1-34. For further discussion of the influence of Herder's ideas on Humboldt see Sapir, E., *Herders Ursprung der Sprache*, in *Modern Philology*, vol. v (1907), pp. 109-42; Haym, R., *Wilhelm von Humboldt* (Berlin, 1856), p. 494 *et seq.*

[4] Sturm, W., *Herders Sprachphilosophie* (Breslau, 1917), p. 71.

[5] ix, 524.

[6] i, 266; xxxii, 152.

of anthropology.   The study of man, as Herder saw it, was truly in a sad state.   The footnotes of the *Ideen* indicate how widely conversant he was with the literature of his day. For a knowledge of the nations and peoples of all parts of the globe books of travel were the most popular sources and they were unreliable.   Many of them contained accounts of half-men, satyrs and nymphs, and belief in their existence was still widespread.[1]   Herder urged that the study of mankind be put on a basis at least as accurate and as scientific as the study of lower animals.   He was irked and exasperated at the neglect of the study of man and suggested that men had " sought after the wonderful and dealt in fiction " long enough;[2] that they had given too much attention to zoölogy and botany and not enough to man.

Is human nature [he asked] alone unworthy of that accurate attention with which plants and animals are drawn?   Yet, in modern days the laudable spirit of observation has begun to be excited toward the human species, and we have delineations of some national groups, though but few, with which those of De Bry or Le Brun, not to mention the missionaries, will bear no comparison; it would be a valuable present to the world if anyone who has sufficient abilities would collect such scattered delineations of the varieties of our species as are authentic, and thus lay the foundations of a perspicuous *natural philosophy and physiognomy of man*.   Art could not easily be employed in a more philosophical pursuit; and an anthropological map of the earth, similar to the zoological one sketched by Zimmermann, in which nothing should be noticed except real varieties of man, but these in all their appearances and relations, would crown the philanthropic work.[3]   When the genealogy of the nationalities, the state and quality of their extensive country, and more

---

[1] See xiv, 146.

[2] See especially the footnotes in vol. xiii, p. 255 *et seq.*

[3] xiii, 251. Italics are Herder's.

especially the variations in the internal physiology of these people, are more thoroughly investigated, we shall not fail to obtain new ideas on the subject.[1] With the assistance of a few maps for the convenience of inspection, we should obtain a *physico-geographical history of the descent and diversification of our species* according to periods and climates, which at every step must afford us important results.[2] That every national group was in its time and place whatever it could be, that we all know, but at that we know very little.[3]

It is in the opinion of the writer no exaggeration to say that in response to the call of Herder, and in his spirit, a large array of naturalists, historians, philologists and eth-nologists ransacked every corner of the earth in search of wider and more accurate knowledge concerning the history of man. Alexander von Humboldt's *Kosmos,* Friedrich Ratzel's *Anthropogeographie* and Lotze's *Microcosmos,* to mention but three works, are, in a sense, elaborations of some of Herder's ideas.[4] He it was, indeed, who initiated the modern comparative study of literature, language, reli-gion and art. In stimulating fellow scholars and others who followed to inaugurate movements for research in phil-ology, anthropology and literature, Herder stimulated an in-terest in racial and cultural problems in general. Due to this interest the knowledge of nationality soon became or-ganized in the different disciplines, above all in anthropology and ethnology, and much of the knowledge gathered by the scientist was later appropriated by the nineteenth-century

[1] xiii, 220. Italics are Herder's.

[2] xiii, 285. Italics are Herder's.

[3] xviii, 149.

[4] See Posadzy, L., *Der entwicklungsgeschichtliche Gedanke bei Herder* (Münster, 1906), p. 105; Ratzel, F., *Anthropogeographie,* vol. i (Stuttgart, 1882), pp. 6, 25 *et seq.,* 44 *et seq.*; Witte, J., *Die Philosophie unserer Dichterheroen* (Bonn, 1880), p. 249.

nationalists to bolster their cause. Wilhelm Scherer, the literary historian, said of Herder,

He took in at a glance the limits and interrelation of the various sciences; and whoever advances to the highest problems in any of the sciences of the human mind, whoever studies history, or the science of language, mythology, or ethnology, whoever collects popular traditions or explores German or Hebrew antiquity, or would trace the development of national peculiarities in all spheres of life, and understand the formative influence of nature upon man—each one of these must reverence Herder as a seer of extraordinary powers.[1]

Finally, in giving expression to his conception of nationality Herder not only used, but in many instances coined words and phrases which nineteenth-century nationalists could, and many of which they undoubtedly did, borrow. If it is true, as Ernest Barker writes, that " literature also influences life through the magic words and phrases with which it stores the mind and by which it moves the imagination ",[2] then the influence of Herder in also this respect must have been considerable. Herder used such terms as *Nationalerziehung, Nationalschatz, Nationaltraditionen, Nationalprodukte, Nationalwerk, Nationalneigungen, Nationalmeinungen, Nationalvorteile, Nationalvorurteil, Nationalpublicum, Nationalsitten, Nationalheiligtum, Nationalsprache, Nationaldenkart, Nationalcharakter, Nationalgeschichte, Nationaltugenden, Nationalismus, Nationalism* (sic).[3] Herder not only used the word nationalism, but he also defined it and seems to have put his stamp of approval upon the idea of nationalism as he conceived it.

[1] Scherer-Walzel, *Geschichte der deutschen Literatur*, p. 370.

[2] *National Character* (New York, 1927), p. 222.

[3] iv, 371; ii, 13; xxxii, 150; ix, 528; v, 259, 510; i, 264, 265; v, 216; xvii, 286; ii, 161; xiv, 426; ii, 13; x, 12; xvii, 318; ii, 160; v, 550, 528; iv, 202; v, 558; xx, 234; v, 510.

The Greek [he wrote] appropriates from the Egyptian, the Roman from the Greek, what he needs; he is satiated, the rest falls upon the ground and he has no desire for it! Or if in this development of peculiar national inclinations toward national happiness the difference between national group and national group has become too pronounced: see, how the Egyptian hates the shepherd, that rover! How he despises the light-minded Greek! Thus whenever two national groups and their inclinations and circles of happiness come into conflict, it is styled prepossession! vulgarity! narrow nationalism! This prepossession is good in its time, for it makes for happiness; it presses each of the nationalities toward its center, establishes it more firmly upon its stem, makes it more florid after its own manner, more ardent and thus happier in its inclinations and purposes.[1]

In summary, Herder regarded the development of humanity or, in other words, the development of the highest and best in man, as the purpose of human existence. In order, however, to attain the fullest development the individual must be an integral part of a national group, for the nationality, not the individual, is the unit in the development of humanity. In the development of humanity each nationality functions as an organic unit, and each branch of culture is an organic part of the larger unit. Inherent in each national organism there is a creative and regulative force, the national soul. This force constitutes the group a single being, an individuality, a personality, and the sum of the expressions of each personality comprises its culture. Culture, then, is not the work of the different individuals as such who make up the group, but of the corporate individuality. But as no two peculiar expressions of individuals are identical, so also no two cultures, the peculiar expressions of national individualities. All cultures differ in greater or lesser degree, and the differences are due to a number of influences, different in each case, which act upon the national soul.

[1] v, 510.

Outstanding factors responsible for the differences are physical environment, mode of education, intercourse or non-intercourse with other nationalities, tradition and heredity. By and large, Herder regarded each nationality as a work of nature, and hence criticised the supporters of the *Aufklärung* because they refused to recognize the national lines that nature had drawn. Since every nationality is a product of nature, man cannot set the limits for the development of a nationality, but he can develop it within the bounds set by nature. Moreover, it is his duty to do this. Each nationality, therefore, has a mission, the development of its national characteristics.

But Herder's ideal was universal despite the fact that he urged the cultivation of the national individuality. The distinctive culture of each nationality represents the special contribution of that group to humanity at large. Therefore the development of the peculiar national cultures is necessary in the development of humanity. Therein lies the fundamental difference between Herder's ideal of humanity and the universal ideals of his predecessors and contemporaries. Whereas the universal ideals of Lessing, Rousseau, Leibniz and others rested on man as an individual, the determining factor in Herder's philosophy of history was the nationality. Although this idea was neither worked out methodically nor expressed in unambiguous terms, it had a stimulating influence, and was applied by others to the different branches of knowledge. Since the development of humanity, as Herder saw it, was dependent upon the cultivation of national characteristics, he wished the information concerning national characteristics to be as authentic as possible, and therefore earnestly urged the importance of scholarly research and advocated the further development of archeology, anthropology, philology and, in general, the comparative study of cultures.

CHAPTER IV

NATIONALITY AND GERMANY

HERDER'S sense of nationality rested on his German national sentiment. He was one of the most, not to say the most, patriotic of the German writers of the eighteenth century. He was a German patriot in an age when the feeling of national patriotism was dormant. Whilst among his contemporaries men like Ramler, J. G. Jacobi, Gleim, Kleist, Uz and Denis were provincial patriots, each one working for the welfare of his respective state, Herder was animated by a patriotism which rose above the narrow provincialism of his time. "National pride", he wrote "is absurd, ridiculous and dangerous; but it is everyone's duty to love his country and it cannot be loved if it is despised and allowed to be disparaged; it must be defended and each of us must contribute the utmost in his power to its honor and its welfare".[1] At all times the love of Germany as a fatherland was uppermost in his heart and mind. While on a visit to Italy he wrote to Frau von Diede, "Slowly I am drawing nearer to Germany, a country and a people whom, since I have become acquainted with Italy and have seen the spirit and activity of the Italian people, I love still more than before".[2] At the end of his catechism of the year 1779 Herder appended twelve rules of conduct, and of these the

[1] xxxii, 519.

[2] Herder, C., *Herders Reise nach Italien: Briefwechsel mit seiner Gattin* (Giessen, 1859), p. 246.

113

tenth reads, " Love your fatherland, for to it you are indebted for your life, education, parents and friends, in it you
have enjoyed the happiest years of your childhood and youth.
Be an asset to it and worthy of it; concern yourself about
its laws.   Be not however its judge but its supporter.   He
who contributes to the common good is a worthy child of
his fatherland.[1]

In 1773 a Frenchman named Cacault journeyed to Germany to study the character of the Germans.   When after
a sojourn of three months at Wolfenbüttel he had not found
anyone, as he thought, with a true German mind, the Hanoverian physician Zimmermann, author of the treatise *Ueber
den Nationalstolz,* advised him to go to Bückeburg and in-
terview Herder if he wished to find an original German
mind.[2]   Gleim styled Herder " father of the fatherland ".[3]
In a letter to Herder in 1793 Gleim wrote, " According to
my ideal you are the only truly genuine German ".[4]   Wilhelm Grimm wrote, " Herder loved and esteemed his people,
and devoted himself whole-heartedly to the task of educat-
ing them ".[5]   But the greatest tribute was paid him by Carl
Friedrich of Baden who, wishing to establish an academy to
foster a common spirit in Germany, chose Herder as the best
fitted to draw up the plan for it and also as the most capable
of putting the plan into execution.[6]

Motivated by an ardent patriotism, Herder's nationalism,
as well as his romanticism, came as a protest against the
state of affairs in Germany at his time.   The tendency of

[1] xxx, 391.

[2] *Aus Herders Nachlass,* vol. ii, p. 330.   See also Jonetz, A., *Ueber
Herders nationale Gesinnung* (Brieg, 1895), p. 3.

[3] *Von und an Herder,* vol. i, p. 130.

[4] *Ibid.,* p. 159.

[5] *Kleinere Schriften,* edited by Hinrichs (Berlin, 1881-87), vol. i, p. 278.

[6] *See infra,* pp. 128-33.

his ideas was pedagogical. He considered it his duty to point out the weaknesses of his time and to incite his countrymen to undertake the task of improvement.[1] As we have seen, Germany was divided politically into many little states, and the culture of Germany gave evidence of this division. In the realm of the mind there was little originality, little creative spirit. The cultural leaders of Germany were chiefly imitators. To the disparagement of their own national life, they sought perfection in foreign writings, foreign manners, foreign culture. In art, for example, imitation, it seems, was taken for granted. Almost all of the German painters of this period were imitators.[2] It was against these conditions that Herder protested.

Above all, the cultural and also the political division of Germany was a matter of great concern to him. What, he asked in effect, is the cause of the division which exists in Germany? "Certainly", he answered, "it is not the difference in religions, for in all the religions of Germany there are enlightened, good people. It is also not the different dialects or the beer-and-wine lands which separate us and keep us apart. It is a pitiful lack of interest in the state, the adoption of different spirits, of different cultures ".[3] " We are working in Germany as in the confusion of Babel; sects in taste, parties in poetry, schools in philosophy contend against one another; no capital and no common interest; no powerful patron and no common legislative genius ".[4] " Why is it that our literature is such a medley? We are in eternal conflict among ourselves and with other nationalities who use us and despise us, whom we serve and honor. The

---

[1] See for example ii, 218; iv, 197.

[2] See Stöcker, H., *Zur Kunstanschauung des achtzehnten Jahrhunderts* (Berlin, 1904), p. 4.

[3] xvii, 25.

[4] i, 141.

literature of Germany is like its government and its history ".[1] " We are Germans, and when it comes down to it, we are again not Germans, but Brandenburgers, Silesians, Saxons, Swabians, Bavarians ".[2]

In order to end this divided condition of Germany and to curb the separatist tendencies of the time, Herder worked to create and to intensify a national spirit in Germany. This national spirit, he believed, would also effect a unity of action. " For, tell me, what prevents us Germans ", he wrote, " from acknowledging, honoring and helping one another as co-workers on the same structure of humanity? Have we not all one language? A common interest? One reason? One and the same human heart? "[3] " The prophecy of Leibniz is an old tested truth. A community without a common spirit will fall ill and die; a fatherland without inhabitants who love it will become a desert ".[4] In the *Briefe das Studium der Theologie betreffend* he made an impassioned plea for coöperation between the religions of Germany. " How nice it would be ", he wrote, " if the Catholic provinces also would draw nearer to us, and all the Germans as brothers, as members of one nationality and speech, would know one another better and work together for the common good ".[5] " What harm ", he wrote in the *Adrastea,* " has not been done to science in Germany because this country is torn and divided into religious factions! Are we not all Germans? Are there Catholic and Protestant physics, mathematics, morals, etc., which are different in principle? Should they exist? And again I say it, are we not

[1] ix, 362.
[2] viii, 425.
[3] xvii, 26.
[4] xvii, 319.
[5] xi, 204.

all Germans?"[1]   "He is deserving of glory and gratitude",
Herder wrote in the *Humanitäsbriefe,* "who seeks to promote the unity of the territories of Germany through writings, manufactures and institutions; he will facilitate the
coöperation and mutual recognition of the several and most
diverse powers; he will bind the provinces of Germany with
spiritual and hence with the strongest ties".[2]   Herder said
that if the German people would unite, "the German name
which many nationalities now regard with contempt would
perhaps appear as the first name of Europe, without noise,
without presumption, just strong, firm and great in itself".[3]

Furthermore, Herder wished to establish a common culture fostered by and in turn fostering a common spirit and
unity of action.   Since, as Herder taught the German people, culture, in the real sense of the word, is the expression
of the life of a nationality, German culture must also be the
expression of the life of the German people.   In other
words, it must be a characteristic culture built on German
foundations.   The German people must look to themselves,
for "every nationality has its center within itself".[4]   They
must immerse themselves in their native folk ways, folk
customs, folk literature and folk language.   In them they
must discover that which is best in a typically German sense
and then cultivate it.   A vital, healthy and enduring culture,
he told them, can be built only on a native foundation.

The solidity of a nationality [he wrote] which does not forsake
itself, but builds and continues to build upon itself, gives to all
the aspirations of its members a certain direction.   On the contrary, other peoples, because they have not found themselves,

[1] xxiii, 551.
[2] xvii, 26.
[3] xvii, 27.
[4] v, 509.

must seek their salvation in foreign nationalities, serving them and thinking with their thoughts—such nationalities forget even the times of their glory and their own proved endeavors, always *desiring*, never *achieving*, always tarrying on the threshold.[1]

Besides, this culture must be a spontaneous culture, not a culture that is constructed forcibly according to arbitrary rules. " Not revolutions ", Herder wrote, " but evolutions are the quiet process of the great mother [nature], whereby she awakens the slumbering powers, develops innate possibilities, rejuvenates premature old age and changes apparent death into new life ".[2] In short, Herder desired to bring the German people back to German foundations of culture and to foster whatever was truly expressive of national qualities in the culture of Germany.

Hence Herder's vigorous opposition to the imitation of foreign culture and to the idea of building a culture on foreign acquisitions. There was for Herder no ideal culture which could serve as a model for all times or for all nationalities. Imitation of foreign culture he regarded as a national aberration. Concentration upon the imitation of foreign culture, Herder told his countrymen, was responsible for the adulteration of the culture of Germany. " Of all the nationalities ", he said, " the people of Germany are most unlike themselves ".[3] Germany

has ever been devastated by foreigners who took with them whatever was valuable and gave alms in return; these the kind-hearted Germans accepted humbly and in admiration of these paltry gifts they forgot the better endowments which they themselves possessed. Thus Germany remained a divided country; always interested in the welfare of others and always imitating

[1] xxiii, pp. 160-61. Italics are Herder's. See also xviii, 115.
[2] xiv, 117.
[3] i, 217.

others. It was never able to marshal all its powers and to
realize its true self or to benefit by its own merits.[1] What
indeed is an imposed foreign civilization, a culture which does
not grow out of native conditions and necessities? It oppresses
and misforms or it will engulf.[2]

The desire to build a culture on foreign acquisitions was to
Herder an indication of " disease, flatulence, abnormal sur-
feit and approaching death ".[3] Although with Lessing and
Winckelmann he shared the enthusiasm for classical culture,
he, nevertheless, wished to assign to it a subordinate place in
the cultural life of Germany.

In our time [he wrote] the most fruitful subjects of history, the
most living characters, all feeling of specific truth and precise-
ness are overshadowed by antiquity. Posterity will stand before
this affectation of word and theory in amazement and will not
know how and in what kind of time we lived, and what led us
to the terrible delusion of endeavoring to live in another age,
in another nationality and climate, thereby casting aside the
whole order of nature and history or miserably ruining it.[4]

" When will our public ", he asked, " cease to be this three-
headed apocalyptic beast, poorly Greek, French and British? "[5] " Is it possible that the German people were destined from the beginning only to translate and imitate? "[6]
In consequence of the long period of imitation, Herder
believed, the German people had lost their national character
and he, therefore, urged them to rediscover it. " Now seek
in Germany ", he wrote, " the character of the nationality,

---

[1] viii, 423.
[2] xviii, 223.
[3] v, 510.
[4] viii, 34.
[5] i, 217.
[6] ix, 510. See also v, 360; xiii, 351; xiv, 141; xviii, 333.

the thought which is peculiar to it, the real mood of its language; where are they?"[1]   The loss of its character he regarded as a great calamity to the German nationality.   He even doubted that the German had gained anything by adopting Christianity since thereby they had lost their national character.[2]   "Read Tacitus", he wrote, "there you will find its character; the tribes of Germany who have not been dishonored by intermixture with others, they are a true, unadulterated original nationality which is the original of itself.   Even the formation of their bodies is still the same in a large number of people".[3]   In the *Humanitätsbriefe* he wrote:

Read Otfried, read the old song of victory from the time of Louis; the good-natured and honest character of the nationality is already recognizable throughout. . . . He that has doubts concerning the character of the German nationality might peruse a dictionary or a book of proverbs, Agricola, Frank, Kaisersberg, Brandt, Luther, Rollenhagen, Opitz, Logau, Dach, Tscherning, etc.; this mind and instructive genius speaks on every page.   Compare our minnesongs with those of Provence.[4]

In the introduction to his collection of folk songs Herder, in a sense, summed up the whole situation in Germany as he saw it.

Everyone of my readers [he wrote] knows the sad or fortunate fate—what should I call it?—which Germany has had since the beginning, to have been the mother and servant of foreign nationalities, their regent, their lawgiver, the determiner of their fate, and almost always at the same time their bleeding slave and self-exhausting wet-nurse who was rewarded with evil.

[1] i, 366.
[2] i, 367 *et seq.*
[3] *Ibid.*
[4] xviii, 115.

Naturally the mode of thinking and the quiet folk ways of the Germans had to partake of the eternal discord, the eternal projection among the foreigners or, which is still worse, the injection of such foreigners into their land. O that we had a real history of the German national spirit and we knew how, where, when and whereby the debilities and infirmities which have made us the household word of all surrounding peoples were caused; all that would show itself better than I can express it. When a tree branches out prematurely into many wild branches, is divided into stems which cannot and will not remain on friendly terms with one another on the same root, where will the manner and fruit, richness and sweetness, strength and growth upon its root and in its stem be and remain? A restless wild thorn-bush from which enough fire often emanated to consume cedars, on which everything caught, and which tore in pieces and trampled everything under foot— I wish that the picture in many periods of history were not drawn by our Germany according to the set laws of fate Therefore it [German culture] was naturally a mixture and an imitative stammering of foreign voices, lands and times from the beginning. And if that, alas, can be shown about centuries almost from the beginning of every new branch of culture, is it a wonder that the most original language of Europe has almost the least original content, the least self-elaborated peculiar materials. . . . How happy I would be if I were actually refuted by the discovery of many really precious national works.

But now! Again I cry, my German brethren! But now! The remains of all genuine folk thought are rolling into the abyss of oblivion with a last accelerated impetus. The light of the so-called culture [1] is eating round about itself like a cancer. For the last half century we have been ashamed of everything that concerns the fatherland. [2]

In order to wean his countrymen from their unreasoning

[1] Herder is here undoubtedly referring to the *Aufklärung*.
[2] xxv, 10.

imitation of other nationalities Herder tried to stimulate national self-respect and a national pride and also to excite a spirit of national independence in Germany. The German people, he said in effect, have held everything German in contempt so long that they have lost their self-respect almost entirely. Not only have they borrowed of the culture of other nationalities, but they have also served most of the peoples of Europe with their blood and have, in turn been despised for it. The great need of the Germany of his day, as Herder saw it, was "a common spirit, a noble pride which will not permit others to regulate its affairs, but which would regulate its own affairs as other nationalities have always done; to be Germans on our well-defended soil ".[1] " It is easy to become the slaves of others, but not always will a Moses appear to free his people and to reward them for their servitude with the spoil of Egyptian legislation ".[2] " Everyone loves his country, his manners, his language, his wife, his children; not because they are the best in the world, but because they are absolutely his own, and he loves himself and his labors in them ".[3] He told the German people that they must discontinue disparaging their national life. " A nationality ", he said, " which does not esteem itself— how can others regard it as worthy of esteem. Self-defence is the root of all human and national worth ".[4] " Our language is in possession of older poetry than that of which the Spaniards, Italian, French and Britons can boast; it is only because of our form of government that we have left this field uncultivated for centuries. We wandered about Italy and other parts of Europe." [5]

[1] ix, 362.
[2] xvii, 317.
[3] xiii, 26.
[4] xviii, 345.
[5] xviii, 112.

If, however, the German people are to achieve a unity of spirit and action, if they are to be successful in developing a common characteristic culture, if, in short, they are to develop a vigorous national life, Herder said in substance, every individual must coöperate for the common good. Every individual must merge his individuality with that of the group. The well-being of the nationality must be set above the well-being of the individual. In the complete coöperation of all lies the way to the future greatness of Germany and the German people. It is, therefore, the sacred duty of every individual to defend his nationality and to add to its honor wherever he can; he must work to preserve and perpetuate the national traditions; he must strive to build and to perfect national institutions; he must aid in developing the national resources of Germany; he must work to reveal and to cultivate the genius of the German people.[1] In the *Humanitätsbriefe* he spoke to his countrymen in the form of a parable:

Everyone who is on the ship in the turbulent waves of the sea feels himself bound to assist in maintaining and saving the ship. The word fatherland has set the ship afloat at the shore; and he cannot, he must not, as if he were on shore, stand idle in the ship and count the waves. His duty calls him (for all his companions and loved ones are with him in the ship); if a storm rises up, if danger threatens, if the wind changes or if another ship hurls itself again his ship threatening to run it down, his duty calls him to help and to call. Softly or loudly, according to his rank as boatsman, helmsman or shipmaster; his duty, the common welfare of the ship calls him. He does not seek only his own safety; he must not dream that he is in the boat, which is here not at his disposal, of a select society upon the shore; he goes to work and becomes, if not the savior of the ship, at least a loyal compatriot and watchman.

[1] iv, 197, 365, 400; xiv, 149; xvii, 211.

Why was it that many a class once highly honored sank and is still sinking into contempt and disgrace? Because not one of them espoused the common cause, because each one lived as a class privileged either in regard to property or to honor; like Jonah they slept quietly during the storm, and the lot fell upon them as upon Jonah. O that human beings who have seeing eyes do not believe in a nemesis. To every injured or neglected duty there is attached not only a deliberate, but a necessary punishment which accumulates from generation to generation. If the cause of the fatherland is sacred and eternal, then according to the nature of things every neglected opportunity avenges itself and augments the venegeance with every corrupt affair or generation. It is not your duty to engage in melancholy meditation over your fatherland, for you were not its creator, but you must be of assistance to it wherever and whenever you can, encourage, save, improve and even though you were the goose of the Capitol.[1]

"Devotion to the fatherland is a great human virtue".[2] "He that has lost his patriotic spirit has lost himself and the whole world about himself".[3] "Who", he asked mournfully, "is willing to make sacrifices in our time? The loudest patriots are often the most narrow-souled egotists ".[4]

Despite the disunion, the imitation, the artificiality and the slavish submission to arbitrary rules which characterized his age, Herder was optimistic about the future. He had a firm faith in the future greatness of the German people and this faith he wished to instil in the hearts of his countrymen. The thought that the disruption was but outward and temporary consoled him. "Almighty time", he was sure, "would overcome the division".[5] "Perhaps", he said,

---

[1] xvii, 315-16.
[2] xiii, 149.
[3] xviii, 337.
[4] xvii, 95.
[5] xvii, 25.

" under the ruins and crumbling gigantic works Germany is now working toward an age of high philosophical taste, to which everything, faults and virtues, theory and practice, which still oppose each other blindly, will contribute ".[1] In the *Humanitätsbriefe* he wrote:

Raise your eyes and see. Everywhere the seed has been sown; here it decays and sprouts, there it grows and ripens for a new sowing. There it lies under snow and ice; be hopeful! The ice will melt; the snow warms and covers the seed. No evil which has come upon mankind can and should be anything but salutary; for vices, mistakes and weaknesses of man are as natural phenomena regulated by rules, and are such or can be regarded as such. That is my credo. Let us hope and work.[2]

Why mourn, he said in effect, let us be up and doing. " Let bygones be bygones; they have happened. If the upper classes of Germany had taken a fancy to speak Kalmuck instead of French what could you do about it? The centuries are lost; and not you but they bear the blame ".[3] He believed that the *Gallomania* and the imitation of other nationalities generally would soon go out of style and that German culture would come back into its own.

We have almost run the gamut of imitation; all possible mistakes [he wrote] have been made, and better things must now follow. To be sure, Germany will have no Homer as long as he must celebrate in song the contracted servile expedition of his brethren to America and no Tyrtaeus will be found at the head of such an army. To be sure, as long as our poems are regarded in the light of goods that are bought and sold at the fairs or as birthday songs, every genuine poet will like Chiron go into the cliff and perhaps teach only a young Achilles to sing. Also, as

[1] v, 646.

[2] xvii, 122

[3] xvii, 204.

long as religion, the interest of the nationality and the fatherland are so divided, so overburdened and so overshadowed, the harp will sound muffled and will be surrounded by mist. But, poor, torn, crushed Germany, be hopeful! Your misery will end, benefactors and true patriots will be moved to pity. National feeling in itself will produce poets who because of their sympathy with their brethren will be loving poets and since we, despite all hindrances and oppressions (to say nothing of a lack of support), have progressed so far, have done so much, and especially since we have fixed our gaze upon the right point, upon truth, religion, simplicity, which even our despisers will not deny, it will be well with us if we continue onward and keep our paths clean and our eyes fixed upon the goal, striving to reach it by stimulating the people to action.[1]

He called to the German people, " Let us, my brethren, work with courageous and happy hearts, even under the cloud; for we are working toward a great future ".[2]   " Noble Germany ", he wrote in a poem, " away with your sorrow! Your enemies are fleeing! You will soon be a happy country to the envy of all ".[3]   But he also spoke in sharper tones. In the ode *Germania* he wrote:

" Germany, are you still slumbering? See what happened round
          about you,
      What happened to you.   Feel it and awake,
          Before the sword of the victor
               Scornfully uncovers your head!

Look at your neighbor, Poland, how strong once upon a time
          And how proud! Oh, it kneels, bereft of its honor and
               adornment,
          With its breast torn,
               Before three mighty ones, and is silent." [4]

[1] viii, 433.

[2] v, 580.

[3] *Die eigenwillige Leier*, xxvii, 105.

[4] xxix, 210.

In urging his countrymen to develop a characteristic national culture, Herder stressed chiefly literature, language and thought in general, but seemed somewhat reluctant about advocating the development of a national religion. To be sure, he regarded the primitive religions as the natural outgrowths of the life and thought of the respective nationalities.

Now whence [he wrote] is the religion of these peoples derived? Can these poor creatures have invented their religious worship as a sort of natural theology? Certainly not, for, absorbed in labor, they invent nothing, but in all things follow the traditions of their fathers.[1] Naturally these theological traditions were as national as anything in the world. Everyone spoke out of the mouth of his forbears; he observed the world that surrounded him; he made up his explanations of things which appeared to him at the most remarkable, and in that manner in which they could best be explained according to his climate, his nationality, his training up to that time.[2] As every religion is more efficacious in a political view the more its objects, its gods and heroes and their various actions are indigenous; so we find every firmly rooted ancient nationality has adapted its cosmogony and mythology to the country it inhabited.[3]

But Christianity, to him the highest expression of humanity, he regarded as a world religion. It was to him an exotic religion imposed upon the indigenous forms of religion of the European peoples.[4] He felt that Christianity was to a large extent responsible for the loss of the German character, and that it had done irreparable harm " to the tales, songs, customs, temples and monuments of paganism among

[1] xiii, 388.

[2] xxxii, 150.

[3] xiv, 88. See also xxxii, 49; iv, 352, 357, 401; i, 144; iii, 59, 90, 226-43.

[4] xxiv, 42 *et seq.*

the Germans ".[1] And yet he saw distinct differences in the conceptions which each nationality had of Christianity. He stated that when Christianity became a world religion " every nationality clothed the conceptions which it received after its own manner ".[2] He permitted a character in one of his dialogues to say, " Do not nationalities differ in everything, in poetry, in appearance and tastes, in usages, customs and languages? Must not religion which partakes of these also differ among the nationalities? " [3] The same character laments the fact that Luther was unable to establish a German national church.[4] In the *Humanitätsbriefe* Herder wrote:

O that Germany had not unhappily divided itself in the century of the Reformation. O that the nationality had adhered to one Christ and to one confession as to one God and to one Bible. Yet much has remained; and perhaps it will depend only on the turn of events that Germany will have for its mind and heart a national religion, the religion of Christ, which in a human way gives the mind and heart true freedom.[3]

In a study of Herder's efforts to arouse and to intensify national feeling in Germany his plan for a patriotic academy which was to foster a common spirit and stimulate a national consciousness merits consideration. Herder prepared this plan in 1788 at the request of Carl Friedrich of Baden (1728-1811) who deserves to be ranked high as a German patriot and as one who attempted to bring about the political unification of Germany. He was one of the chief supporters of the idea of a league of princes (*Fürstenbund*) as a

[1] i, 367 *et seq.*; xiv, 384; xxxii, 143.
[2] xx, 147.
[3] xxiv, 49. See also xvii, 125.
[4] xxiv, 47.
[5] xviii, 347.

means of affecting a political unity in Germany and he also felt that an association of learned men would contribute much toward unifying the spiritual endeavors of the German people. Hence he requested Herder, as the best fitted for the task, to draw up a plan for the proposed academy. Herder began work on the plan immediately and before many months had passed, it was delivered to Carl Friedrich who, in turn, sent it to Duke Carl August of Weimar, to Baron von Dalberg and to Schlosser [1] for their approval. Some time was spent in discussing and amending the plan, so that when Carl Friedrich was ready to enter upon its execution and suggested Herder as the most capable of making it a reality, because " everyone would gladly join an undertaking which is earnestly sponsored by him ", Herder was about to depart on his journey to Italy.[2] Before it could be set on foot after Herder's return, the French Revolution centered all attention upon itself and everything else was forgotten for the time being. Hence the plan remained a patriotic dream. The plan, of which an abstract follows, was published shortly after Herder's death in 1803.[3]

PLAN FOR THE FIRST PATRIOTIC INSTITUTE TO FOSTER A COMMON SPIRIT IN GERMANY [4]

From the time when Germany was the tilting-ground for the tribes and nomadic peoples, through the centuries during which the different territories and provinces fought, worked and invented, to the present time, our fatherland was a political body which did not always know its own powers and therefore could not use them for a common end with any degree of constancy.

[1] Goethe's brother-in-law.

[2] *Erinnerungen*, vol. ii, p. 231 *et seq.*

[3] Whenever possible Herder's exact wording has been retained. Condensation is mostly by omission.

[4] xvi, 600 *et seq.*

On the contrary, it often employed them for purposes harmful to itself. In the present state of our organization all efforts are laudable which spread light, but especially those which seek to unite the light so that it may become a common flame. All efforts therefore which tend to aid the different peoples and provinces of Germany in knowing and in understanding one another more intimately, and which aim to assist in uniting all to work for the common welfare so that one law of reason and fairness may reign and blind partisanship be enfeebled, will render immortal service to the whole nationality. It should be the earnest concern of every sovereign and his country to put an end to the unfriendly relations of the German provinces. It must be of importance to them that whoever lives in Germany should belong to Germany and should speak and write a pure German.

Our language, whether it be considered as a learned or a political tool, deserves a center of union for the different provinces which might become the center for the development of this indispensable tool. Our nationality can boast that since the most ancient times of which we know its language has remained unmixed with others, just as our people were not conquered by any other national group and in their wanderings carried their language into different parts of Europe. Hence it is just that this language not only be preserved as long as the nationality exists but that it also be clarified and strengthened just as the organization of the national group is strengthened. A purified language, regulated by definite rules, contributes incredibly much toward a set mode of thought. History shows that all the ruling peoples of the different periods of world history have ruled not with arms, but especially with reason, art and a highly developed language, often for thousands of years; nay, even after their political power had passed, the highly developed tool of their thoughts and organization remained as an example and sanctum for others. The Greek, Latin and Arabic languages are examples of this in the ancient and middle period; in the modern period, first the Spanish, then the French language have proved what advantages, nay what a secret superiority a nationality whose language has become a dominant one may attain. Just it is, therefore, that the German language be the prevailing one at least within the confines of the nationality, that the German sovereigns understand it, speak it correctly and love it, that the German nobility and every cultured social group, spurred on by their example, endeavor to give it the elasticity and elegance which distinguishes the French language. This will come to pass when our purest book language seeks to become ever more the language of polite society and of every public discourse. To the present it has been far removed from such common use. It is a known fact that our book language, taken in the best sense of the word, is spoken hardly anywhere. Since the taste of our fatherland is anything but established and certain, every person of culture must welcome the establishment of a public institution which, without despotism, would promote the welfare of our fatherland. The exaggerated imitation of other nationalities of which we are accused would then be curbed and transformed into emulation which, with the united support of all, must produce good results.

These and other causes have moved several sovereigns of Germany to reflect upon the idea of establishing and supporting a German academy in which some and perhaps all of the German provinces are to be represented. Our immortal Leibniz already attempted to establish German academies in different provinces and then to unite them. In Berlin he was successful; but the state of affairs at that time and finally his death thwarted the completion of the venture. Since that time diverse academies have been established in various provinces, but there is a great need for a place where the diverse and scattered efforts of the academies can be united for the common welfare. The academy will concern itself with anything that aims to effect this. All petty partisanship, every disdain of other provinces and religions will be rigorously excluded; for everyone who lives in Germany will and must work and think for Germany. No divided political interest of the sovereigns or of the classes shall knowingly disturb the peace of its circle, the clarity of its judgment or the zeal of its efforts; for Germany has but one interest, the life and happiness of all Germans.

Several lines of endeavor would be:

1. Language. The members of the academy will not only endeavor in their writings to give examples of the purity, strength and that unaffected simplicity which are most becoming to the character of our nationality; but they will also, each in his province, name and denote with due honor the writings which bear this stamp. The academy hopes thereby, and especially through its common efforts, to promote the dissemination of these writings. With the greatest care it will avoid all despotic laws concerning language; and it will sedulously endeavor, through observations, suggestions and critical rules, gradually to provide that security which in comparison with other languages it sadly lacks. The academy will attach importance to everything that belongs to the history of the language, to its development in the different provinces, its grammar, its style and its dictionaries, and it will consider no product of the German mind and industry, be it poetry or prose, translation or original work, unworthy of its attention.

2. History of Germany. Although the learned men of our fatherland have applied much diligence to the elucidation of individual points and periods of German history, it is a matter of common opinion that, disregarding several of the important newer works, we are far behind our neighbors in the study of the history of the individual provinces as well as the general history of Germany, at least in the fact that the patriotic study of this history is far from being a common interest of this nationality. And yet this study is indispensable for the creation of a common spirit. The superb examples of the writers who have prepared studies of the history of provinces and also portions of the general history of Germany permit us to hope that the missing parts will soon be supplied and the whole can be brought to an irreproachable perfection as soon as the public of the whole fatherland turns its eyes upon it. Compared with other national groups we may appear tardy, but we are better

prepared and more thoroughly tested. The auxiliary sciences of history, the antiquities, natural history, geography, legislation and political philosophy of the different periods have already been elaborated in part. With its eyes fixed upon the patriotic history of the entire fatherland, the academy will endeavor to promote further development of the auxiliary sciences. The more unpartisan the spirit in which this work is done, the more it will contribute toward the extirpation of the sectional spirit.

3. Everything that belongs to the active philosophy of national development and national happiness will be the ultimate and highest purpose of the academy; and nothing which might in any way contribute thereto will be excluded. Every clear truth which decreases or puts an end to ruling prejudices and bad habits; every practical attempt and suggestion for the improvement of the education of the rulers, the nobility, the peasants and the burghers; improvements in all public institutions in allotting justice, in the mutual relations of the classes, in the organization of churches and schools, in a rational political economy and human political wisdom, will become matters for consideration, deliberation and practical knowledge in the academy. It cannot be denied that in our fatherland prejudices and follies hold sway which in the neighboring lands are openly recognized as such. It cannot be denied that the division into many states, sects and religions has retarded the development of human reason in general, of the common prudence and reasonableness whose principles have long been the moral and political calculus in other countries. The members from the different provinces will at each meeting present an accurate report concerning the efforts of each province in behalf of the common welfare. The strong will inspire the weak, the experienced will teach the well-meaning and the different provinces and different religions will learn to know, tolerate and love one another.

In summary, Herder gave evidence of a fervent national feeling such as few, if any, of the writers of eighteenth-century Germany exhibited. This national feeling found an outlet in his endeavors to excite in his countrymen as a whole a common national feeling and in urging them to develop a common culture on a native foundation. Imitation of foreign cultures he regarded as a national aberration and, therefore, vigorously opposed the imitation of the ancients which had become a tradition since the Renaissance, and also the more recent tendency of imitating the French. In consequence of centuries of imitation the German people, he told them, had lost their national character or that which was characteristic of their life and thought. In the discovery, the preservation and the cultivation of the characteristics of the life and the thought of the German nationality he saw the way to national greatness for the German people. But in order to do this effectively, Herder said in substance, the German people must, as nature had prescribed, become a living homogeneous whole. Every member of the group must merge his individuality with that of the group and work for the common welfare. In a word, Herder worked to make more profound every influence which might tend to mold the German people into a compact group and which would keep them conscious that they were members of this group. The mission of this group, as he saw it, was the cultivation of its innate faculties and of its idiosyncratic gifts. Cheerfully he said to his countrymen, " Let us, my brethren, work with courageous and happy hearts, even under the cloud; for we are working toward a great future ".

Herder was indeed the high priest of nationality who preached the gospel of nationality as the royal road to strength and greatness. In an age when the political and economic foundations for national unity were lacking, Herder endeavored to make the German people conscious of their cultural ties. Despite the political and economic division he saw a spiritual unity and sketched the symbols of this unity for his countrymen in unmistakable terms. More than this, he endeavored to strengthen the cultural ties which existed and also to create new ones which would assist in binding the German people into a compact group. The goal of the German people, he told them, must be self-realization. In this way he set up for his countrymen an ideal of future achievement which was to serve as a psychological basis in the struggle for political and economic unity. In a word, Herder formulated the idea of German nationalism.

The ideas which Herder proclaimed were to have a wide influence. Although a large number of men had a share in exciting a national feeling in Germany and in laying the foundations for a characteristic German culture, the name of Herder stands out prominently. The influence, however, of Herder's ideas upon the masses was more indirect than direct. The direct influence of his ideas was chiefly upon the writers of his and the following generation. " To any nation ", George Saintsbury writes, " Herder must have been a useful and stimulating teacher; to the Germans at this time he was simply invaluable ".[1] According to Horst Stephan, " We may regard him as the man who in the second half of the eighteenth century exerted the widest and most profound influence ".[2]

It was chiefly due, for example, to Herder's conception of national culture that Goethe became interested in Gothic architecture. The Enlightenment regarded Gothic architecture as barbarian, and the term Gothic was used to label everything that was ludicrous or grotesque. Goethe previous to his association with Herder had been, in his own words, " a declared enemy of the confused arbitrariness of Gothic ornamentation ".[3] " Under the rubric Gothic ",

[1] *History of Criticism*, vol. iii (New York, 1904), p. 298.

[2] *Herders Philosophie* (Leipzig, 1906), p. ix.

[3] *Von deutscher Art und Kunst* (Hamburg, 1773), p. 127.

Goethe wrote, " I heaped up all synoymous misunderstand·
ings about the indefinite, subordinate, unnatural, hashed-up,
patched-up and overladen that had ever passed through my
brain ".[1]   But during the winter of 1770-1771 which he
spent at Strassburg his attitude toward Gothic architecture
changed and the change was due chiefly to the influence of
Herder's ideas.   As a result, Goethe learned to see Gothic
architecture as the characteristic expression of the German
spirit.   His delight with Gothic architecture now became so
great that he gave utterance to it in the essay *Von deutscher
Baukunst*.   In this essay, which Herder included in his small
collection of essays entitled *Von deutscher Art und Kunst*
published in 1773, Goethe defended Gothic architecture in
terms of a glowing patriotism against the cold antagonism
of the Enlightenment.   He attempted to open the eyes of
his contemporaries to the naturalness and originality of
Gothic architecture in contrast to the so-called classical
architecture of his time which he regarded as a poor imitation of the ancient forms.   As the characteristic art of the
German spirit he believed Gothic architecture to be the only
true art.   The German " should thank God ", he wrote,
" that he is privileged to proclaim in a loud voice that this
is German architecture, our architecture.   The Italians cannot boast of an architecture that is really their own, and
much less the French ".[2]   In his autobiography he wrote
concerning the Strassburg Cathedral:

Since I now found that this building had been built on German
ground, and had grown thus far in genuine German times, and
that the name of the master, on his modest gravestone, was likewise of native sound and origin, I ventured, being incited by the
worth of this work of art, to change the hitherto decried appella-

[1] *Ibid.*
[2] *Werke*, Cotta ed., vol. xxiii, pp. 130-31.

tion of ' Gothic architecture ', and to claim it for our nationality
as ' German architecture '; nor did I fail to bring my patriotic
views to light, first orally and afterwards in a little treatise
dedicated to the memory of Erwin Steinbach.[1]

Goethe's *Von deutscher Baukunst* was the first of a number of writings which were to elevate Gothic architecture,
regarded with contempt since the Renaissance, to a place of
honor. Although the enthusiasm which Goethe felt for
Gothic architecture soon left him, others became interested
in it. Both August Wilhelm and Friedrich Schlegel, and
also Sulpitz Boisserée, soon cultivated a love for the long-
despised architecture. As a result Gothic architecture rose
in the esteem of the German people until it reached its zenith
in the reconstruction of the Cathedral of Cologne.[2]

Herder's vision of a Germany unified at least culturally
did not remain the isolated vision of one man. Others soon
shared the ideas which he had posited and also developed
them. In 1806 Friedrich Schlegel wrote to Schleiermacher,
" I feel it clearly how it is my sole calling to be a writer,
author and historian of my nationality ".[3] Herder's idea
of the German people as a cultural nationality was further
developed by Fichte and Jahn.[4] Both Fichte's *Reden an
die deutsche Nation* (1808), and also his other works, and
Jahn's *Das deutsche Volkstum* (1810) stressed the cultivation of native gifts, native materials and native manners.
Contemporary with Fichte and Jahn and also subsequent to
them came the romantic philosophers of nationality who
were indebted to Herder for many of their ideas. In 1810

[1] *Ibid.*, p. 206.
[2] See Klenze, C. von, *From Goethe to Hauptmann* (New York, 1926)
p. 73.
[3] Cited in Kluckhohn, P., *Die deutsche Romantik* (Leipzig, 1924), p. 132.
[4] For Herder's influence on Fichte see Wundt, *Fichte*, pp. 86, 165;
Janson, *Fichtes Reden an die deutsche Nation*, p. 5.

Josef Görres, who was influenced directly by Herder, published his essay, *Ueber den Fall Deutschlands,* in which he admonished his countrymen not to betray " German manners and customs ".[1] Stein, the Prussian reformer and German patriot, lauded Herder's efforts to awaken a national spirit in Germany.[2] Herder was one of Stein's favororite authors, and from him Stein adopted the idea of the national character.[3] Furthermore, Stein's national feeling seems to have been intensified by the reading of Herder's works. In the *Historisch-politische Betrachtungen* he wrote, " The cosmopolite is among the citizens of a state what the polyhistor is among the learned; the former belongs to all states and does nothing for anyone, the latter studies the sciences and achieves nothing in any one ".[4] He then went on to quote the passage from Herder's *Ideen,*

The savage who loves himself, his wife and child with quiet joy and glows with activity for his tribe as for his own life is in my opinion a more real being than that cultivated shadow who is enraptured with the shadow of the whole species. The former has room in his hut for every stranger. . . . The inundated heart of the idle cosmopolite is a home for no one.[5]

According to Stettiner, Herder, because of his statements regarding coöperation and unity of action, was also an influ-

---

[1] See Stern, A., *Der Einfluss der französischen Revolution auf das deutsche Geistesleben* (Stuttgart, 1928), p. 214 *et seq.*

[2] See Lehmann, M., *Freiherr vom Stein* (Leipzig, 1921), p. 388.

[3] For statements regarding the influence of Herder on Stein see Lehmann, *op. cit.,* p. 383; Elster, H. M., *Freiherr vom Stein* (Berlin, 1920), p. 197; Stein's *Briefe und Schriften,* ed. by Pagel (Leipzig, 1927), p. 138; Pertz, G. H., *Das Leben des Ministers Freiherrn vom Stein,* vol. ii (Berlin, 1850), p. 442 *et seq.*

[4] *Briefe und Schriften,* p. 141.

[5] Herder, *Werke,* xiii, 339.

ence in the formation of the *Tugendbund*.[1] " Herder ", he wrote, " was the great champion of the idea of coöperation ".[2] During the Napoleonic period, in general, the ideas regarding nationality were made dynamic among the German people at large; they became the slogans of the German people, calling the attention of the people to the real and also to the imaginary ties which united them and forming the foundations for the national strivings which were to culminate in economic and political unity. In 1812 Wilhelm Grimm said of Herder, " Though we mourn that physically he was taken from our midst, his spirit still lives among us and is active and effective ".[3]

[1] Stettiner, P., *Der Tugendbund* (Königsberg, 1904), p. 5.
[2] *Ibid.*
[3] *Kleinere Schriften*, vol. i (Berlin, 1881), p. 278.

CHAPTER V

NATIONALITY AND LANGUAGE

The fashionable language among the gentry and the wealthy bourgeoisie of Germany during the seventeenth and the larger part of the eighteenth century was, as has already been stated, the French tongue. The German language was regarded as crude, inelegant, undeveloped, and for a time French threatened to displace German entirely as the language of the upper classes. But, though neglected and despised by the upper classes, the German language soon found a number of champions who not only defended it, but who also worked for its improvement. These men wished to cultivate the German language so that in regard to elegance of expression it could take its place beside French and the other languages of Europe.

Just before the Thirty Years War broke out Martin Opitz (1597-1639) introduced the great movement of reforming the German language and of restoring its purity by publishing his *Aristarchus, sive de contemptu linguae Teutonicae* (1617). This work, written in Latin so that it would be read by the learned men of Germany who, generally speaking, despised the German language, was an earnest protest against the neglect of the mother tongue. In it the ancient Germans, their heroism, their virtues and their language are glorified, and the German people are petitioned to cast the foreign words out of their language and to respect and to cultivate it. Opitz concluded the treatise with the earnest plea:

140

You must love it [German language] if you do not wish to foster enmity against the heaven of your fatherland or, in other words, against yourself; you must work for its cultivation and therein show yourselves as men. Here is Rhodus, dance here. And if you believe that one must yield to supplications and entreaties, then I pray and entreat you for the sake of your well-beloved mother Germany and your illustrious forbears, show an interest worthy of your noble people, defend your language with the same persistence with which they defended their borders. Your ancestors, the brave and far-famed Semnonians, died for altar and hearth without hesitation. Necessity now demands of you that you do the same. See to it that you express in a pure language the noble sentiments which you have preserved in all their purity in your noble hearts. See to it that you bequeath to your children the versatility of speech which you have received from your parents. Finally, see to it that in excellence your language is not inferior to the language of those whom you excel in bravery and fidelity.[1]

Das Buch von der deutschen Poeterey which appeared in 1624 discussed the use of the German language in poetry. In this work also Opitz pleaded for a purified German. "It is very untidy", he wrote for example, "to patch all kinds of Latin, French, Spanish and Welsh words into the text of our speech ". [2]

Before the end of the Thirty Years' War Justus Georg Schottelius (1612-1676) published his *Deutsche Sprach-kunst* (1641) for which among other things he had collected a number of statements which foreign and native authors had made regarding the German language. With seeming pride he quoted the statements which pointed out the excellences of the German language, but when the state-

---

[1] *Aristarchus, sive de contemptu linguae Teutonicae und Buch von der deutschen Poeterey*, edited by Georg Witkowski (Leipzig, 1888), pp. 117-18.

[2] *Ibid.*, p. 162.

ments were unfavorable he tried to defend the German tongue against them. He also vigorously attacked those who believed that the German language contained many elements which had been borrowed from the other languages of Europe and endeavored to show, on the contrary, that almost all of the European languages had taken over much from the German. Furthermore, he drew up a comprehensive plan for a German dictionary, a plan which Leibniz, who was directly influenced by Schottelius, restated in his *Unvorgreifliche Gedanken*. In 1663 Schottelius published his chief work entitled *Ausführliche Arbeit von der deutschen Haubtsprache* in which he combined all the ideas on the German language and on German poetry which he had previously expressed. As a whole it was a plea for the historical study of the German language and for the preservation and cultivation of its purity. Both works were to be invaluable at a later time to students of Germanic philosophy.[2]

In 1670 in the treatise *Ueber die beste Vortragsweise des Philosophen* Leibniz stated that German of all languages is the best suited for philosophy, and urged the German people to uncover its buried treasure and to use it as the means of literary and oral communication. In the pamphlet entitled *Unvorgreifliche Gedanken, betreffend die Ausübung und Verbesserung der teutschen Sprache* (1697) he wrote:

It now appears that the evil has become worse and a medley has ignominiously gained ground with us, so that the preacher in the pulpit, the judge in the seat of justice and the citizen in his ordinary writing and conversation all seem bent on corrupting their mother-tongue with wretched French. It would

---

[1] *Unvorgreifliche Gedanken*, edited by Schmarsow (Strassburg, 1877), p. 59. For influence of Schottelius on Leibniz see *ibid.*, introduction, p. 6 *et seq.*

[2] See Jördens, K. H., *Lexikon deutscher Dichter und Prosaisten* (Leipzig, 1809), vol. iv, p. 614 *et seq.*

almost seem that if this is continued and nothing is done to stop it the German language may ultimately be lost in Germany as the Anglo-Saxon was in England.[1]

But, though he advocated the use of German as the literary language of Germany, Leibniz himself in order to reach a larger public wrote most of his own works in French or Latin. He was known and renowned because of his French and Latin works, but only a few of his contemporaries knew that he had written works of excellent content and form on scientific subjects in German. Leibniz did not publish them, and it was only after his death 1716 that they reached the public.[2] In the eighteenth century Klopstock, in his eagerness to establish German as the literary language of Germany, proposed that the writings of Leibniz be banished from the national republic of letters because their author had written so extensively in French and Latin.[3] But the pleas of Leibniz were not entirely in vain, for his disciple, Christian Wolff (1679-1754), wrote his philosophical works in German. Written in a popular style, Wolff's works were for a time read widely and contributed much toward making the German people familiar with a philosophical vocabulary.[4]

In 1687 Christian Thomasius threw the gauntlet to Latin as the language of the lecture room in the universities when he posted on the bulletin board of the University of Leipzig an announcement written in German which invited the students to a course in which German was to be the language

[1] Schmarsow, op. cit., pp. 51-52.

[2] See Rückert, H., Geschichte der neuhochdeutschen Schriftsprache (Leipzig, 1875), vol. ii, p. 321 et seq.

[3] Mackie, J. M., Life of Godfrey William Leibnitz (Boston, 1845), p. 206.

[4] See Steinhausen, G., Der Aufschwung der deutschen Kultur (Leipzig, 1920), p. 6.

of the classroom. The posting of this announcement on the black bulletin board which, as a biographer of Thomasius ironically wrote, " had never before been profaned by the German language," [1] created a furor both among the teachers and the students of the university. The very idea of using German as the language of the lecture-room seemed to them proposterous, and the myth was circulated that Thomasius intended lecturing in German because he knew no Latin.[2] The students were so prejudiced against the use of German in the discussion of learned subjects that at first few attended his lectures. Although after a time the number of students attending his classes increased, the opposition to the use of German did not disappear.[3] At the University of Halle where he was given a chair in 1694 Thomasius continued to lecture in German. Soon his example was followed by some of his colleagues and also by teachers in other schools. The influence of the movement started by Thomasius was far-reaching. When the University of Göttingen was founded in 1737, for example, most of the lectures were given in German. By the end of the eighteenth century Latin lectures were the exception, at least in Protestant universities.[4]

Besides introducing German into the lecture-room of the universities Thomasius also extended his efforts in behalf of

---

[1] Luden, H., *Christian Thomasius nach seinen Schicksalen und Schriften* (Berlin, 1805), p. 15.

[2] Raumer, K. von, *Geschichte der Pädagogik* (Stuttgart, 1843), vol. ii, p. 103.

[3] Luden, *op. cit.*, p. 12.

[4] See Stötzner, P., " Christian Thomas und sein Verdienst um die deutsche Sprache", in *Zeitschrift des allgemeinen deutschen Sprachvereins*, vol. iii (1888), p. 86 *et seq.*; Hodermann, R., " Universitätsvorlesungen in deutscher Sprache", in *Wissenschaftliche Beihefte des allgemeinen deutschen Sprachvereins*, no. viii (1895), pp. 99-116.

the German language to other fields. In 1688 he published the first German monthly journal. (*Monatsschrift*) and thereby became, in a sense, the father of German journalism.[1] The publication of a German journal was a momentous move against the use of French and Latin and must have contributed indirectly to the growth of German sentiment. He also wrote philosophical works in German and thereby excited no small indignation. " The College of Censors ", we are told, " actually sent back one of his books with the message that it was impossible to pronounce judgment on a work treating of philosophical matters in the German tongue ".[2] In general, although his innovations were by many regarded with open hostility, Thomasius continued to champion the use of the German language. Its use in all phases of German life, he thought, would be the best means of obliterating the sharp lines which separated the learned and lay classes.[3]

In the early part of the eighteenth century Johann Christoph Gottsched (1700-1766) continued the reform which Opitz had started. In his *Ausführlich Redekunst* he wrote:

It is an unfounded assertion that our mother-tongue is indeed too poor, and that it is necessary to borrow words from neighboring peoples. He who knows his German thoroughly will certainly not find it necessary to call upon the tongues of the whole world for assistance in order to speak and to write clearly, emphatically and pleasingly. It was only a stupid love of foreign languages which gave our countrymen the idea that the German language sounds better when a little Italian, French or even Latin is mixed with it. We will gladly recognize the

---

[1] Prutz, R. C., *Geschichte des deutschen Journalismus* (Hannover, 1845), vol. i, p. 295.

[2] Höffding, H., *A History of Moral Philosophy* (London, 1908), vol. ii, p. 3.

[3] Luden, *op. cit.*, p. 10 *et seq.*

excellences of the foreign languages; but our German language is certainly not entirely devoid of them.[1]

In his *Lobrede auf Martin Opitz* he said, " He renders no small service to his fatherland who gains honor for it by useful and ingenious writings, written, to be sure, in his mothertongue ".[2] Gottsched also opposed the practice of mixing provincialisms with literary German. Most of the writers of his time who wrote in German interspersed their writings with words and phrases taken from their local dialect, and it was therefore easily recognizable whether a writer was a native of Saxony, Swabia or of some other province. To put an end to this localism in German literature Gottsched sponsored the establishment of the provincial dialect of Meissen as the standard literary language of Germany. He was, however, unsuccessful in effecting this reform.[3]

In general, the reform movements which both Opitz and Gottsched sponsored were purely intellectual. Their efforts were directed toward making the language conform to a certain set of rules based largely on the theories of Scaliger, Ronsard and Boileau. The grammatical rather than the artistic perfection of the German language was the goal toward which they were striving.[4] Herder with his insistence upon spontaneity felt that Gottsched and his followers had done violence to the language with their reform movement.[5] And yet, despite all criticism of their aims and methods, it must be conceded that Opitz and Gottsched

---

[1] Cited in Reichel, E., *Gottsched der Deutsche* (Berlin, 1901), p. 114.

[2] *Ibid.*, p. 64.

[3] Biedermann, *Deutschland im achtzehnten Jahrhundert,* vol. ii, pt. i, p. 464.

[4] Paul, H., *Grundriss der germanischen Philologie* (Strassburg, 1891), vol. i, p. 42.

[5] ii, 40.

purged the German language of many foreign idioms and also worked for a wider use of German.[1]

In the second half of the eighteenth century a number of writers contributed toward the development of the language and were also instrumental in arousing a deeper interest in it. Klopstock, in the ode *Unsere Sprache,* praised the German language as the most flexible and resourceful of languages. It is capable, he said, of giving expression to the finest and strongest emotions of man, and, furthermore, since Arminius saved the independence of Germany, German had remained an unmixed language.[2] Despite his laudations, however, Klopstock found the German language too impoverished to express his ideas and hence created a new terminology to meet his need. This new poetic terminology, according to Herder, gave the German language a new vigor and a new power of expression.[3] Herder celebrated Klopstock as " the genius who ushered in a new period in the history of the language ".[4] But Klopstock's language was the language of the poet, not of the people; a wide gulf separated him from the masses. In a letter to Herder in 1772 Friedrich Nicolai wrote, " No one can follow an original mind like Klopstock unless he is just as original. In the end our authors will cater only to the cooks and not to the guests ".[5] Lessing, whose dramas raised the dignity of the German language, also raised his voice in behalf of a purer German. Regarding the borrowing of foreign words he said, for example, that " *Licenz, visiren, Education, Discip-*

---

[1] See Sperber, H., *Geschichte der deutschen Sprache* (Berlin, 1926), p. 103 *et seq.*

[2] *Werke*, Kürschner ed., vol. iii (Berlin, 1884), p. 249.

[3] i, 165.

[4] ii, 42. See also Jenisch, D., *Vergleichungen der Sprachen Europas* (Berlin, 1796), p. 258. His praise of Klopstock, however, is rather lavish.

[5] *Von und an Herder*, vol. i, p. 335.

lin, Moderation, Eleganz, Aemulation, Jalousie, Corruption, Dexterität—and a hundred more of such words do not say the least bit more than the German, and excite a feeling of nausea even in such as are anything but purists ".[1]

The importance of Herder lies in the fact that he stimulated a wide interest in the German language. Others before him, we have seen, encouraged the study of the German language and its use as the medium of literary communication, but Herder did more than simply advocate its use; he endeavored to give his countrymen an intelligent reason why they should study, use and cultivate the German language. He developed a philosophy of language in its relation to the group and gave it to the German people as a foundation for the study, use and cultivation of the German language.

Each national group, Herder believed, has a peculiar language which, like every other phase of culture, is a characteristic expression of the national soul. Just as all men had their origin from and in one race, so all languages have developed from a common source.[2] Physical environment, custom and other factors acting upon the national soul modified the original language and the result was many languages. In his essay *Ueber den Fleiss in mehreren gelehrten Sprachen* (1764) Herder wrote:

When the children of dust undertook to build the structure that menaced the clouds, the Tower of Babel, then the pleasure-cup of confusion was poured out over them; their families and dialects were transplanted in divers regions of the earth, and there came into being a thousand languages according to the climate and the customs of a thousand nationalities. If the oriental burns here under a hot zenith, then a fervid and impassioned language

---

[1] *Sämmtliche Schriften*, Lachmann-Muncker ed., vol. viii, p. 31.

[2] xxx, 8; v, 134.

also emanates from his impetuous mouth. The Greek flourished in the most voluptuous and mildest climate; his body is, as Pindar expresses it, suffused with grace, his veins are filled with a gentle fire, his members are all nerves, his organs of speech are fine, and among them therefore originated that fine Attic speech. The Romans, those sons of Mars, had a more vigorous language, and in order to beautify it, they gathered flowers from Greece. The martial German speaks still more stoutly; the sprightly Gaul invents a saltatory and softer speech; the Spaniard imparts to his a softer appearance, even though it be only mere sounds; the slothful African stammers brokenly and droopingly, and finally the Hottentot is lost in a babble of Calcuttian accents. Thus this plant, human speech, transformed itself according to the soil that nourished it and the celestial air that drenched it, and became a Proteus among the nationalities.[1]

Peculiar language is the most precious possession of the group. " Has a nationality ", a character in one of Herder's dramas asks, " anything more precious than the language of its fathers? In this language dwell its whole world of tradition, history, religion and principles of life, its whole heart and soul ".[2] Language " is the bond of souls, the vehicle of education, the medium of our best pleasures, nay of all social pastimes ";[3] it expresses the most distinguishing traits of the character of each nationality, and is the mirror of its history, its deeds, joys and sorrows;[4] " it is generally acknowledged to be the means for transmitting human ideas, inclinations and deeds; by means of it we bequeath the treasures of former times to later generations; through a common language all the members of a national group partici-

[1] i, 1. See also i, 167, 272; ii, 19; v, 123 *et seq.*
[2] xvii, 58.
[3] xviii, 384.
[4] xi, 225; xviii, 337.

pate one in another to a greater or lesser degree ".[1]   Briefly,
the native language is the purest expression of the spiritual
character of a national group.[2]

Moreover, peculiar language is not only the most precious
possession of the nationality, it is so indispensable that a
nationality cannot come into existence without it.[3]   " Without a common native tongue ", Herder wrote, " in which
all classes are raised like branches of one tree there can be
*no true mutual understanding, no common patriotic develop-
ment, no intimate common sympathy, no patriotic public* ".[4]
" A national group which neither knows nor loves and hon-
ors its own language has robbed itself of its tongue and its
brain, i.e., of the organs for the development of itself and the
most precious national honor ".[5]

As the most precious and indispensable possession of the
national group it stands in the same relation to the individuals who constitute the group.

What better vehicle of expression [Herder wrote] is there than
the mother-tongue?   Like the charm of the fatherland, her
charm surpasses all other languages in the opinion of him who
was the son of her heart, the infant of her breasts, to whom
she is now the joy of his best years and should be the hope and
honor of his old age.[6]   She is the guide without which he
would lose his way in the labyrinth of many foreign languages;
she is the bark which saves him from sinking in the vast ocean
of strange dialects; she effects unity in the otherwise confusing
variety of languages.[7]   Whoever writes in a foreign language

[1] xvi, 46.
[2] xvii, 59.
[3] xviii, 387.
[4] xvii, 288-89.   Italics are Herder's.
[5] xviii, 346.
[6] i, 400.
[7] i, 401.

must have a mother-tongue in which he is brought up. If he despises this mother he must have been reared so badly by her that the first impressions of his education did not mature; otherwise the early impressions upon the soul would be indelible.— How much does a writer not lose whose mind has not been mightily moulded by his native language.! His later learning will but paint the surface of his mode of thought; he will wander about in foreign regions without fatherland and household gods; he can never be an original writer for whom thought and expression coincide to make a complete picture of his soul.[1] Since the mother-tongue is the best adapted to our character and fills out our mode of thought, nature, it seems, has given us ability only for our mother-tongue.[2] Hence one can see that if a writer does not wish to be a complete failure he must write in the mother-tongue; for if the thought should form the expression, the whole range of the language, like the field of thought, must be under my mastery; otherwise I cannot express my real thoughts or else I will sin incessantly against the language.[3]

Since he deemed the mother-tongue so indispensable in the development and expression of national individuality, Herder implored the German people not to despise the German language. " He that despises the language of his nationality ", he told them, " dishonors its most noble public; he becomes the most dangerous murderer of her spirit, of her honor at home and abroad, of her sentiments, of her finer morality and activity ".[4] " The honor of a nationality is dependent upon its mother-tongue; the latter is the vehicle of the honor of a country. It must be guarded more closely, and its purity protected more zealously than the honor of the

[1] i, 402.
[2] i, 2.
[3] i, 403.
[4] xvii, 287.

most tender loved-one ".[1]   The German language, alone, he
wished to impress upon the minds of his countrymen, is
adapted to the needs of the German people and it alone can
express their innermost thoughts.   It is impossible, therefore, for the German people to develop a vital and lasting
culture except on the basis of their native language.[2]

And for what [Herder wrote] can our mother-tongue be more
indispensable than for poetry and rhetoric; for the greatest
thunder of their power, the brightest beauties of their elegances
died with the dead languages.   The Homers, Ciceros, Voltaires,
Popes,—did they write in foreign languages?   Except Terence
among the ancients, and some writers among us, no one despised
his own language.[3]

The chief reason for the neglect of the German language,
Herder thought, was the fact that the German people were
ashamed of their language.   He, therefore, tried to excite in
them the pride of ownership by extolling the virtues of the
German tongue.   He told his countrymen that they had
every reason to be proud of their language, for it had, despite
all the changes, always been and still was an original, peculiar
national language " filled with the life and blood of our
forefathers ".[4]

The German language [he wrote] has always remained an
original language.   No one can rob her of that merit.[5]   To be
sure, we are not Greeks whose language is sweet chords and soft
strains like the music of stringed instruments in the pure ether
of Olympus. . . . Nor do we wish to be Greeks.   Our language
is strong and redoundingly brave like the people which speaks

[1] xvii, 120.

[2] xvii, 59.

[3] i, 6.

[4] iv, 116; ii, 30.

[5] ii, 248.

it, and only to weaklings does it seem fearful and terrible.[1] Of all the cultivated languages of Europe flourishing at the present time it is ours which, free of the shackles of rhyme, is most like the language of the Greeks and Romans. An obvious excellence which should make it dear to us.[2] The German language seems to be more perfect for philosophy than any other of the living languages. It is sufficiently rich and specific to express the finest thoughts of the metaphysician in their true beauty and it is also sufficiently emphatic and figurative to animate the most abstract doctrines.[3] You say, 'My language disgraces me!' Take heed that you do not disgrace your language.[4] What man among us will explain to us its history and show us its beauty? Who will take the cloud from our eyes?[5]

The decade from 1760 to 1770 during which Herder's *Fragmente* appeared saw the number of French books published in Germany reach its maximum. From the lists of the publishers it has been calculated that during this decade thirteen per cent. of the total literature published in Germany was in French and the ratio of Latin was about the same.[6] In the *Fragmente* and in all of his works which followed Herder took a determined stand against the use of foreign languages in Germany as the medium of literary and oral communication.[7] "The best culture of a nationality", Herder wrote, " does not develop quickly; it cannot be forced by a foreign language. It thrives best, and I should like to

[1] ii, 32.

[2] xxvii, 172.

[3] i, 196.

[4] i, 186; ii, 33.

[5] i, 196.

[6] See Frederking, A., "Unsere Muttersprache unter Fremdherrschaft", in *Wissenschaftliche Beihefte zur Zeitschrift des allgemeinen deutschen Sprachvereins*, no. 14/15 (1898), pp. 148-166.

[7] See, for example, v, 360; xiii, 351; xiv, 141; xviii, 333.

say only, on the native soil of the nationality and in the language which the nationality inherited and which continues to transmit itself ".[1] In the poem *An die Deutschen* he wrote :

> Look at other nationalities! Do they wander about
> So that nowhere in the whole world they are strangers
> Except to themselves?
> They regard foreign countries with proud disdain.
> And you German alone, returning from abroad,
> Wouldst greet your mother in French?
>
> O spew it out, before your door
> Spew out the ugly slime of the Seine.
> Speak German, O you German.[2]

In the *Adrastea* he said :

This slavish mania of imitation in the use of foreign languages cannot be counteracted most effectively by banishing individual words, but by permitting the soul of the nationality to become a force in speech and in thought. . . . The rich man does not borrow; he lends, and the poor readily borrow of him. When one nationality thoughtlessly imitates another, it does not think the borrowed thoughts after its own manner; but confesses itself to be a servile captive who cannot speak except in the manner and with the mouth of its captor. The great difference in the character of the two nationalities is shown by the fact that the elegances of the French language can be translated only with great difficulty.[3]

In the *Fragmente* he said emphatically, " This language [German] is the true national mood, you Germans! If you must imitate, please imitate the people of your own country

---

[1] xvii, 59.

[2] xxvii, 128.

[3] xxiii, 85.

and do not make yourselves ridiculous or contemptible by imitating foreign nationalities ".[1]

In place of imitation Herder advised emulation. He told his countrymen to develop their language so that it would stand on the same plane with the other languages of Europe. He tried to impress upon their minds that a nationality which had a poor and mean language could not produce great poets or philosophers.[2]

If language [he wrote] is the tool of the sciences, then a nationality which without a poetical language has had great poets and without an elastic language fortunate prose writers and without an exact language great philosophers is a monstrosity.[3] Therefore learn to know your language, you censors, and develop it for poetry, philosophy and prose. For then you are building a foundation which will hold a building. More than that, you are furnishing tools for the writer, forging thunderbolts for the poet, furbishing the armor of the orator and sharpening the weapons for the philosopher. It is more than a tool; words and ideas are very intimately related in philosophy, and how much in the criticism of the fine arts is not dependent upon the expression.[4] A purified language, regulated by definite rules, contributes incredibly toward a set mode of thought.[5] Little reasoning has been done about the German language; Breitinger, Bodmer, Bödicker, Heinze, Oest, Klopstock have made only disjointed remarks; and of the many German societies only two or three have shown that they have been able to produce anything.[6] Caesar wrote about the similarity of languages; Varro concerning etymology; Leibniz was not

[1] i, 137.
[2] i, 147.
[3] ii, 8.
[4] *Ibid.*
[5] xvi, 604.
[6] ii, 149.

ashamed to occupy himself with the study of language, and we, despite our German societies, have done little or nothing in the matter.[1] The Greeks, the Romans, how did they not work to develop their language. The Arabs who named grammar the salt of knowledge, had so many critics that a certain rabbi could load sixty camels with dictionaries, as an Arabic writer has informed us with accuracy.[2] You industrious Germans! We need someone who will do for the German language what Johnson [3] did for his.[4] He who elevates the language of a nationality and improves it so that it can express every feeling, every clear and noble thought in the most powerful terms, helps the widest and best public to expand or to unite itself and to establish itself more firmly.[5]

For the true foundation upon which they must rest the development of their language if it is to be natural Herder urged the German people to look into their past history. Although German as the language of learning, he told his countrymen, may have been forced to give way to Latin, in the mouths of the people and in the literary monuments of the past it has been preserved in all its original vigor and beauty. " The language of the Germans ", he wrote, " as we find it in Otfried and his followers has, despite its still undisciplined harshness, . . . a power, a fullness and a pliability which we might envy in many respects ".[6] In the Minnelieder there is a language so sweet and noble that its equal is difficult to find.[7] He asked his countrymen to go back to the language of the *Meistersänger,* of Opitz, of

[1] i, 166.
[2] i, 148.
[3] Samuel Johnson (1709-1784).
[4] i, 217.
[5] xvii, 287.
[6] xvi, 195.
[7] ii, 248.

Logau and of Luther.[1] " Luther, for example ", he wrote, " spoke the simple, vigorous, plain language of good reason; he spoke from his breast and heart, and not from his head and memory ".[2] In Klopstock he saw the original vigorous German spirit.[3] Klopstock was to him " the first poet of our nationality ".[4] " The study of an original poet like Klopstock ", he said, " opens the way for the student of philosophy to grasp the genius of a language ".[5] Lessing also was held up as a model by Herder:

As long as German has been written, methinks, no one has ever written German like Lessing. Let some one come and tell me in what respect his turns, his sense of language is not the true sense of the language itself. Since Luther no one has used it so well in this respect or has understood it so well.[6] Let us Germans read him; he was a master of the language both theoretically and practically.[7]

In an attempt to stimulate an interest in the German language and its cultivation Herder proposed problems which he thought worthy of being investigated. Among others were the following:

In what degree has the natural mode of thought of the German people an influence on their language? And the language upon their literature? How much of the language can be explained from the nature of their circumstances and organs of speech? In what measure, according to the testimony of history, can its

[1] i, 165.
[2] x, 320. See also xvi, 230.
[3] xxvii, 172. See also v, 175.
[4] ii, 42.
[5] i, 165.
[6] xv, 487.
[7] xviii, 202.

wealth and its poverty have resulted from their mode of thinking? To what extent can the etymology of their words be explained by views which they had in common with other nationalities or which were peculiar to them? To what extent also do the grammatical rules keep parallel with the mode of thinking? And how can the idioms be explained from their mode of thinking? What revolutions has the German language had to undergo in its vital parts? And how far developed is it for the poet, the prose-writer, and the philosopher? [1] Our words which imitate sound are often powerful words; in this respect we are still rich and strong; but were richer and stronger in the past. Since it is impossible to overlook this power and magnificence of the ancients in the oldest remains of the German mode of writing, why is it that so little is thought about reconquering them? [2]

As a special means of developing the German language Herder suggested conversation.

Language and speech are developed most intensely through conversation, but, I am sorry to say, we Germans hardly make use of conversation for the development of our language and speech; therefore other nationalities often style us mute or clumsy-speaking coarse barbarians. . . . Language originated through intercourse and not in solitude; through conversation every expression is sharpened and polished. In conversation also one should not permit oneself a barbarism. All educated classes in other nationalities speak their language correctly in conversation; the German is the only one who does not; he speaks and narrates like the midwife in Shakespeare. [3]

Herder also made a special appeal for the preservation of the idioms of the German language.

[1] i, 148 *et seq.*
[2] ii, 40.
[3] xxx, 223.

The idioms are the elegances of which no neighbor can deprive us and they are sacred to the tutelary goddess of the language. They are the elegances woven into the spirit of the language, and this spirit is destroyed if they are taken out.[1]   Take the idiomatic out of a language and you take its spirit and power.[2] The idioms of the time of the *Meistersänger,* of Opitz and Logau, of Luther, etc., should be collected.[3]   And if they are good for nothing else they will at least open the way to the student of language so that he can understand the genius of the language, compare it with the genius of the nationality, and explain one by the other. . . . The idioms of every language are the impressions of its country, its nationality, its history.[4]

But much as Herder urged his countrymen to study and to cultivate their native language he did not wish them to do so to the exclusion of all other languages.   On the contrary, he felt that the German language might be enriched as a result of the study of other languages.   Hence he wrote:

The German language can learn much from the other languages even if only scolding for which the best Latin is generally used. It can learn simplicity and dignity from Greek, neatness from Latin, precision from English, vivacity from French, a soft picturesqueness from Italian.[5]   How much could we not learn from the British and how little have we learned.[6]

In the study of foreign languages, however, the mother-tongue must always be the starting point and its enrichment the goal.

Ordinarily we think only in the language in which we were

---

[1] i, 162.
[2] ii, 46.
[3] i, 165.
[4] ii, 49.
[5] i, 220.
[6] i, 217.

brought up, in which we first received our deepest sensations, in which we loved, in which we dreamed, asleep or awake. And yet this does not prevent us from learning ten other old and new languages later on or from loving their beauties and from collecting from them all the fruits of their spirit. An educated man of our time must do this, but let him have and hold the native language of his fatherland. On this tree let him graft everything, for under it he was born and under it he should live and die. A man who has lost his patriotic feeling, has lost himself and the world.[1] Not to forget my own do I learn other languages, not to exchange the customs of my rearing do I travel among foreign peoples, not to lose the civic rights of my fatherland do I become an acclimated foreigner, for then I should lose more than I gain. But I walk through strange gardens merely to get flowers for my language, the betrothed of my mode of thought. I see strange customs so that I may bring mine, like fruits ripened by a foreign sun, as an offering to the genius of my fatherland. When I leave my native country to graze in strange languages, I imitate Kleist's bees who fly humming through the air in scattered swarms and then light on clover and blooming plants and return to the hive laden with the sweet spoil and furnish us with the honey of wisdom.[2]

But Herder was the great apostle of the use of the German language in the schools as well as in social life. Some of the schools of Herder's day still gave to Latin, because it was considered the language of learning, the most important place in the curriculum, and there were still some people who believed that facility in the use of Latin was the chief goal of education. Writing in 1795 Friedrich Gedike described the conditions in the schools of his time and of the decades which immediately preceded it as follows:

Greek and Latin writers were read and expounded, but it was

[1] xviii, 336.
[2] i, 401.

considered a pedagogical sin to read and expound German authors in a public school. The young were even forbidden to read privately a book for the cultivation of style, and at the present time there are schools in which the reading of a German author by a pupil is forbidden under severe penalties.[1]

In a book-review of Bodmer's *Die Grundsätze der deutschen Sprache* (1769) Herder wrote, " It is worthy of being introduced into all schools where German is taught; but in how few is German taught. They teach languages which neither teachers nor pupils have ever used or will ever use in their daily life rather than the language which is spoken and written ".[2] Granted that the foregoing statements are in some respects exaggerated, and granted that in the first half of the eighteenth century German had gone a long way toward supplanting Latin in the schools, yet it remains a fact that there were still schools in which Latin was either the medium of instruction or in which to the neglect of German it occupied the most prominent place in the curriculum.

Against this old type of Latin school Herder raised his voice in protest. This type of school, he believed, did not satisfy the need of the day and was not an aid in the development of innate characteristics. He feared that the Latin schools and a Latin education would make the children Romans and that the knowledge which was necessary to make good German citizens of the children might become merely incidental.[3] The Latin schools were, therefore, in his opinion, hindrances in the development of humanity and could but pervert the German mind.

Even now the Latin tongue is the medium of our learned tuition

[1] Cited in Matthias, A., *Geschichte des deutschen Unterrichts* (Munich, 1907), p. 194.

[2] iv, 301.

[3] xxx, 129.

from our early youth, and we who possess so little of the Roman mind and spirit are destined to form an acquaintance with the Roman ravagers of the world before we are introduced to the milder manners of more gentle nations or to the principles that conduce to the happiness of our country. The names of Marius and Sulla, of Caesar and Octavius become familiar to us before we know anything of the wisdom of Socrates or of the institutions of our forefathers.[1] Since Latin shackles our culture should we give it so prominent a place in our schools and in our education?[2] Away with Latin as a means of learning grammar; for that there is no other language but our mother-tongue. Through Latin we become clever in our speech and drowsy in our thinking; we speak words of a strange nationality and wean ourselves from our own thoughts.[3] He who loves mankind must sigh when he sees how in the schools that vaunt the name *Latin Schools* the first youthful ardor is dampened, the first fresh vigor is repressed, the talent is buried in the dust, the mind is retarded until like a spring which has been repressed too long it loses its power. Who ever conceived the idea that this method of language instruction is suitable for our youth? . . . Oppressed minds! Martyrs of a purely Latin education! Oh, if you could only make your complaints known in a loud voice![4]

Herder also protested most emphatically against the custom of sending German children to French schools or of employing French tutors to give the German children a French education. During his early life he was more lenient toward the French. In the *Journal meiner Reise* he still respects the French language enough to write:

After the mother-tongue the French should follow, as it is the most universal and indispensable in Europe and, according to

[1] xiv, 152.

[2] i, 378.

[3] iv, 388.

[4] i, 380-81. See also i, 2, 406. Italics are Herder's.

our modes of thought, the most finished and the most complete in beauty of style and tasteful expression. . . . Our state of society requires that it should come immediately after our own language before any other, even before Latin. I would rather have men of learning know French than Latin.[1]

After a short sojourn in France, however, his attitude underwent a change. His preference for the French language changed to antipathy. " I am now in Nantes ", he wrote in a letter to Hamann, " where I am learning to know the French language, French manners and the French mode of thinking. I am learning to know them, but I am learning not to accept them, for the nearer I see them, the less I like them ".[2] In the *Humanitätsbriefe* he vigorously opposed the use of French as a medium of instruction in Germany, and, in general, the imitation of the French:

Since language is the organ of our mental faculties and the chief means of our training and education, we cannot be well-taught except in the language of our nationality and country. What is termed French education (a term actually in use) in Germany must of necessity deform and pervert the German minds. Methinks this truth stands out as clearly as the sun at noon.

By whom and for whom was the French language constructed? By Frenchmen, and for Frenchmen. It expresses ideas and relations which are peculiar to their world, and to the course of their life; it expresses them in the manner which their local circumstances, the fleeting moment and the mood of their soul at that moment indicate. Outside of this area the words are only half understood or not at all; they are ill applied or, where the subjects are wanting, altogether inapplicable and thus uselessly learned. Since fashion rules as despotically in no language as in French; since no other language

[1] iv, 372.

[2] Cited in Haym, *Herder*, vol. i, p. 338.

is so entirely a reflection of variableness and of a changeable succession of shades and customs, opinions and relations; since no other language equals it in expressing soft shades of meaning and in plays upon a color-piano of brilliant meteors and refractions of light; with these qualities what can it be for the education of Germans in their peculiar circumstances? Nothing—or a will-o'-the-wisp. It leaves the mind empty of ideas or gives it, in place of the truths and actualities of our own country, false expressions, erroneous terms, unnatural representations and affectedness. Wrenched out of its proper place, such results must of necessity follow even if it were a language of angels. Neither is it going too far to say that in those classes of our own nationality where it has been the vehicle of education, and still more where it has constituted the whole education, it has distorted the understanding, devasted hearts and, which is worse, left the mind void of such qualities as are most essential to the enjoyment of pleasure in our people, in our circumstances, in our calling; and are these not the sweetest of pleasures?

And yet the whole value of a man, his usefulness in society, his happiness as a man and as a citizen, depend upon this, that he understand thoroughly and clearly from the days of his youth the world in which he lives, his employment and relations, and their means and purposes, that he gain secure possession of ideas on these subjects, sound in the strictest sense, and sincere and cheerful views; and that he train himself in them, unperverted, immovably, without any unnatural or false ideal in his mind and without any squinting toward foreign manners and relations. One who has not attained to this will find his ways of thinking distorted and his heart uninterested in the situation in which he is placed or, as it might better be represented, his heart will have been stolen from him in his youth, for his whole life, by a courtesan.

What can be more precious than a real world of real hearts and minds, than a condition in which we know our own thoughts and feelings in their truest form and express them to others in the truest and most natural way; in which others communicate to us in return their own thoughts and feelings; in short, where every bird sings as nature taught it to sing? If this light be extinguished, this flame quenched, this primeval bond between souls broken or weakened, then, instead of all this, nothing would be heard but mere memorized, foreign, poverty-stricken phrases. O the misery of everlasting superficiality and false-hood, a heart-and-soul-shrivelling drought and frigidity.[1]

In place of the study of Latin and French Herder advised the intense study of the mother-tongue. A thorough knowledge of the mother-tongue and skill in its use he deemed indispensable in the training for German citizenship.

I can perhaps stammer imperfectly the language of a foreign nationaliity without penetrating to the heart of its idioms. I can perhaps with great effort learn the words of dead languages from their monuments, but the spirit will evade me. . . . And to these foreign languages we offer up our best days, our most vigorous memory and the fire of our youth, just as the flower of youth was put into the glowing arms of the idol. Would not subject-matter instead of words, and ideas instead of symbols nourish us far better.[2] What a limitless sea I see before me into which I dare not venture without a guide—a labyrinth of tongues in which I should lose my way without a guide. And this guide is my mother-tongue to which I must, therefore, first of all devote myself.[3]

Hence " the first class in language should be devoted entirely to the mother-tongue " and " the instruction in the mother-tongue should last as long as the instruction in the sciences is continued ".[4] " He who is well informed in foreign languages ", Herder said, " and remains a barbarian in his own, hardly understanding the writers of his nationality, is a

[1] i, 2.
[2] i, 5.
[3] iv, 389, 400.
[4] i, 7.

ridiculous know-all ".[1] It must not be thought, however, that Herder wished to exclude Latin and French from the curriculum entirely. He desired only that they give place to German as the medium of the classroom and as the foundation of education.

In Bückeburg (1771-1776) and in Weimar (1776-1803) Herder put some of his theories into practice. He remodelled the school curriculum so as to make it a more practical preparation for German citizenship.[2] A school, Herder believed, must be characterized by its " national color ".[3] He replaced the strict Latin regime with thorough instruction in the mother-tongue. The addresses which his predecessors had been accustomed to deliver in Latin Herder delivered in German. In these addresses he repeatedly stressed the cultivation of the mother-tongue. In a school address of the year 1796 he said:

Alcibiades gave a slap on the face to the schoolmaster in Athens who did not have the works of Homer, the foremost classical author of his language, in his school, and how diligently did not the Greeks read their best authors. . . . In Italy the educated part of the nationality knows its classical authors almost from memory; in the newer English writings they are constantly quoted and praised with true British pride; how proud the French nationality is of its language and its mode of writing everyone knows. We Germans, however, fall short also in this respect. Our school and pulpit style and our style of chancery, not excluding that of Regensburg, are wooden styles, often not even formed of genuine German oaks and beeches, with which we will hardly attract any nationality or kill an enemy. Our noble German tongue is a far way from becoming what it could be; our best authors are unknown in the homes, often also in the

[1] xviii, 157-159.

[2] See Haym, *Herder*, vol. ii, p. 361.

[3] iv, 400. See also Andress, J., *Herder as Educator* (New York, 1916), *passim*.

schools, and despised at the courts where they should mold the thought of the youth and sweeten and enliven their intercourse. Which of you youths knows Uz and Haller, Kleist and Klopstock, Lessing and Winckelmann as the Italians know and honor their Ariosto and Tasso, the British their Milton and Shakespeare, the French so many of their writers.[1]

But Herder was not satisfied with the mere reading of the German authors in the schools; he desired that they be read aloud, memorized and recited, for this he said, " will awaken, if that is possible among us, a national character ".[2] In another address he said:

It is evident how little German the German people know; not only the peasant and not only the artisan, for the most part, speak a confused, abominable, atrocious German, even when they wish to express themselves well; but the higher one goes in the social rank, the worse it often becomes, until one reaches the peak of the mountain where they are ashamed of German and speak it only to servants and chamber-maids. . . . Learn German, O youth, for you are German; learn to speak it, to write it; learn to say what you think and desire.[3]

In his endeavors to introduce a wider use of the mother-tongue Herder also included the church. Worship, he told his generation, must be in the mother-tongue; worship in a learned tongue is a mere formality.[4] " Every nationality ", he wrote, " has its own language of worship and must have it; a strange language which has been forced upon it will be unintelligible and inapplicable. . . . And thus let the Anglican and the Gallican, the Spanish and the German church worship God, each in *her* words ".[5] " The lan-

[1] xxx, 222.
[2] *Ibid.*
[3] xxx, 241-42.
[4] xxiv, 43.
[5] xxiii, 126. Italics are Herders.

guage in which we make love, pray and dream, that is our most intimate language, our language of worship ".[1] Herder specifically asked the preachers of Germany to set a good example for the people by using the language of Luther in the pulpit.   He endeavored to impress upon them that they could contribute much toward making the language of Luther the common language of the German people.[2]   To his sorrow he found that the German which was most commonly used in the pulpit was not the language of Luther, but a hybrid jargon.   Even the pulpit, he observed, was infected with the *à la mode* disease.   Deeply moved by this condition, he wrote in a spirit of bitter irony:

Our newest book language which has forced its way into the pulpit was certainly not taken from the writings of Wolff, for they are no longer read; but from France, England, Italy and I don't know where. . . . Our inherited character, that is the mania for imitation, causes us to beg and borrow continuously, and if it is not easy to bring over the things themselves, we take with us at least the words, that is, the empty wooden vessels and afterwards display them in the most puerile manner. . . . When Klopstock first became prominent, every youth who wished to be illustrious preached in mutilated hexameters.   If the *Bardenlustrum* had lasted a little longer, they would have preached after the manner of the bards.   Several years back when everyone wished to know something about art, art appeared in the pulpit.   Now that the young sirs use biblical expressions in their romances and moonlight verses, it would be very ungrateful if the pulpit were not to follow their example and in time borrow the tone of the romances and moonlight verses.   *O Luther,* when I think of you and your pure, fixed, intelligible language![3]

[1] xxiv, 43 *et seq.*
[2] x, 320 *et seq.*
[3] x, 322.   Italics are Herder's.

In summary, each national group, Herder believed, has a peculiar language which, like every other human manifestation, is a characteristic expression of the national soul. This language is the most precious possession of the national group, in fact, a nationality cannot come into existence without it. Since it is so indispensable to the existence of a nationality, nature has given us ability only for our mother-tongue. Herder, therefore, pleaded with the German people not to despise their native language, endeavoring at the same time to excite the pride of ownership by extolling the virtues of the German tongue. He repeatedly pointed out the harm that was being wrought in Germany through the use of French and Latin, and suggested that, as the first step toward the rehabilitation of the German language, French and Latin as a medium of literary communication be banished from Germany. He advised his countrymen to cultivate their language so that it would be on a level with the other languages of Europe. For the true foundation of their language Herder pointed the German people to their past history. There, he told them, they would find it preserved in all its original vigor and beauty. This original vigorous German must serve as the basis for further cultivation of the language if the development was to be vital and lasting. As much as Herder urged his countrymen to study and to cultivate their native language, he did not, however, wish them to do so to the exclusion of all other languages.

But Herder was the great apostle of the use of the German language in the schools of Germany as well as in the social life. He raised his voice in protest against the old type of Latin school which, he believed, did not prepare the youth for the practical needs of German citizenship. He also protested most emphatically against the custom of sending German children to French schools or of employing

French tutors to give German children a French education. A French education, he contended, must of necessity deform and pervert the German mind. Instead of spending so much time and effort in the study of French and Latin, the German people, Herder urged, ought to devote themselves to a more intensive study of the mother-tongue. Above everything else Herder considered a thorough knowledge of the German tongue necessary for German citizenship. To his theories Herder also added practice. In the schools of Bückeburg and Weimar he remodelled the curriculum so as to make it more characteristically German. He also insisted that worship must be in the mother-tongue if it was to be more than a mere formality, and asked the preachers to set a good example for the people in general by shunning the *à la mode* jargon and by using the language of Luther in the pulpit.

*   *   *   *   *   *   *   *

It is difficult to overstress the importance of the establishment of a common language in the development of a common feeling. Although a nationality can exist without the possession of a distinct national language, language is, nevertheless, one of the prime factors in the development of a nationality and in its continued existence. Uniformity of language tends to produce like-mindedness which in turn tends to develop group consciousness. The more uniform a language, the greater are the possibilities that the members of a group will be bound together more intimately. By means of a common language thoughts, hopes, desires can be communicated more quickly and can be understood and assimilated more easily. They become the thoughts, hopes and desires, so to speak, of the group. In the words of Wirth, "Language is and will remain the most important part of the national organism, for it is the cement which holds the human beings together; it is the means whereby all

can participate in the products of the mind ".[1] " It is doubt-
ful ", the historian Dietrich Schäfer writes, " if of the factors which promoted a common feeling among the people
[of Germany] any one was more decisive than the fact that
one language was established as the literary language of
Germany, from the North Sea to the Carpathians and from
the Alpine passes to the Finnish Gulf ".[2]

In order to appreciate rightly Herder's influence upon the
cultivation and use of the German language, one must keep
in mind that when he began his literary activity the German
tongue was not held in high regard by scholars, men of
learning and by the upper classes generally. Latin, generally speaking, was still the language of learning and
French the language of many courts. The German language was not regarded as being fit to express learned ideas
or elegant enough to be used at court; neither was it looked
upon as being susceptible of greater refinement. By the
time of Herder's death, however, the German language had
supplanted French and Latin almost entirely. The change
which had taken place was due in no small degree to the
efforts and influence of Herder. Second to none as a spiritual force in his time, he aided materially in ensconcing
German as the literary language of Germany, as the language of the classroom and, in general, as the foundation
of German culture. He was untiring in his efforts to impress upon the minds of the German people that the German
language is the necessary road to a genuine and lasting culture; that no foreign tongue could possibly take the place
of the mother-tongue as the foundation of this culture; that
a culture built upon a foreign language is like a house built
on sand. In addition, Herder was lavish in his praise of the

[1] Wirth, M., *Die deutsche Nationaleinheit* (Frankfort, 1859), p. 363.
[2] *Deutsche Geschichte*, vol. ii (Jena, 1919), p. 232.

various qualities of the German language. In his praise, it seems, he went beyond everything that had been written up to that time, and his enthusiasm for the language was greater than that of any writer preceding him.

Contemporary with Herder or soon after his death the great literature of Lessing, Goethe and Schiller appeared and gave point to the statements of Herder. In the works of these authors the German people could see the actual confirmation of many of Herder's ideas regarding the German language. The writings which made their appearance rapidly raised the German language to an equal power and dignity among the modern tongues and filled the German people with pride. It was an age of the greatest importance for the national life of Germany. It was due in large part to the influence of Herder that Goethe turned away from French and centered his attention upon his mother-tongue. During the occupation of his native town by French troops Goethe had as a boy learned French and at a later time had even attempted to write French plays. At Leipzig Goethe had been under the influence of the French " school" which had taught him to regard French authors and French taste as authoritative.[1] His interest in and liking for French grew to such a degree that, as he stated in his autobiography, he chose to continue his studies at the University of Strassburg because he desired to perfect his command of French. " But alas ", he wrote, " I was destined to experience there just the opposite ".[2] Up to that time he had considered himself half a Frenchman and had written much of his correspondence in French and had even interspersed it copiously with French verse. Here in Strassburg he was destined to be drawn away from the French. He fell in with a group

[1] See Weissenfels, R., *Goethe im Sturm und Drang*, vol. i (Halle, 1894), pp. 31-37, 224-33.

[2] Goethe's *Werke*, Cotta ed., vol. xxiv, p. 38.

which was under the spiritual leadership of Herder and soon abjured the French language. The influence of Herder upon this group was so great that Goethe wrote, " We resolved to give up the French language altogether and to devote ourselves with more earnestness and zeal to our mother-tongue ".[1]

The ideas which Herder had expressed were also powerfully reëchoed in the works of those who followed him. Soon after Herder's death Fichte held up language as the outstanding mark of a nationality. In his *Reden,* for example, he said, " Wherever a separate language is found, there a separate nationality exists which has the right to take independent charge of its affairs and to govern itself ".[2] In 1810 August Wilhelm Schlegel said of the German language, " It is the palladium of our culture which we now, more than ever before, have cause to guard carefully and to hold sacred ".[3] In 1813 Ernst Moritz Arndt, in the poem, *Des Deutschen Vaterland,* asked the question, " What is the fatherland of the German? ", and in answer said,

> The whole of Germany it must be,
> As far as the German mother-tongue sounds.[4]

Schenkendorf celebrated the German language in the poem *Muttersprache* (1814) which began with the lines,

> Mother-language, mother-tongue!
> O how winsome, thou, and sweet![5]

Noteworthy also is the fact that with his essay *Ueber den*

---

[1] *Ibid.*

[2] *Werke,* vol. v (Leipzig, 1910), p. 564.

[3] Cited in Verschoor, A. D., *Die ältere deutsche Romantik und die Nationalidee* (Amsterdam, 1928), p. 54.

[4] *Gedichte,* vol. iv (Leipzig, 1892), p. 20.

[5] Schenkendorf, M. von, *Sämmtliche Gedichte* (Berlin, 1837), p. 266.

Usprung der Spache (1772) and other writings, and by continually advocating the cultivation and study of the mother-
tongue, Herder laid the foundations, although they were
rudimentary, for Germanic philology. Rudolf von Raumer
writes in his *Geschichte der germanischen Philologie,* " It
was the epoch-making views of Hamann and Herder which
exercised the greatest influence upon the development of
Germanic philology ".[1] He goes on to say that the influence of Hamann was indirect in that Herder sowed many
seeds which he received from Hamann. " Where, however,
it is a question of a direct and comprehensive influence upon
the science of Germanic philology", Raumer continues,
" there we must preferably side with Herder ". The ideas
which Herder expressed in a fragmentary way in his first
larger writings were in the following years developed by him
in an ever more profound and comprehensive manner. In
the essay *Ueber den Ursprung der Sprache* it is not only the
rejection of the divine origin of language, but rather the
manner in which Herder proved the origin of language that
was to be of incalculable influence upon Germanic philology.
In 1773 Lavater wrote to J. G. Zimmermann, " Have you
read Herder's *Ursprung der Sprache?* If you have not done
so, go and sell all your books and buy this book—and mark
that no such thing has ever happened in Germany hitherto,
and that a great prophet has arisen among us and true heav-
enly wisdom would again visit us ".[2] Herder's call for
men to study and write the history of the German language
was answered by Jacob Grimm who published his *Deutsche
Grammatik* in 1819. This was followed several decades
later by the appearance of the famous *Wörterbuch* of the
Grimm brothers. Walking in the path which Herder had
charted Friedrich Bopp (1791-1867) became the founder

[1] (Munich, 1870), pp. 276-77.
[2] *Nachlass,* vol. ii, p. 331.

of comparative philology.[1] Herder's wish for a "Johnson who would do for the German language what he did for his "[2] might be said to have been fulfilled by the appearance of Wilhelm von Humboldt. Humboldt was profoundly influenced by Herder's writings.[3] He read Herder's *Ursprung der Sprache* and the *Ideen* soon after their publication and at a later time said, " I love Herder's writings very much and esteem him highly also as a man ".[2] Due, at least in part, to influences emanating from Herder, Fichte and his followers championed the idea that a vital and lasting culture must rest on the bed-rock of the mother tongue.[5] Adelung borrowed many ideas on the origin and development of language from Herder and incorporated them with but slight modification in his *Grammatisch-kritisches Wörterbuch der hochdeutschen Mundart* (1774-1786).[6] Also the *Kulturgeschichte* (1782) of Adelung is built up in part on ideas expressed by Herder.[7] One might

[1] See Martin, E., "Zur Geschichte der deutschen Sprache", in *Zeitschrift des allgemeinen deutschen Sprachvereins*, vol. xxi (1902), pp. 1-11.

[2] i, 217.

[3] In his zeal for Humboldt, Steinthal, himself an enthusiastic follower and developer of Humboldtian views, most emphatically denied any indebtedness on Humboldt's part to Herder. See Steinthal, H., *Der Ursprung der Sprache* (Berlin, 1858), p. 12. This contention, however, has been disproved by several writers. See, for example, Sapir, E., *Herders Ursprung der Sprache*, in *Modern Philology*, vol. v (1907), pp. 109-42, and also Schultz, W., "Das Erlebnis der Individualität bei Wilhelm von Humboldt", in *Deutsche Vierteljahrschrift für Literaturwissenschaft und Geistesgeschichte*, vol. vii (1929), p. 656.

[4] W. von Humboldt's *Werke*, vol. vii (Berlin, 1908), p. 372.

[5] See, for example, Fichte's *Werke*, vol. v (Leipzig, 1910), p. 425; also Wundt, M., *Fichte Forschungen* (Stuttgart, 1929), p. 93.

[6] See *Allgemeine Deutsche Biographie*, vol. i (Leipzig, 1875), p. 83.

[7] *Versuch einer Geschichte der Kultur des menschlichen Geschlechts* (Leipzig, 1782). For influence of Herder see especially pp. 9, 10, 12, 20 *et seq.*

say, then, that Herder aroused a wide interest in the origin and development of language. As among the Czechs, the Bulgars and the Finns at a later time this interest in linguistic and literary studies stimulated national ideals also among the German people.[1]

If then, on the one hand, it is established that Herder was instrumental in arousing a wide interest in the cultivation and use of High German as the foundation of German culture, and, on the other, that a common language is a factor of the greatest importance in the development of national sentiment, national ideals and national aspirations, the importance of Herder in the development of nationalism in Germany through his efforts in behalf of the German language, both directly and indirectly, becomes immediately apparent.

[1] See Koch, M., *Nationalität und Nationallitteratur* (Berlin, 1891), p. 6 *et seq.*; Joseph, B., *Nationality: Its Nature and Purpose* (New Haven, 1929), pp. 54-70.

CHAPTER VI

NATIONALITY AND LITERATURE

I.

GERMAN literature was an effective agent in welding together the diverse peoples of Germany. It provided a point of contact during a time of political and economic division and also created the demand for political and economic unity. It created common characters which tended to draw the German people together. Moreover, it became the vehicle of national traditions; it voiced the national hopes of the German people and inspired them to further the interests of their nationality. In a word, it assisted in awakening to life in Germany the dormant national feeling.[1]

The golden age of German literature, however, was not ushered in until the last half of the eighteenth century. The favorite forms of German literature in the seventeenth and in the larger part of the eighteenth century are characterized by a dull formalism. Since the second half of the sixteenth century German literature had gradually become barren of national feeling, and, in regard to content, had lost touch with the life of the people. Hence the literature of this period, with few exceptions, was a spiritless and meaningless mass of words compiled according to formal rules or copied from foreign models. Opitz in the seventeenth and Gottsched in the early eighteenth century were the leaders and the most

---

[1] Joseph, *op. cit.*, p. 113 *et seq.*; Rose, J. H., *Nationality in Modern History* (New York, 1906), p. 47 *et seq.*; Koch, *op. cit., passim.*

representative types of this tendency.   Both were earnest in
their endeavors to raise German literature to a level with
the literatures of England and France.   Neither felt, however, that the German writers were capable of producing
original works by themselves.   Both believed that the foundation for this national literature must be laid through imitation.   The former advocated the imitation of French and
Latin writers, and the latter prescribed the French writers
of the age of Louis XIV to his countrymen as models of
imitation.[1]   " Perhaps we will be so successful ", Gottsched
said, " that in a short time we will no longer need the help
of our neighbors ".[2]   Opitz felt that there was in German
literature a great lack of epithets and suggested that a selection be made from Greek and Latin literature to fill the need.
Gottsched, on the other hand, sought to improve the German
stage by translating, in conjunction with his wife, many
French dramas into German.   In their endeavors to improve
German poetry both concentrated their attention on formal
rules for the composition of poetry.   In his *Buch von der
deutschen Poeterey* (1624) Opitz laid down the laws for the
composition of poetry and about a century later Gottsched
gave expression to his ideas in his *Critische Dichtkunst*.
The rules and ideas set forth by these men were authoritative to most writers and established the prevailing literary
taste of the period.   The spiritless formalism which they
made fashionable is to be found in most of the writings of
this period including the works of such authors as Philip von
Zesen, Buchholz, Ziegler, Lohenstein, Gryphius, Hoffmanns-

---

[1] See Braitmeier, F., *Geschichte der poetischen Theorie und Kritik*
(Frauenfeld, 1888), vol. i, p. 134 *et seq.*; Francke, *Social Forces in German Literature*, p. 172 *et seq.*; Gervais, E., *Die antike und die fran-
zösisch-klassische Tragödie: Die Nachahmung beider von Gottsched und
seinen Schülern* (Hohenstein, 1864), p. 32 *et seq.*

[2] Cited in Reichel, *op. cit.*, p. 67.

waldau, Besser and König.[1] In 1740 Mauvillon, a Frenchman residing in Germany, published a series of letters [2] in
which he discussed the question, " Why is it that the Germans have no good poets? " The German men of learning,
he said in effect, are pedants; the poets occupy themselves
with poems for particular occasions and with chronosticha,
and even the writings of the most noted of them are filled
with dull and spiritless statements. " Show me ", he wrote,
" show me in your Parnassus a creative spirit; name, I defy
you, a German poet who out of his own materials has produced a work of some reputation ".[3]

About the time of the Seven Years War a group of writers who were instrumental in combating some of the basic
ideas upon which the literature of the seventeenth and the
first half of the eighteenth century had been built appeared
on the scene. Yet even these writers, Herder alone ex-
cepted, either recommended the imitation of foreign models
or formed their own writings according to foreign patterns.
The inspirations which gave rise to Wieland's works were
derived largely from the literature of France, England,
Greece and Italy. The German people, he said in effect, cannot have an original literature because of their form of
government and must, therefore, use the literatures of other
nationalities as models.[4] Although Klopstock rebuked the
German writers for their imitation of foreign patterns, he
was often guilty of this himself. Lessing, the most influ-

[1] See Francke, *op. cit.*, p. 172 *et seq.*

[2] *Lettres françoises et germaniques, ou Réflexions militaires, littéraires
et critiques sur les François et les Allemands* (London, 1740).

[3] p. 362. Cited in Strauss, D. F., *Gesammelte Schriften* (Bonn, 1878),
vol. x, p. 13.

[4] See Wieland's review of Christian Schmidt's *Ueber den gegenwärtigen
Zustand des deutschen Parnassus* in *Teutscher Merkur*, vol. ii (1773),
p. 176 *et seq.*

ential member of the group, played a large part in the emancipation of German literature from the yoke of French rules, but could not free himself entirely from the spell of the ancients. Nevertheless these men, unlike many of the writers who preceded them, were by no means mere imitators. Their writings, characterized in a marked degree by originality, helped to prepare the way for those who were to throw off the foreign yoke entirely. Wieland's writings aroused an interest for German literature among those classes in Germany which had been nurtured on French literature. After centuries of decline Klopstock was the first to earn for poetry a high place in German life. His poems are, as it were, harbingers of the new national spirit in German literature.[1] Lessing's *Minna von Barnhelm* painted a picture of German life and was prophetic of the new gospel of German literature which was soon to be heard. By undermining the influence of the rules of French classicism which up to his time had been authoritative in literary matters, Lessing cleared the path for the onward march of Herder's ideas. With these writers, it may be said, the period of transition and preparation for a new national literature came to an end, and to Herder, if to any one individual, credit may be given for ushering a new spirit, the national spirit, into German literature.

Vital and lasting literature, according to Herder, is the expression of the national soul conditioned by environment and tradition. As such it is the reflex of the life of the group, a mirror of its joys and sorrows, its hopes and disappointments, its faults and virtues; it is a true picture of the characteristics of the group and the embodiment of its highest ideals. In brief, it is the revelation of the whole soul of the nationality.[2] Hence it is not solely the expres-

[1] See Adler, F., *Herder and Klopstock* (New York, 1909), p. 58 *et seq.*
[2] i, 262; ii. 160; ix, 318; xi, 175; xviii, 58, 136.

sion of the individual, it is rather the expression of the higher organism of which the individual is an epitome. The individual must permit the soul of the nationality to speak through him if the literature which he produces is to be significant, and only in the measure in which it is rooted in the life of the nationality can a literary product become a vital and permanent influence.[1] The chief criterion, then, of a literary work is, to what degree does it reveal the spirit of the age in which it was written and of the nationality for which it was written? The greatest authors of the past, Herder observed, were usually the greatest national authors, for thy knew how to portray the spirit of their age and the mode of thought of their nationality. They were great because they wrote for and of their age and nationality.[2]

This idea that vital and lasting literature is the expression of the entire national personality as it was molded by its environment Herder illustrated with great force. In the *Fragmente,* his first great work, for example, he wrote:

The Greek, Roman, oriental and bardic poets of ancient times— how they were stimulated by the spirit of their nationality, of their age and of their language! Especially the Greek poets, historians, philosophers,—how prominent is their national and temporal mode of thought! Almost every one is excellent in the degree to which he drew from his age, his nationality and his language, and almost every one was also the favorite of his nationality and the god of his age to the same degree.[3]

The treatise *Aelteste Urkunde des Menschengeschlechts* rests on the fundamental idea that the poetry of the Old Testament, the story of Creation, the story of the flood and the

[1] xii, 56; ii, 40, 160.
[2] ii, 160; iv, 425; xi, 175.
[3] ii, 160. See also i, 262.

story of Moses must be regarded in the light of the national character of the Hebrew people if they are to be understood.[1] In the essay *Vom Geist der Ebräischen Poesie* he stated that Hebrew poetry is the natural expression of the Hebrew nationality.[2] The writings of Homer, Pindar, Sophocles and Shakespeare, he wished to impress upon the authors of his time, were characteristic of their respective nationalities. They reflected the life which surrounded the authors. These men wrote about the things which they saw and heard. Therein lies their importance for all time.[3] " The poetry of the Arabians ", he stated in *Blumen aus morgenländischen Dichtern,* " sprouted from a peculiar root, and is the pure expression of the nationality which composed it, of its language, its mode of life, its religion and its mode of perception.[4]

This idea, that genuine literature is the expression of the national soul and that literature is significant only in so far as the author permits the national soul to work through him, Herder wished to impress upon those writers who felt that the imitation of the classical writers was the only sure method of raising German literature to a level with the literature of France or England. Many of the writers of Herder's day, and some who came after him, were filled with the hope that a new Hellenic life would blossom forth in Germany, and in order that this might come about, they set up Greek poetry and art as the goal of German poetry and art. Klopstock, Winckelmann and Lessing, for example tried to make Greek poetry and art the standard according to which the productions of German writers were to be measured. " The only way for us to attain greatness, nay

---

[1] vi, 197 *et seq.*

[2] x, 213 *et seq.*

[3] ix, 543-44.

[4] xvi, 13. See also iv, 357 *et seq.*; 425 *et seq.*; v, 214; viii, 208; xi, 247.

to become inimitable ", Winckelmann wrote, " is to imitate the ancients, in particular the Greeks ".[1] Of this tendency Korff says:

Every important or minor poet of the time was either like Klop-stock a modern Homer, like Willamov a German Pindar, like Uz a new Anacreon, like Gleim a new Tyrtaeus, like Gessner a risen Theocritus or even like the worthy Madam Karsch a modern Sappho, and his whole worth was evaluated according to the measure in which he approximated or even excelled his model.[2]

The German writers not only imitated the style, but they also used the ideas and narratives of their prototypes. Thus Hagedorn, for example, used the Greek gods in his fables. Lessing, too, introduced the ancient gods into his fables, as, for example, in *Zeus und das Pferd*.[3] Willamov, Gleim, Gessner, Gerstenberg and Ramler made wide use of classical mythology. Generally speaking, Greek art and literature were regarded as the absolute standard of all time by the German writers of this group.[4]

Despite the feeling that Greek culture was the most finished that had as yet appeared upon the earth Herder tried desperately to dispel the dream of making Germany a new Greece. In the *Abhandlung über die Ode,* one of his earliest writings, he vigorously attacked those who wished to make Greek poetry the standard according to which all other poetry was to be judged and evaluated.[5] The main theme

---

[1] Cited in Vaughan, *The Romantic Revolt,* p. 196. In general, see Hettner, *Geschichte der deutschen Literatur im achtzehnten Jahrhundert,* part iii; Lehmann, *Die deutschen Klassiker,* p. 50 *et seq.*

[2] *Geist der Goethezeit,* vol. i, p. 147.

[3] *Sämmtliche Schriften,* Lachmann-Muncker ed., vol. i, p. 197.

[4] Strich, F., *Die Mythologie in der deutschen Literatur* (Halle, 1910), vol. i, p. 34 *et seq.* See also Herder, *Werke,* vol. i, p. 296.

[5] LB, vol. i, pt. i, p. 61.

of the *Fragmente* is opposition to the imitation of the classical writers. Here Herder attempted to show those writers
who saw in the imitation of the Greeks the panacea for all
the ills which were afflicting the literature of Germany, first,
that for natural reasons it was impossible for them to imitate
the classical writers with any degree of success; secondly,
that even if they did succeed in producing something which
outwardly resembled the writings of the classical authors, the
product would be an imitation and not genuine literature;
and thirdly, that the very fact that they were endeavoring to
imitate the writings of the classical authors was a hindrance
to the development of a genuine literature. Classical literature, he told them in substance, is the product of national and
cultural factors which differ widely from those of eighteenth-century Germany. The Greek writers were nothing
more and nothing less than national; they " wrote with a
Greek pen, on Greek faith, for Greece ".[1] " Homer,
Aeschylus and Sophocles ", he wrote, " could never have
written their works in German in our environment, in our
times and with our present customs ".[2] Even though one
might succeed in producing copies which were outwardly similar to the original model, the relation of the copy to the original would be about the same as that of a wooden horse to a
real horse. In a work of imitation the true poetic spirit is
necessarily absent, for the product is not the expression of
the true poetic spirit, but of the spirit of an imitator. Moreover, the very fact that a writer concentrates upon the classical works paralyzes his power of self-expression. Hence
the constant efforts of German writers to copy foreign,
especially Greek, models had had but one result: the intellectual life of the German people had been adulterated until the

[1] ii, 113 *et seq.*
[2] i, 297.

original German spirit was hardly recognizable. Herder execrated the word " classical " because, as he stated, it had crowded out all genuine culture and had deprived the fatherland of " many blossoming fruit trees ".[1] " Curses," he wrote, " on the German mania for imitation and thoughtless writing ".[2]

In the same spirit he opposed the imitation of the French. " Why is it ", he wrote, " that this imitation of the French, whose national character is so different from ours, has become so terribly predominant? "[3] " Will you with your German mode of thought which has coalesced with your mother-tongue, will you beg your way through French literature with your German slowness." [4] " If the spirit of Germany had only, like the Italian spirit, resisted the French spirit! ".[5]

Another point which, generally speaking, the writers of eighteenth-century Germany before Herder stressed was that the composition of poetry must be guided by certain arbitrary rules. Their attempts to develop German literature was based on the idea that there is an arbitrary set of rules which must be universally acknowledged. In general, it was the policy of the period of the Enlightenment, with its mechanical conceptions, to reduce, if possible, everything to rational rules, to regard everything as motivated by reason.

[1] i, 208.

[2] i, 254. Herder came back repeatedly to this question in his later writings. See iii, 26, 202; v, 209, 213, 491; ix, 543; xiv, 98-99; xviii, 150. In like manner he inveighed against the imitation of the literatures of other nationalities and peoples. See i, 258, 382-83; v, 635; xi, 292; xviii, 134-35.

[3] xviii, 333.

[4] iv, 435.

[5] xxiii, 14. See also i, 254, 261, 278, 362, 382; iv, 280; v, 360; xiv, 141; xviii, 333; xxxii, 151.

Opitz, as we have seen, in his *Buch von der deutschen Poet-erey,* set up as a standard of correctness certain rules which he had gathered from a study of the masterpieces of poetry. No more than strict conformity to these rules was required of a poet. These laws which he laid down remained the accepted literary canon until the appearance of Gottsched's *Critische Dichtkunst.* Based essentially on Boileau's *Art poétique,* it also emphasized mechanical methods of writing poetry, but with a stronger leaning toward French rules. Gottsched was horrified at the idea of writing poetry without arbitrary rules. Lessing, it is true, rejected the French canons of poetry, but instead of banishing all arbitrary rules from literature, he pointed his generation back to the teachings of Aristotle. In the seventeenth *Litteraturbrief* he stated, for example, that judged by the standards of the ancients Shakespeare was greater than Corneille, and the former would therefore be a much better model for emulation than the French writers.[1] Even though Lessing was more liberal in the application of the rules, he still belonged to that group which held that art is regulated by rational rules or that poetry is " the imitation of classical models ".[2]

Herder revolted against the authority of arbitrary rules and conventional forms, both in art and in life. He not only rejected the French poetical rules, as did Lessing, but he rejected all rules. It was he who opened in Germany the controversy of spontaneity *versus* arbitrary rules. Like Rousseau, Herder was impatient of all rules and restrictions except those imposed by nature, and he, therefore, insisted that to be genuine a literary product must be the spontaneous expression of the national soul. What men express instinctively was for him of infinitely greater value than that

[1] *Sämmtliche Schriften,* Lachmann-Muncker ed., vol. viii, p. 43.

[2] See, for example, the last article of the *Hamburgische Dramaturgie* in *Werke,* vol. x, p. 214 *et seq.* In general, see Korff, *op. cit.,* p. 144 *et seq.*

which they produce by deliberate effort according to arbitrary rules. Conventional rules and arbitrary regulations, he believed, interfere with the spontaneity of the national soul and retard the progress of the national group toward the coveted goal of humanity.[1] " The expression of poetry ", he wrote, " must be in harmony with the times, the customs, the mode of thought of a nationality. The description must be suitable to the deed itself; the mode of expression is regulated by the inner feeling ".[2] Herder wished to free German literature from the restrictions of conventional and artificial rules, so that the German writers could give expression to the " inner feelings ". He desired German literature to be the unreflective expression of the heart, for the greatest writers and poets, he stated, as for example Luther, spoke " from the heart " and not " from the head ".[3] Literary productions based on arbitrary rules, he tried to impress upon the German writers, lack the essential element which gives to the poet's work the true stamp of genius.[4] " If Homer and Sophocles, Ossian and Shakespeare, Milton and Dante had been professors who taught the art of poetry or had been paid princely sums for their poetry ", he wrote, " they would hardly have become what they are ".[5] " The artful use of rules by them was not artifice, but nature ".[6] Homer, he said in substance, did not make up his mind to write poetry according to the rules of Aristotle. He described what he saw and had seen, and sang about those things which he heard. " His rhapsodies are, so to speak,

[1] v, 214 *et seq.*; viii, 174 *et seq.*; xviii, 134.

[2] xi, 176.

[3] x, 320; v, 182 *et seq.*

[4] ii, 98, 156; iii, 94, 157, 438; viii, 208; ix, 329, 530; xviii, 138 *et seq.*; xxix, 230, 234, 258; xxxii, 234.

[5] viii, 216.

[6] v, 211.

impromptus".[1] Shakespeare, whose writings are excellent examples of originality and spontaneity, he stated, was not guided by arbitrary rules in his writings.[2]

In opposition to the spirit of imitation which was rampant in his day, it was Herder's deliberate aim to foster the creation of a literature which would come from and give expression to the spirit of the German nationality. When he was but little more than twenty he told the German people in unmistakable words how to develop a literature which in influence would equal that of the other nationalities, and during the rest of his life he did not grow weary of entreating them to produce it. He desired a national literature which would be characteristic of the German nationality in both form and content. " Let us be characteristic writers ", he said, " characteristic of our nationality, our subject and our language, and posterity may decide whether or not we are classical ".[3] " Let us awaken emulators, not imitators. The better we know the ancients, the less we will plunder them ".[4] The Greeks, he said in substance, excelled because they were original and the only way in which the Germans can attain to their excellence is by also being original.[5] " Of a nationality which has no *national songs* ", he wrote " it can hardly be said that it has a national character ".[6] The Germans are indebted to their heroes and their bards for the fact that the Romans were unable to conquer them. As long as the Germans had bards, their national spirit was indomitable and their customs and manners ineradicable.[7]

---

[1] ii, 64; v, 182; i, 275; ix, 453; xxv, 314.

[2] v, 208, 238, 242; viii, 340, 419, 433; ix, 525, 544.

[3] ii, 57. See also vi, 45.

[4] ii, 162.

[5] ii, 265.

[6] xxvii, 180. Italics are Herder's.

[7] viii, 389.

I am ashamed [he wrote] when the best German authors make so much of favorable comment, for example, in the *Journal étranger* and do not notice the reservations with which the praise is given. God prevent every German from writing for French or English glory! Methinks we will stay on our own path and make of ourselves what we possibly can. Let them speak evil and good about our nationality, our literature and our language; they are at least *ours*.[1]

In summary, although many of the elements of Herder's ideas can be found in the writings of Klopstock, Winckelmann, Hamann, Lessing and others who helped to prepare the soil for the growth of a national literature, Herder's ideas show a marked advance over the ideas of his predecessors and contemporaries.

1. Throughout his active career Herder opposed the imitation of foreign models, in regard to both content and form. Neo-classicism was to him the great bane of German literature. Klopstock, Wieland and Lessing, despite their originality, still belonged in a class with those who held up foreign patterns as models. As Lessing had ridiculed the eagerness of the German writers to imitate the French, Herder regarded all imitation as ridiculous and degrading. In attacking the prevalent neo-classical spirit, Herder, so to speak, aimed a thrust at the last foe that prevented the rise of a national spirit in German literature. His first contribution, then, toward the development of a literature which was to be national in form and in content was that he labored assiduously to clear of all obstacles the ground on which the foundation for the new type of literature was to be laid.

2. But Herder did not stop at clearing the ground; he laid the foundation for the new type of literature. Great preacher that he was, he not only pleaded with the German

---

[1] xviii, 206. Italics are Herder's.

writers to repent of their evil ways, but pointed out the
way in which they were to walk. Taking the words
originality and spontaneity as his perennial text, he tirelessly
expounded it again and again with profuse illustrations
from life and history. He was the first, it seems, to expound to the German people, in a way both large and impressive, the idea that literature is the evolutionary product
of national conditions. Time and again he stressed the
point that the criteria for judging a literary production must
be sought in the environment from whence it came. He
it was, evidently, who put the expression " national literature " into circulation in Germany.[1] He endeavored to
persuade the German people to return to original and spontaneous forms of literary expression. He gave to the German people the positive philosophy which was to form the
basis of the new national literature. He it was, above all,
who gave a powerful impulse to the introduction of a national spirit into the literature of Germany.

The appearance of the *Fragmente,* in which Herder first
stated the revolutionary view that the literature of a nationality is the expression of its entire personality as shaped
by its *milieu,* caused a sensation in the literary circles of
Germany. Although they were published anonymously
because Herder feared the effect of his ideas, the name
of the author was soon known throughout Germany.
Since these ideas were so antipodal to ,the ideas of the
time, criticism of and opposition to them were, of course,
not wanting, but, in general, they were favorably received
and their effect was tremendous. Upon reading the first
and second parts of the *Fragmente* Friedrich Nicolai wrote
and asked Herder to become a contributor to his *Allgemeine deutsche Bibliothek,* adding the words, " I assure you

---

[1] See Koch, *Nationalität und Nationallitteratur,* p. 16.

that everyone holds you in high esteem ".[1] " The *Fragmente* ", Suphan writes, " as is generally known, opened a new epoch in the history of our literature; they became the canonical book of the younger generation for aesthetic criticism, and with the freshness of a morning breeze they ushered in the period of the renaissance of a genuinely national literature ".[2] The literary historian Koch writes, " The author of the *Fragmente,* which revolutionized the old and laid the foundations for new ideas, contributed more than any one else to prepare the way for the golden age of our literature ".[3]

3. By his insistence upon originality and spontaneity Herder probably contributed more than any one else toward initiating the movement known in German literature as *Sturm und Drang.* This movement was characterized by its revolt against authority of whatever kind. On the one hand it was a reaction against the worship of reason and, on the other, against the prevalent pseudo-classicism. The reaction against both was undertaken in close association with the *Gefühlsphilosophie* and the idea of " back to nature " or, in the words of Herder, spontaneity and originality. Aroused by the gospel of emotionalism which Herder preached the iconoclastic group of writers constituting this movement approximated the extreme of *Gefühl ist Alles.* They decried the traditional view of art and sought to free the German mind from the shackles of neo-classicism, so that the German writers might give free rein to the heart and to the imagination. In Göttingen a number of students in-

---

[1] LB, vol. i, part ii, p. 206. See also Herder's letter to Hamann (1766) in Hamann's *Schriften*, vol. iii (Berlin, 1822), p. 369.

[2] Introduction to vol. i, Herder's *Sämmtliche Werke*, p. xxiv.

[3] Koch, M., " Herders Führerstellung in der Entwicklung der deutschen Litteratur ", in *Jahresbericht der schlesischen Gesellschaft für vaterländische Kultur*, vol. lxxxi (1904), p. 98.

spired by one of Klopstock's odes and by Herder's idea of originality and spontaneity formed the famous *Hainbund*. They met in a grove of oaks to celebrate the memory of Arminius, the " great liberator ", and the Teutonic bards. Their great hero was Klopstock who had revived the poetry of the bards. To show their disapproval of neo-classicism, they built a fire and burned the works of Wieland whom they regarded as the incarnation of artificiality. Although the group soon disbanded, the former members continued to adhere in some degree to the basic principles upon which the group had been founded.[1]

Because of the lack of a definite and deliberate plan, the *Sturm und Drang* movement which Korff has styled " the German form of the French Revolution ",[2] was but of short duration. But its contributions to the rise of a national spirit, though mostly indirect, are not unimportant. In stressing nature and the emotions as the sole source of the poet it contributed to turning the German writers away from the ideals of neo-classicism to native forms and subjects. Goethe's *Götz von Berlichingen* and Schiller's *Räuber* might serve as outstanding examples of the new trend. They introduced a national type of tragedy and gave a powerful impetus to the development of a national theatre. In general, the movement was of the nature of a spiritual revival which, as Klüpfel says, " spread over the whole nationality and violently opposed everything that was antiquated, pedantic or unnatural in school, home and society ".[3]

4. In his exaltation of the native and the national Herder

---

[1] See Hillebrand, *Die deutsche Nationallitteratur*, vol. i, p. 300 *et seq.*; Korff, *op. cit.*, pp. 49, 70 *et seq.*; Bruntsch, M., " Der Geist von Sturm und Drang in der Pädagogik des jungen Herder", in *Pädagogische Studien*, vol. xxv (1904), pp. 190-212, 241-246.

[2] Korff, *op. cit.*, p. 201.

[3] *Die deutschen Einheitsbestrebungen* (Leipzig, 1853), p. 285.

was also the prophet and forerunner of the Romantic movement.[1] Moreover, Herder's spirit was one of the motive powers of Romanticism. Wilhelm Scherer styled the Romanticists " that group of German writers which continued to develop and made the most use of Herder's suggestions ".[2] In setting much store by the spontaneous, the original and the irrational, in their interest in the past of the German people, in their historical sense and poetic intuition, in their enthusiasm for medieval German art and poetry, especially the folk song, in their faith in the mission and future greatness of the German people, in their opposition to neo-classicism, in regarding art and, above all, literature, language, morals and philosophy as the expression of the national or folk soul, and in other respects, the German Romanticists were the epigoni of Herder. The romantic conception of art as expressed by Wackenroder is in the spirit of Herder, and Friedrich Schlegel seems to have borrowed the idea of organic growth from Herder. He merely restated Herder's desire for a national literature.[3] August Wilhelm Schlegel's lectures, delivered in Berling during the winter of 1803-1804, might be regarded as the first comprehensive effort

[1] Because of the magnitude of the task it is impossible for the writer to give in specific detail the influence of Herder upon the Romanticists. There is, so far as the present writer's knowledge goes, no work which attempts to show the relation in any detail. Different authors have, however, alluded to one or more aspects of the relationship. Haym has at different times pointed out various elements in the relationship of Herder to romanticism. See Haym, *Herder*, vol. i, pp. 135, 153, 163, 548, 676; vol. ii, pp. 264, 296, 457, 555, 635, 681, 768. Also Haym's *Romantische Schule*, pp. 149, 155, 169, 178, 192, 273, 438, 555. In recent times O. Walzel, *Deutsche Romantik*, pp. 7-13, 35, 40, 43, 48, 75, 84. For additional references see Schmidt, *Herder und August Wilhelm Schlegel*, p. 9 *et seq.*

[2] *Kleine Schriften*, vol. ii (Berlin, 1893), p. 238.

[3] See Silz, W., *Early German Romanticism* (Cambridge, 1929), p. 5 *et seq.*; Verschoor, *Die ältere deutsche Romantik und die Nationalidee*, p. 76 *et seq.*

since the appearance of Herder's *Ideen* " to consider the history of literature, ancient and modern, as a process of social evolution ".[1] Walzel goes so far as to say that the organic idea which Herder was the first to formulate is the key to the romantic *Weltanschauung*.[2]

When the Romanticists sought their ideals for the future in the past, they were, in a sense, walking in the paths which Herder had opened. His estimation of the ' dark ' Middle Ages clearly characterizes Herder as the forerunner of romanticism. Irving Babbitt writes in *Rousseau and Romanticism*:

The delicate point to determine about Friedrich Schlegel and many other romanticists is why they finally came to place their land of heart's desire in the Middle Ages rather than in Greece. In treating this question one needs to take at least a glance at the modification that Herder (whose influence on romanticism is very great) gave to the primitivism of Rousseau. . . . Any German who followed Herder in the extension that he gave to Rousseau's views about genius and spontaneity could not only see the folk soul mirrored at least as naively in the *Niebelungenlied* as in the *Iliad*, but by becoming a medieval enthusiast he could have the superadded pleasure of indulging not merely personal, but racial and national idiosyncrasy.[3]

In shaking off the yoke of classical imitation and in going back to the Middle Ages the Romanticists were endeavoring to recover that which was primitive in their national past. For that which was alien to them they desired to substitute the native. The fact, therefore, that medieval Germany became the burden of the romantic song played a most important part in the development of national sentiment.

[1] Francke, *op. cit.*, p. 459.

[2] Walzel, O. F., *Deutsche Romantik*, 5th ed. (Berlin, 1926), p. 12.

[3] P. 97.

With Herder the Romanticists also shared the conviction in the future greatness of Germany. " With a slow, but steady gait Germany is passing the rest of the European countries. This advance must in the course of time necessarily give it great preponderance over the others ", wrote Novalis, in *Christentum und Europa.*[1] " In everything, especially in the scientific achievements of the Germans ", Friedrich Schlegel wrote to his brother August Wilhelm, " I see only the germ of a great future time, and I believe that things such as have never happened before in the human race will take place amongst our people ".[2] In short, German romanticism owes no small part of its wealth to the preparatory work of Herder, and the influence which this movement had upon the rise of a national spirit in Germany was, to put it mildly, considerable.

II.

Although Herder was displeased with the literary productions of the neo-classicists, he saw in Germany a type of literature which measured up to his standard. To distinguish this literature from the so-called classical literature of his time Herder styled it folk literature. By the word *Volk* as he used it in connection with literature Herder did not intend to designate the uncultured masses or the crowd. " *Volk* ", he wrote, " does not mean the rabble of the streets, which never sings and creates, but roars and mutilates ".[3] *Volk* was to him the " body of the nationality ",[4] that part of the group which had remained on its national foundations

---

[1] *Schriften*, edited by J. Minor, vol. ii (Jena, 1907), p. 38.

[2] Friedrich Schlegel's *Briefe an seinen Bruder August Wilhelm*, edited by O. Walzel (Berlin, 1890), p. 26.

[3] xxv, 323.

[4] xxv, 10.

as opposed to those who attempted to build a culture on foreign acquisitions. It was that part of the nationality which was working in harmony with the national soul. The literature by means of which the national soul expresses itself is folk literature. Hence it follows that genuine classical literature, as distinguished from the pseudo-classical literature of Herder's time, is identical with folk literature. Technically *Volkslied* is the opposite of *Kunstlied*. The latter term designated poetry that was composed in accordance with a set of rules and which bore the traces of foreign influence.[1]

Folk literature, then, is not a definite class of literature which is to be found only in a certain period of the history of man or of a nationality, neither must a literary production be of and for the rabble in order to be included in the term folk literature; but folk literature to Herder is that literature which is the original and spontaneous expression of the national soul. Irregularity of meter and poor rhyme are no criteria.[2] Whether or not the name of the author is known matters little, for he is but the means employed by the national soul to express itself. "Not one of these writers", Herder stated, "*fabricated* the fable which he recounted in book language; it had long been in the mouth of the singer of the people and in it had undergone many changes".[3] "The common folk tales, fairy tales and myths also belong here. They are so to speak the product of the beliefs of the folk or of its feelings, power and

---

[1] See Meier, J., *Kunstlied und Volkslied in Deutschland* (Halle, 1906), p. 3. Herder's ideas on folk literature are to be found chiefly in *Fragmente über die neuere deutsche Litteratur* (1767), i, 131 *et seq.*; *Ueber Ossian und die Lieder alter Völker* (1771), v, 159 *et seq.*; *Von der Aehnlichkeit der mittleren englischen und deutschen Dichtkunst* (1777), ix, 522 *et seq.*; and in the introduction to the *Volkslieder*, vols. xxv and xxvi.

[2] v, 189.

[3] xviii, 89. Italics are Herder's.

motives ".[1] Herder spoke of folk literature as *National-stücke*.[2] The criterion, therefore, is: Did the author permit the national soul to speak through him? Was his mind in harmony with the mind of the group? If so, his literary productions may be included under the heading of folk literature; if not, they were not to be regarded as such.

But how is one to know if the author's mind was in harmony with the mind of the group? If the author has permitted the national soul to speak through him the literary product will be characteristic of the nationality. It will present a picture of the inmost heart and ideals of a nationality, of its hopes and fears, its joys and miseries; it will bear the stamp of the environment in which it was created, and not merely the marks of the physical environment will be readily apparent, but also the impress of the social, political and religious environment. It will be a mirror of the culture and life of the national organism which is responsible for its existence.[3]

During his early years when he followed closely in the footsteps of Rousseau, Herder sought the much vaunted originality and spontaneity in the primitive stages of civilization, in the period when the national souls was still free from conventional and artificial rules and unhampered by an artificial civilization. He found this originality and spontaneity in the literature of that stratum of a national group which had remained comparatively free from the burden of conventions and restrictions, in other words, among the unsophisticated masses whose spontaneity had not yet suffered from artificiality.[4] On the journey to

---

[1] ix, 525. See also i, 263; xiii, 307.

[2] ix, 530.

[3] ix, 529; v, 185, 197.

[4] i, 266 *et seq.*

France, however, his conception of folk literature expanded so as to embrace everything which he believed to be an original and spontaneous expression of the national soul.[1] In the introduction to the *Volkslieder* he wrote, " To be a folk poet it is not essential to be one of the rabble or that he sing for the rabble; just as the fact that it was in the mouth of the people does not dishonor the most noble poetry ".[2] The folk poet is no longer an exotic savage or a peasant, but one who sings of and for the national group.

Although Herder was interested in folk literature in general, he was especially interested in folk poetry. To show the relation of the poetry to the word *Volk* he coined the term *Volkslied* (folk song, folk poem).[3] In the *Fragmente* he used the terms *Nationallieder* and *Nationalgesänge* (national songs) to express the same idea.[4] These folk songs were to Herder " the archives of a nationality ", " the imprints of the soul " of a nationality, " the living voice of the nationalities, nay even of humanity itself ".[5] From them, he said, " one can learn the mode of thought of a nationality and its language of feeling ".[6] He believed that Homer, " the greatest singer of the Greeks, was also their greatest folk poet and the content of his poems was folk [national] history ".[7] In Shakespeare's works Herder

---

[1] iv, 357 *et seq.*

[2] xxv, 323.

[3] The three terms *Volkslied, Volkspoesie, Volksdichtung* were coined by Herder, it seems. See Wackernell, J. E., *Das deutsche Volkslied* in *Acta Germanica*, vol. vii (1911), p. 305 *et seq.* First instance of the use of the term *Volkslied*, Herder's *Werke*, v, 174.

[4] i, 266. See also v, 164; xxiv, 263; xxv, 129.

[5] ix, 532; iii, 29; xxiv, 266.

[6] ix, 530.

[7] i, 298; xxv, 314.

saw the primitive and national associations expressed in an original and spontaneous manner. He was profoundly impressed by the fact that Shakespeare made use of the old ballads, the common stories and sayings, the fantastic legends of the *Volk* in his writings.[1] He regarded Dante as the greatest folk poet of Italy and Klopstock as one of the great folk poets of Germany.[2] The two expressions, then, folk poetry and national poetry were identical in Herder's mind.

Because he saw the true spirit of the German people in its folk literature Herder urged his countrymen to collect it so that it might serve as a foundation for a genuinely national literature. "Am I in error or is it true", he wrote, "that even the most beautiful lyrics which we already have, and have had for a long time, are in harmony with this masculine, strong, fixed, German tone or approximate it. What might we not expect from the resurrection of more such".[3] It was self-evident to Herder that the German people had folk songs that were quite as good as those of the English.[4] He therefore urged the German people to collect their folk literature, to ransack the provinces so that the German people would have a collection of folk literature which would be on a par with " the ballads of the British, the chansons of the troubadours, the romances of the Spaniards, the festival *Sagoliuds* of the old scalds ".[5] " The English ", he said to them, " with what relish have they not collected, printed and reprinted, used and read their old songs and melodies ".[6] " The course of romantic poetry

[1] v, 217 *et seq.*
[2] xxv, 323; v, 200, 203.
[3] v, 203.
[4] xxv, 9.
[5] i, 266.
[6] ix, 526.

extends over Europe; but how about Germany in particular?
Can we prove that it really had its favorite heroes, original
subjects, national and primitive mythology, and that it cultivated them in a peculiar manner?"[1]   "But who would
concern himself with the coarse *Volk,* with their dregs of
fables, prepossessions, songs and crude language?   What a
barbarian he would be.   He would come to soil our classical, syllable-counting literature, like an owl among the
pretty, brightly-colored, song birds".[2]   In *Briefwechsel
über Ossian* he wrote:

You believe that we Germans, too, have more poems such as I
quoted with the Scotch ballad.   I do not only believe it, I know
it.   In more than one province I know of folk songs, songs in
dialect, peasant songs which, as regards vivacity, and rhythm,
and simplicity and strength of language, would certainly concede
nothing to many of those of other nationalities.   But who would
collect them?   Who would trouble himself about the songs of
the people on the streets, in the alleys and fish-markets, in the
simple roundelay of the peasant folk, about songs which are
often without scansion and with bad rhymes?   Who would
collect them?   Who would print them for our critics who are
so clever at counting syllables and scansion?   We would rather
read, even though only for pastime, our modern beautifully-
printed poets.   Let the French collect their old chansons!   Let
the English publish their old songs and ballads in magnificent
volumes!   In Germany let Lessing alone concern himself about
the Logaus and Scultetus and the songs of the bards.   Our
modern poets are certainly better printed and therefore easier
to read; in any case we still print the works of Opitz, Flemming
and Gryphius.   The rest of the older, genuine folk literature
can, since so-called culture is spreading daily, perish entirely,
as many such treasures have already perished—we still have
metaphysics and dogmatics ind legal documents — and con-

[1] ix, 524.
[2] ix, 529.

tinue to dream peacefully. And yet, believe me, if everyone would seek provincial songs in his province, we could perhaps still make a collection, perhaps half as many as Dodsley's *Reliques*, but they would be almost equal in value to the latter.[1]

In the essay *Ueber die Aehnlichkeit* he wrote:

Great empire, empire of ten peoples, Germany! You have no Shakespeare; have you also no songs of your forbears of which you can boast? Swiss, Swabians, Franks, Bavarians, Westphalians, Saxons, Wends, Prussians, all of you together have nothing? The voice of your fathers has died and lies silent in the dust. Nationality of brave customs, of noble virtues and noble language, you have no expressions of your soul from the past? Without doubt they have been and still exist; but they are lying under the slime, are unappreciated and despised. Give a hand, therefore, my brethren, and show our nationality what it is and is not, how it thought and felt or how it thinks and feels.[2]

But Herder not only admonished his countrymen to collect folk literature, he himself set an example by publishing in 1778 and 1779 a collection of folk poetry entitled *Stimmen der Völker in Liedern,* generally referred to simply as *Volkslieder.* In the home of his parents Herder had already become intensely interested in one form of folk poetry, the church hymn. He soon learned to know by heart many of the hymns which were sung in his parental home mornings and evenings. During the same period he also learned to know another type of folk poetry, for he says that the country people sang " old heathen ditties which they could not be broken of singing, so that the priests complained at harvest ".[3] In Königsberg his association with Hamann

[1] v, 189-90.

[2] ix, 530.

[3] Cited in Nunns, T., " Herder as Sponsor of the Folksong ", in *Temple Bar*, vol. cxi (1897), p. 535.

served to increase his interest in folk poetry.   At this time
he began collecting folk poetry, continuing his activities during his stay in Riga.   Some of the folk songs which he gathered during this time were later given a place in his collection of 1778 and 1779.   From Caroline Flachsland who
later became his wife, he received a more direct incentive to
collect folk poetry.   In his letters to her Herder occasionally
included bits of folk poetry and these Caroline copied into a
note-book.   This note-book formed the nucleus of the collection which Herder later published as *Stimmen der
Völker*.[1]   The poems of Ossian,[2] which for a time enjoyed
great favor in Europe, exercised a distinct influence upon
Herder.   They increased his interest not only in folk
songs in general, but helped to draw his attention to the
rich store of German folk poetry.   Many of Herder's
theories concerning folk poetry were based in large part
upon these poems.[3]   But the immediate incentive for the
publication of his collection was the appearance of Percy's
Reliques of Ancient Poetry.[4]   Patriotic motives seem to
have entered in here, for he wished to give Germany a collection which would be similar to the *Reliques*.   As has been

[1] LB, vol. iii, 8, 94, 128, 142, 237, 317.

[2] A number of epic poems published between 1760 and 1765 by James
Macpherson as the translations of the poems of a pretended Gaelic bard
of the third century named Ossian.

[3] See v, 166-67. In general, Tombo, R., Jr., *Ossian in Germany*
(New York, 1901), p. 67 *et seq.*

[4] In 1765 Dodsley of London published a collection of English ballads
with the title *Reliques of Ancient English Poetry*. The editor of the
collection was Thomas Percy. In Germany generally both Macpherson's
Fragments of Ancient Poetry (1760) and Percy's *Reliques* aroused a
widespread interest in the tales and poems of the past. Klopstock, for
example, regarded Ossian as a German. See Tombo, *op. cit., passim*;
Blochmann, E., "Die deutsche Volksdichtung in Sturm und Drang und
Romantik", in *Deutsche Vierteljahrsschrift für Literaturwissenschaft
und Geistesgeschichte*, vol. i, (1923), p. 422 *et seq.*

stated, he was sure that the German people had folk songs which were the equals in every respect of those which had appeared in England. So he went at his work of collecting folk songs with renewed ardor, and in September, 1773, sent the collection to his publisher. But before the collection was published Herder withdrew it from the press because of the hostile criticism of Nicolai and others of the ideas on folk poetry which he had expressed in the *Fragmente* and *Kritische Wälder*.[1] He was, however, finally prevailed upon by Boie to return the collection to the publisher, and it appeared in two volumes, the first in 1778 and the second in the following year. The collection was not limited to Germany, but contained folk songs of many nationalities.

During his last years Herder made plans for further collections of folk literature. After the publication of the first collection both Herder and his wife continued to gather folk songs, and in 1803 Herder put an outline on paper which organized the collection according to " countries, periods, languages and nationalities ". These same factors were also to explain the folk songs.[2] But illness and death prevented the plans from being carried out. Herder also made plans for a collection of folk tales. In 1796 Caroline had already begun working on it. She asked Georg Müller's wife to jot down folk tales just as they were told her, without decoration or ornamentation.[3] Herder himself, however, did not find time to take up the actual work.

Herder's purpose in pointing out the beauties of folk lit-

---

[1] See Herder's *Briefwechsel mit Nicolai*, edited by O. Hoffmann (Berlin, 1887), p. 108 *et seq.*; *Von und an Herder*, vol. i, p. 51. In 1773 the historian Schlözer also attempted to ridicule Herder's interest in folk poetry. See Blochmann, *op. cit.*, p. 435.

[2] xxiv, 263.

[3] xxiii, 286.

erature, and in collecting and urging the collection of folk songs and folk literature, was, to show the German people the means whereby their literature might become truly national. He wished to renovate and regenerate the German literature of his time by immersing it in the national life. He said to his countrymen:

From ancient times we have absolutely no living poetry on which our newer poetry might grow like a branch upon the stem. Other nationalities have progressed with the centuries and have built with national products upon a peculiar foundation, with the remains of the past upon the beliefs and tastes of the *Volk*. In that way their literature and language have become national. The voice of the *Volk* is used and cherished, and in these matters they have cultivated a much larger public than we have. We poor Germans were destined from the start never to be ourselves; ever to be the lawgivers and servants of foreign nationalities, the directors of their fate and their servile, bleeding, impoverished slaves. . . . It will remain eternally true that if we have no *Volk,* we shall have no public, no nationality, no language, no literature of our own which will live and work in us. Unless our literature is founded on our *Volk* we shall write eternally for closet sages and disgusting critics out of whose mouths and stomachs we get back what we have given; we shall mechanically compose romances, odes, heroic epics, church and kitchen hymns of a kind that nobody understands, no one wants, no one really feels. Our classical literature is like a bird of paradise, showy in plumage, pert in aspects, all flight, all elevation, but without any true footing on German soil.[1]

He demanded a literature which the majority and not only the educated few could understand. He decried the fact that the weekly journals, religious books and sermons were not suited to the common man, and suggested how they could

[1] ix, 528-29.

be made interesting for all.[1] Characterizing as false the statement that " it is advantageous to Germany when writers write *only for writers* ", he said pointedly that " the cooks cook for guests, not for the cooks ".[2] " How much further we would be ", he wrote, " if we had used these folk ideas and folk tales like the British and had built our entire poetry upon them as Chaucer, Spenser and Shakespeare built upon them took from them and created on the basis of them. Where are our Chaucers, Spensers, Shakespeares? " [3]

Moreover, Herder wished to promote the solidarity of the German people and to stimulate a consciousness of nationality. He saw that the people of Germany were sharply separated into classes and that the upper classes despised the lower. He saw also that there was an appreciable difference in the culture of the classes.[4] This difference Herder wished to eliminate. He desired to bridge the wide gulf which separated the upper from the lower classes and to create a feeling of unity. He worked to excite a national feeling which would not be confined to the upper classes, but which would be shared by all the people. In the *Fragmente* he wrote:

There [in Greece] this name [*Volk*] was honorable; it included all citizens except members of the council and the priests; now it is synonymous with rabble and *canaille*. There all citizens were equal; they were soldiers, farmers and councilors, all in one body; today the peasant is separated from the soldier, and in general the government from the citizens.[5]

[1] i, 392.

[2] xviii, 204. Italics are Herder's.

[3] ix, 525. See also xxv, 8.

[4] i, 18.

[5] i, 18.

" There is only one class in the state, the *Volk* (not the rabble) ", he wrote in the *Humanitätsbriefe,* " and the king belongs to this class as well as the peasant ".[1] " Because there was no difference between the language of the learned and the *Volk,* between the mode of thought of the high-born and the lowly, Homer sang in the language of the gods and at the same time in a refined language of the rabble ".[2]

As Sieyès demanded political recognition for the third estate of France in his famous pamphlet of 1789, Herder, in his writings, demanded cultural recognition for the masses of Germany. Not the educated few, he told his countrymen, but the masses must be the foundation of a national culture. For the rationalists of the eighteenth century, who felt that they had reached a high stage of culture, Herder had the message that their culture was sickly, artificial and unnatural. To be genuinely healthy and natural a culture must be built on the *Volk,* that is, on a national foundation. The *Volk* which has been despised, he told them, is the possessor of a real untainted culture which is the purest product of the national soul. " In Germany ", Herder quoted Realis de Vienna, apparently with approval, " all common sense dwells outside of the schools; with foreigners occasionally in the schools; with them the most learned are often the wisest; in Germany the reverse is true ".[3]

As champion of the *Volk* and of folk literature Herder's influence was far-reaching. Although the collection of folk songs which he published contained but twenty German songs, it was the first collection of its kind which had appeared in Germany, and Herder was in this respect a pathfinder. His collection aroused interest in folk songs gen-

[1] xviii, 308.

[2] i, 298.

[3] xvii, 210.

erally. With the appearance of Herder's *Stimmen der Völker* a movement began to collect the poetic treasures which had so long been disregarded and neglected. Spurred on by Herder's example, Achim von Arnim and Clemens Brentano published a collection of folk poetry under the title *Des Knaben Wunderhorn* in 1806. The first volume, which contained two hundred and ten German songs and ballads, was followed two years later by two more volumes of equal size. The original plan included as a fourth volume Grimm's *Altdänische Heldenlieder, Balladen und Märchen,* but this appeared as a separate volume in 1811.[1]

Herder's influence through his essays on folk literature was wide. When his essay entitled *Ossian und die Lieder alter Völker* appeared in 1773 it aroused almost immediately an interest in folk literature. Soon after its appearance Claudius wrote that Herder had spoken " like a lover after the first hours of love ", and with a force equal " to the Danube which pours forth its water into the sea from seven months ".[2] Bürger, whose interest in folk literature was probably originally aroused by Percy's collection of ballads, was so enraptured that he wrote, " O Boie, Boie, what bliss when I found that Herder taught in a clearer and more definite manner what I had long dimly thought and felt ".[3] Herder's essay kindled such burning enthusiasm in Bürger that he was moved to write his *Herzensguss über Volkpoesie* which was published in 1776. After he had finished the poem *Lenore,* of which Goethe said that " it was received with enthusiasm by the German people ", Bürger wrote to

[1] See Steig, R., " Wilhelm Grimm und Herder ", in *Vierteljahrschrift für Literaturgeschichte,* vol. iii (1890), p. 574 *et seq.*

[2] Cited in Lohre, H., *Von Percy zum Wunderhorn* (Dortmund, 1906), p. 12.

[3] *Ibid.* See also Laas, E., " Herders Einwirkung auf die deutsche Lyrik von 1770 bis 1775 ", in *Grenzboten,* vol. ii (1871), p. 581 *et seq.*

Boie, " I think that *Lenore* will in some degree measure up to Herder's ideas ".[4] Inspired by Herder's writings and by Klopstock's odes Friedrich David Gräter in collaboration with Christian Gottfried Böckh founded a periodical entitled *Bragur, ein literaisches Magazin für deutsche und nordische Vergangenheit* which carried on the work of collecting and publishing folk literature.[2] The plea for a collection of folk tales which Herder sent out was answered when Jacob and Wilhelm Grimm, to whom Herder was a direct inspiration, published their *Kinder und Hausmärchen* in 1812.[3]

Herder's real influence, however, must be measured not by this or that ballad which he included in his collection or by his influence upon this or that individual, but by the force and importance of the entire movement which he started. This movement can be said to have originated in large part as a result of the publication of the essay on Ossian.[4] Herder was a pioneer in pointing out the beauties of folk literature. Before Herder *Volk* and folk literature were generally regarded with contempt and derision by the writers of Germany. *Volk* was to them synonymous with rabble or *canaille* and the language of the *Volk* was classified as distinctly different from that of the classical language. The latter, whenever possible, was purged of terms

---

[1] Cited in Laas, *op. cit.*, p. 582. See also Arnold, F., *Das deutsche Volkslied* (Prenzlau, 1907), p. 22 *et seq.*

[2] See Haym, *Herder*, vol. ii, p. 521 *et seq.*

[3] See Lichtenstein, E., " Die Idee der Naturpoesie bei den Brüdern Grimm und ihr Verhältnis zu Herder ", in *Vierteljahrschrift für Literaturwissenschaft und Geistesgeschichte*, vol. vi (1928), p. 516; Steig, *op. cit.*, p. 581 *et seq.*

[4] See Kircher, E., *Volkslied und Volkspoesie in der Sturm-und-Drangzeit* (Strassburg, 1902), p. 3 *et seq.*; also Lohre, *op. cit.*, p. 33 *et seq.*

which had been borrowed from the language of the people. Folk poetry, the golden age of which falls in the sixteenth century, had not only been mostly forgotten, but was regarded with contempt.[1] This aristocratic attitude toward folk literature was, generally speaking, characteristic of the rationalistic movement. The theoretical poets of the seventeenth and of the first half of the eighteenth century were too proud to take notice of folk literature; they considered it beneath all criticism. This literature in the opinion of the *Aufklärung* was nothing but the crude expression of simple people and primitive conditions. It was condemned by the prepossession that literature must be purely formal and conventional. The attitude of the *Aufklärung* toward folk literature is exemplified by the attitude of Friedrich Nicolai who, in his *Almanach* which appeared in 1776, put down as absurd the idea that the common people have poetic talent. He scoffed at Otfried, and also at Hans Sachs, whom Goethe had just rescued from oblivion. Even Klopstock's circle despised the unpoetic rabble ".[2]

In consequence of the movement which Herder started the attitude of the learned classes toward the *Volk* changed. They began to see more in the *Volk* than just dumb masses from which they must be separated as widely as possible. " He taught us ", Goethe wrote in his autobiography, " that the poetic art is a world, a national gift, not the private inheritance of a few cultured individuals ".[3] The change which came over Goethe as a result of his association with Herder is easily discernible in the writings which he pro-

---

[1] See Kircher, *op. cit.*, p. 3 *et seq.*; also Eichler, F., *Das Nachleben des Hans Sachs* (Leipzig, 1904), p. 156 *et seq.*

[2] See Korff, *Geist der Goethezeit*, vol. i, p. 133; Arnold, *op. cit.*, p. 14 *et seq.*; Lohre, *op. cit.*, p. 70.

[3] *Werke*, Cotta ed., vol. xxiii, p. 233.

duced after that time.[1] It was due primarily to the efforts
of Goethe that the folk poet Hans Sachs was again admitted
into the poetic heaven from which he had been cast out.[2]
Goethe aided Herder by collecting folk songs for him. On
his travels during the summer of 1771 Goethe gathered
twelve Alsatian peasant songs which he gave to Herder for
his collection. In general, the interests in folk literature
which Herder awakened in Goethe did not leave him to the
end of his life.[3] But the influence on Goethe was only a
fraction of Herder's influence. Following the footsteps of
Herder the writers of the *Sturm und Drang* period glorified
the *Volk* as the sole source of genuine poetry, poetry characterized by strength and originality. To them creative
genius and *Volk* became almost synonymous. Soon after
the turn of the century the romanticists centered much
of their attention on *Volk*. Evidence of this interest in the
Volk and its condition is to be seen in fiction, where the
tales about princes and princesses gave way to tales of village
and country life. Moreover, a revaluation took place in the
whole realm of German literature. The older generation
of theoretic and formal poets fell into neglect. Wieland became the object of disparagement and the writings of Lessing were accepted without much enthusiasm. Instead Hans
Sachs and his writings were exalted and praised, an interest
in the *Minnelieder* became manifest, and many became interested in the bards of the early Germanic period.[4] The

---

[1] See Suter, J., *Das Volkslied und sein Einfluss auf Goethes Lyrik*
(Aarau, 1897), *passim*.

[2] Jastrow, *Geschichte des deutschen Einheitstraumes*, p. 92.

[3] See Waldberg, M. von, *Goethe und das deutsche Volkslied* (Berlin,
1889), p. 23 *et seq.*

[4] See for example *Der teutsche Merkur*, April, 1776, p. 75 *et seq.*; also
Wackenroder, W. H., *Werke und Briefe* (Jena, 1910), vol. i, p. 323
et seq.; and Eichler, *op. cit.*, p. 165 *et seq.* In general, see Korff, *Geist
der Goethezeit*, vol. i, p. 144.

interest in *Volk* and folk literature was probably an influence in the liberation of the serfs in Prussia early in the nineteenth century.[1] Poets of a later date like Uhland, Eichendorff and Heine owe much to the folk song.[2] Wackernell writes, " The folk song became in fact the fountain of youth which rejuvenated our national lyric poetry and which incessantly supplied it with new nourishment".[3] " Most of the Germans poets ", in the words of another writer,[4] " who lived after him, beginning with Goethe, the prince of poets, up to our time, must acknowledge themselves as his pupils; for almost all have drawn from the source which he first opened to German poetry, from the inexhaustible spring of living folk poetry ". Another German writer in attempting to sum up the influence of the revival of interest in German folk literature said in part:

Furthermore, the recognition of the great value of the German folk song awakened an interest in the other creations and expressions of the German folk soul. With equal zeal, legends, fairy tales, manners and customs began to be investigated, collected and studied. The influence of the folk soul upon the other fields of human development — law, state, religion, all forms of life—were recognized and traced. From this, assisted by many other factors, there arose not only a science of German antiquity, not only an entirely new conception of the history of civilization, but above all a reverence and love for our people, such as had long been lost in Germany. The recognition that the individual must be rooted in his own people, that he must feel himself at one with it and with its spirit, and that only on this sod must he ripen to independence, blossomed

---

[1] See Blochmann, *op. cit.*, p. 423 *et seq.*

[2] See Karsten, G., *Herder und das Volkslied*, in *Washington University Bulletin*, vol. iii (1905), pp. 101-122.

[3] *Op. cit.*, p. 42.

[4] Reinke, J., *Herder als Uebersetzer altdeutscher Gedichte* (Münster, 1902), p. 5.

into full consciousness, into shape and into active life. It became evident where they had erred and what ignominious consequences the lack of patriotism had incurred. The feeling of duty toward the nationality grew strong with the love for it. The whole people became engrossed in the idea of marshalling all its powers to regain the independence so nearly lost and to make secure its nationality by means of the reestablishment of its unity.[1]

[1] Benfey, T., *Geschichte der Sprachwissenschaft und orientalischen Philologie in Deutschland* (Munich, 1869), p. 318.

CHAPTER VII

NATIONALITY AND HISTORY

IN Germany, as in France, many writers of the Enlightenment regarded the past, especially the period since the decline of Roman civilization, with contempt. History had little to teach them. The age of the Enlightenment, in general, desired to stand on its own feet; it viewed itself as the wise, the enlightened age in contrast to the " dark barbarian" ages of the past. The writers of the Enlightenment, therefore, desired to free man from the shackles of tradition. Many phases of Greek and Roman civilization, it is true, were held in high esteem, but it was because they were regarded as the embodiment of reasonableness. Whatever in their opinion was not rational had no *raison d'être* and it became a practical ideal of the day to demolish the historical in order to make room for the rational. Hence most of the deeds and achievements of the past were dismissed as inferior to the standards of their time. They vented their ridicule upon such monuments of the past as, for example, Hebrew poetry. The descriptions of Homer were looked upon as being naive.[1] Wieland went so far as to append to his translations of Shakespeare apologies to the " enlightened " public of his day for the crudeness and artlessness of the great Briton.[2] In the opinion of many of the writers of the Enlightenment history was " mostly a chapter of acci-

[1] Heinemann, K., *Die deutsche Dichtung* (Leipzig, 1914), p. 114.
[2] *Uebersetzungen* (Berlin, 1909), vol. i, pp. 10-11.

dents, a chronicle of names and dates, of wars and intrigues, of frauds, and deceptions ".[1]   In the words of Hibben:

The sense of historical continuity and the appreciation of its debts to the past were wholly foreign to the thought of that age. While there was no revolution in Germany, the ties with the past were but lightly regarded and there was a general declaration of independence in reference to all the historic phases of thought, as well as to all thinkers who were not of the living present.[2]

This unhistorical tendency of the Enlightenment Herder was one of the first to call in question.   Although profoundly influenced by Rousseau and by the Enlightenment generally, he yet gave evidence of a profound historical sense which was antipodal to the spirit of Rousseau and, in general, to that of the Enlightenment.   Much of the treatise *Auch eine Philosophie,* for example, is a diatribe against the self-glorification of the Enlightenment at the expense of the past.

The common, philosophical philanthropic tone of our century [Herder wrote] willingly bestows upon every distant nationality, upon every ancient age of the world ' our own ideal ' of virtue and happiness which thus becomes the sole judge and passes judgment upon their customs solely according to itself.[3] Why deceive ourselves with the idea that our means of education have affected this [enlightenment] ?   Why is this ' romance of a one-sided scornful lie ' carried into all centuries and why

[1] See Saunders, T. B., " Herder ", in *Hibbert Journal,* vol. ii (1904), p. 686.

[2] Hibben, J. G., *The Philosophy of the Enlightenment* (New York, 1910), p. 201.   See also Windelband, W., *Geschichte der Philosophie* (Leipzig, 1919), vol. i, p. 545; Schmalenbach, H., *Leibniz* (Munich, 1921), p. 41; Preuss, *Die Quellen des Nationalgeistes der Befreiungskriege,* p. 29.

[3] v, 511.

are the customs of all nationalities and ages ridiculed and disfigured therewith so that a sane, sensible, unsympathetic person
finds nothing to read in almost all of the so-called pragmatic
histories of the world but the disgusting rubbish of the ' highest
ideal of his time '.[1] Nothing appears more important to us than
the present; nothing more unusual and greater than that which
we experience.[2]

Nevertheless, Herder insisted, the past was not to be despised or looked upon as a dark age, for " whatever could
be has been according to the situation and wants of the
place, the circumstance and occasions of the times and the
native or generated character of the nationality ".[3] " Everything that could blossom upon the earth, has blossomed;
each in its due season, and its proper sphere ".[4] " In Hin-
dustan, Egypt and China, in Canaan, Rome and Carthage
took place what would have occurred nowhere else and at
no other period. The law of necessity and convenience,
composed of power, time and place, everywhere produces
different fruits ".[5] Each age and each nationality has lived
its own life and must serve as its own standard.[6] Hence
" we cannot judge everything according to our enlightened
time " and must free ourselves from the arrogant presumption that " every nationality even in the earliest times should
think, speak, feel and compose according to our desires ".[7]
" We do not do justice to any nationality of the earth by
forcing upon it a foreign standard of knowledge ".[8]

[1] v, 555.
[2] xxiii, 214-15.
[3] xiv, 83.
[4] xiv, 203.
[5] xiv, 86.
[6] v, 505, 509; xvi, 395.
[7] xvi, 396; xii, 5; xxxii, 104.
[8] xiv, 124. See also v, 485; viii, 398; xvi, 393; xviii, 249.

If the past is to be understood, Herder told his age, it must be approached sympathetically. Not abstract reasoning, but a sympathetic approach and patient inquiry is the key to the past. As early as the *Fragmente* Herder insisted that if the ideas and events of the past are to be understood, they must be " regarded in the spirit of their age ".[1] One must become a " regenerated contemporary " of the past; " one must sympathize with a nationality in order to feel a single one of its inclinations and deeds as a part of the whole "; " one must go into the age, into the region, into the whole history and feel one's way into everything ".[2] In a book-review of Schlözer's *Universalgeschichte* Herder criticised the author, who was a disciple of the Enlightenment, for not having entered into the spirit of the past.[3] In his plea for historical-mindedness Herder went so far as to demand that the Bible he treated as a historical document. In order to understand the Old Testament, he stated, and to " enjoy these writings in their original atmosphere " one " must become a shepherd with shepherds, a peasant with an agricultural people, an oriental with the primitive inhabitants of the East ".[4] Homer, Herder said in effect, can be understood only by studying the environment in which he wrote and the nationality of which he was an integral part.[5] " If the past is approached in this way ", Herder wrote, " our age will soon open its eyes. We will learn to appreciate periods which we now despise ".[6]

In his demands for a sympathetic approach to the past

[1] i, 137.

[2] ii, 118; v, 502. See also ii, 258; v, 503; vi, 56, 357.

[3] v, 436-38.

[4] x, 14. See also v, 211; vi, 74 *et seq.*; xii, 5.

[5] v, 167; iii, 202.

[6] v, 567.

Herder included the Middle Ages, the period which the Enlightenment considered the darkest and most barbaric period of history.[1] In contrast to Voltaire's contempt for the ages of the Crusades, Herder conceived the Middle Ages as a necessary link in the development of man. Herder, according to his own statement, had no desire to defend the Middle Ages, but simply asked that they be considered in the spirit of their time. It was his intention to "explain them". "How differently", he wrote, "I see those times in that light. How much do I not learn to forgive them! Much of the slander concerning them is actually false" and, he added, in effect, the abuses which have been read into them fictitious.[2] "How foolish to brand them with the blackest devils of your century, with fraud and stupidity, superstition and slavery, to fabricate an army of priest-devils and tyrant-apparitions which exist only in your mind".[3] In opposition to his time he went so far as to say that the Middle Ages possessed many virtues for which his age might envy them.[4] He loved the German literature of the Middle Ages, of the *Meistersänger* and the *Minne-sänger*. "Why is it", he asked concerning Bodmer's collection of *Minnelieder*, "that these remarkable and mostly pleasing poems have up to the present produced so little effect, nay even aroused so little attention in our fatherland".[5] The poetic age of the *Minnelieder*, he said, "is and

[1] So, for example, Isaak Iselin (1728-82) and related historians. See Iselin's *Geschichte der Menschheit*, 5th ed. (Basel, 1768), pt. vii, p. 22; pt. viii, p. 2 *et seq.*

[2] v, 526.

[3] v, 485.

[4] v, 526. At times Herder also spoke disparagingly of certain phases of medieval life in a spirit closely akin to that of the Enlightenment. See, for example, xiv, 462.

[5] xvi, 214. Concerning Bodmer's collection see xxv, 6. When Bodmer

will remain a phenomenon in Germany history ".[1]   In the *Fragmente* he had already written, " Do not the times of the Swabian emperors deserve to be set forth in their true light in accordance with the German mode of thought? "[2] He urged that the legends of the Middle Ages be collected and interpreted, for they, he believed, would contribute much toward an understanding of that age.   " A complete critical study of the chronicles and legends of the Middle Ages ", he wrote, " impartial and honorable, written on the knees of truth and dictated by truth herself, still remains a good wish ".[3]   He also expressed a desire for a history of the arts in the Middle Ages.[4]   So great was his admiration of the Middle Ages at times that on one occasion he is reputed to have said, " I wish I had been born in the Middle Ages ".[5]

Herder not only demanded recognition of the inherent worth of each nationality and age, but he also wished to impress upon his age the idea that history is not a series of accidents or disconnected events, but a continuous coherent development.   " All things ", he said, " rest upon one another and have grown one out of another ".[6]   He spoke of history in terms of a " stream which flows unceasingly toward the ocean of humanity " and " of a drama which is being enacted on our planet ".[7]   He saw the same orderly

published his *Sammlung der Minnesinger* in 1758-59 his star was already waning and the collection was not accorded the hoped-for reception. See Körner, J., " Die Renaissance des germanischen Altertums ", in *Zeitschrift für den deutschen Unterricht*, vol. xxvii (1913), p. 18.

[1] xvi, 214.

[2] i, 368.   See also xvi, 212.

[3] xvi, 389.

[4] xiv, 422.

[5] *Erinnerungen*, vol. i, p. 111.

[6] v, 565.

[7] v, 512 *et seq.*

growth in history that was visible in nature. This development was to him so continuous, so orderly, that not even a
god could change it without " destroying the nature of all
things and thereby himself ".[1] He could see this development in the earliest times and in the most distant regions,
and it was visible to him especially in language, in literature,
in religion, in the history of culture as a whole.[2] The culture of the Enlightenment, he said in substance, did not rise
overnight; it arose through a long process of development.
Progess in history is a gradual continuous development, not
a sudden leap out of a dark past into an enlightened present,
as the writers of the Enlightenment are wont to picture it.
This development is regulated by laws of nature which are
more powerful than all the conventions of man which the
philosophers might enumerate.[3] " Philosophers ", he said
to them, " if you wish to honor and to utilize the position of
your century, the book of the past lies open before you ".[4]

Unsystematic as Herder was, the idea of historical development is, nevertheless, to be found running through his
manifold writings. He gave so much attention to the evolutionary treatment of civilization in general that he is regarded by some as the precursor of the Darwinian conception of evolution.[5] To demonstrate the idea of historical
continuity, Herder wrote the *Ideen*. As has already been
stated, the main idea of this work is the progress of mankind

[1] v, 250.

[2] i, 151 *et seq.*; xiii, 352.

[3] v, 118.

[4] v, 561.

[5] See Bärenbach, F. von, *Herder als Vorgänger Darwins und der
modernen Naturphilosophie* (Berlin, 1877) ; *Encyclopedia Britannica*, 14th
ed., article on evolution; Lovejoy, A. O., " J. G. von Herder, an Eighteenth-century Evolutionist ", in *Popular Science*, vol. lxiii (1903), pp.
229-38; Headstrom, B., " Herder and the Theory of Evolution ", in
Open Court, vol. xliii (1929), pp. 596-601.

toward humanity, and the chief factor in this development is the national group. History is no longer an account of abstract ideas or of detached individuals, but of ethnic groups or nationalities considered as historical, genetic, organic entities. In each national group there is an active power which, influenced by environment and tradition, effects an orderly development or historical continuity.

When Herder, however, bade his countrymen study the history of their nationality, he did not mean thereby only a study of political events or of the deeds of great men. What the writers preceding him had considered the whole of history was to Herder only a small part.[1] The term history must include not only a few lines of human endeavor, but all that the nationalities do and think or, rather, did and thought.[2] "Where", he wrote, "is the history of the German people? Not the German emperors, not German princes and princely houses, but the German nationality, its organization, welfare and language".[3] All the manifestations of the national mind, including language, literature, art, music and religion, even fairy tales, myths, legends, were embraced in his meaning of the term history.[4] Poetry and language he considered the purest expressions of the national soul; they, as he thought, manifest the very essence of the national character and must therefore be studied especially. "Poetry", he wrote, "is the expression of the weaknesses and perfections of a nationality, a mirror of its sentiments, the expression of the highest to which it aspired".[5] From a study of national literatures

[1] iv, 465 *et seq.*; ix, 340; xiii, 387.
[2] xi, 226.
[3] xviii, 382.
[4] ix, 525; xvi, 388; xviii, 157, 384.
[5] xviii, 137.

we learn to know the ages and nationalities more profoundly than on the disappointing sorrowful path of its political and military history. In the latter we seldom see more than the manner in which it was ruled and how it permitted itself to be killed; in the latter we learn how it thought, what it wished and wanted, how it enjoyed itself and how it was led by its teachers or by its inclinations.[1]

He pleaded with his countrymen to read and study the old poets. " They ", he wrote, " are our fathers, their language is the source of our language and their crude songs are the mirror of the ancient German soul and of the simplicity of their character ".[2] " There could hardly be a more patriotic yearning than to wish for the songs of the bards which Charlemagne collected. What a treasure for the German language, poetry, customs, mode of thought and knowledge of antiquity—if only this wish did not always remain a wish ".[3] He never ceased to draw attention to the *Minnelieder* which he considered the spontaneous expression of the German spirit. In them, he told his contemporaries, they would find the true national spirit of the German people.[4] He urged them to search out the gnomic poems of the *Meistersänger,* for they " really contain German wit and sense ".[5] In the same work he wrote:

I give no credence whatsoever to the rumor that the Germans have less feeling than the other nationalities for the achievements of their ancestors. The germ of the old honesty, loyalty and fidelity is still in them, even though in ancient and modern times they have often been led astray and have nearly always been deceived, because of their good faith, by the glitter of

[1] *Ibid.*
[2] ii, 246.
[3] xxv, 5.
[4] ii, 248; ix, 532; xvi, 214.
[5] xvi, 228.

several foreigners. Methinks I see the time coming when we shall return to our language, to the merits, the principles and purposes of our fathers in earnest and consequently learn to value our old gold.[1]

Herder himself saw the dawn of this new age in the appearance of romanticism.[2]

In his endeavors to arouse an interest in the national past Herder also reproached his countrymen for neglecting the prominent figures of German history and their writings.

Just why [he wrote] are the opinions of meritorious German statesmen of former times so enveloped in darkness? The English, French and Italians have dressed theirs in gorgeous attire. In this matter we are almost behind Poland and Hungary. And yet the realm of thought and activity of meritorious, experienced men of a nationality is, so to speak, the nucleus without which it hardly deserves to be styled a nationality, to say nothing of a carefully planned sympathetic political body. The geographic boundaries alone do not constitute the whole of a nationality; a diet of princes, a common language do not effect this alone; nay the last is so different in the different provinces of Germany that when this is taken into consideration, one cannot take it amiss that the schoolmasters still dispute *pro gradu* upon the whole theme, 'What form of government has Germany?' or whether the Germans constitute a nationality. The taunting opinions of foreigners on this matter, even though they do justice to our diligence, our fidelity, our loyalty, are well known. Is it not the smallest debt of gratitude which can be paid a sainted servant that the thoughts which he expressed are not withdrawn from posterity with his activities. The faithful servants will then at least form a chain, spanning the centuries, to which new faithful servants might attach themselves. The century of the Reformation permitted

[1] xvi, 132.
[2] ix, 524.

itself to think aloud about patriotic matters; since then everything has become rank, form and class or, as soon as a native idea appears, it is consigned to the oblivion of the archives. For that reason we have been without a history of Germany for so long a time and in some respects shall not have one for a long time.[1] A most singular nationality are we Germans. Our neighbors boast of their authors and collect their works, essays, letters, fragments with great diligence, regarding them as a precious possession, as a national honor. Thus (to mention only a few) in France the works not only of Corneille, Racine, Molière, Voltaire, Rousseau, Fénelon, Bossuet, but also of Motte le Vayer, Motte Huoudart and others, in England Shakespeare's, Bacon's, Milton's, Swift's, Pope's, Hume's works have appeared; some in such splendor that even the most vain author himself would have been satisfied with them. And whenever a letter, a thought, an anecdote of this one or that one was found, the author was made known and glorified. Our German journals relate, glorify and praise; only in respect to our own merits are we ungrateful, despising that which comes before us in the most comely attire after the most diligent efforts and withholding even from the dead his just due.[2] Our Westminster, I am sorry to say, is the last page of a sordid journal.[3]

In a book-review he wrote:

A splendid edition of Leibniz' works has been announced—but where?—in Paris. We have also just read of one announced in Turin! *Proh Dii!* The greatest man whom Germany has had in modern times, the pride of Germany, whom Germany can set over against Newton, has received neither memorials nor monuments from his compatriots. We leave it to a Fontenelle to laud him and to a Jaucourt to write his biography; Paris and Turin adopt his works so that they do not fall into decay.[4]

[1] xviii, 254.

[2] xviii, 201-02.

[3] xi, 90.

[4] iv, 224.

He also wrote an essay on Hutten which he published in *Der teutsche Merkur*. In this essay he chided the German people for neglecting Hutten and his works. "Hutten's writings", he wrote, "are scattered; no one has as yet collected them. You Germans, what is wrong with you? What is wrong with Hutten's writings that you do not collect them, permit them to live again, preserve them?".[1]

As has already been indicated Herder also asked his countrymen to write history. In the essay *Ueber die Reichsgeschichte* Herder asked:

Why do we not proclaim our history in the same manner [as the Greeks and Romans]? Why do we not make the tone of our voice worthy of our fatherland and time? We have rules aplenty. Historical societies have been organized. Everyone is working on the art of history, but on history itself—but few. And even among the few, where are the Thucydides, the Xenophons, the Livys, the Tacituses, the Humes of our Germany?[2]

In 1795 he propounded the question, "Why have we as yet no history of the German people?" The writings of his time on the past of the German people with which he was acquainted, Herder, with few exceptions, did not think worthy of being styled history. He consoled himself with the thought that a history of the German nationality would be written as soon as it was possible to write one. "Meanwhile", he wrote, "let everyone endeavor in so far as he can

[1] ix, 494. Herder, it seems, regarded Hutten more as a German patriot and as an original German mind than as a Protestant reformer. Wieland in whose *Teutscher Merkur* the essay on Hutten was published in 1776 stated in an editorial note that Herder's patriotic enthusiasm had probably made him oblivious to the fact that only about half of the German people regarded Hutten as a hero. But at the same time Wieland made a plea for a general acceptance of Hutten as a great German mind. ix, 496.

[2] iii, 362.

to write the history of particular states. Möser has shown the way with his history of Osnabrück, Spittler with his histories of Württemberg and Hanover, and others with the history of their states have followed, and as a beginning what more do we desire?" After the history of the individual states had been written Herder desired historians to continue along the path which had been opened and, among other works, to write *A History of the German National Spirit*.

Möser [he continued] wrote several pages on that subject; they contradicted him and stated that Germany never had a national spirit. He opposed these statements good-naturedly in his *Patriotische Briefe* which, however, were according to the custom addressed to the great German Nobody. Since according to the ideas of the Americans [1] every river, every tree, every meadow has a spirit, should not the German rivers and mountains also have one? Let someone, therefore, defend the national spirit against such slanders and show by examples that Germany has since the earliest times had a fixed national spirit in all classes, still has it at the present time, and according to its organization will have it everlastingly.—The writer of such a history deserves more than one civic crown; a wreath of oak, beech, spruce and linden boughs; only — he must braid them himself.[2]

Herder, however, did not stop at telling his compatriots to write history; he also told them how to write it. Since it was most important to him to get the true spirit of a nationality from its history, Herder asked that the accounts of the past be accurate. Leibniz had known and fostered the principle of the use of primary sources, and Mascov, Gatterer and Schlözer had used them in their writings.[3] On the

[1] American Indians.

[2] xviii, 380.

[3] See Lamprecht, K., "Entwicklung der deutschen Geschichtswissenschaft vornehmlich seit Herder", in *Beilage zur Allgemeinen Zeitung*, no. 83 (Munich, 1898), p. 2 *et seq.*

whole, however, many of the writers of the time were still unfamiliar with the principle, or the sources which they used were unreliable.[1] Satryrs, nymphs, half-men of different kinds and other fanciful creatures still cavorted in many of the books of travel.[2] Although he himself did not always carry out the principles which he laid down,[3] Herder throughout his life made many pleas for accuracy in the writing of history. The past, Herder asserted, must not be approached with preconceived ideas, principles or maxims, but the events of the past must be pictured " as they happened ".[4] The facts in each case are to be diligently sought out.[5] " Where shall we get to ", he asked, " if we despie sources and records, etc., and compose beautifully in the French manner? "[6] " The more history rests upon actual facts and data, the more probable it is ", and this with special reference to the history of a nationality.[7] " With all our dressing-up of history for good taste, it ought to be a primary rule to show the reader exactly where history stops and supposition begins, nay even the degree of certainty in every step ".[8] " The history of Germany ", he wrote, " is not to be treated in a semi-Greek or semi-French manner "; it " must be as original as Germany's organization ".[9] Fiction must be ruled out in an-

[1] See viii, 46; iv, 202 *et seq.*

[2] See xiv, 146.

[3] See, for example, xiii, 140, 270.

[4] iv, 201. Compare Herder's demand that events be depicted *wie sie geschehen* and conditions *wie sie gewesen sind* with the later dictum of Ranke, *wie es eigentlich gewesen.* See also i, 290; iii, 466; v, 202, 357, 433; viii, 418, 467; xvii, 321.

[5] vi, 354.

[6] iv, 467.

[7] iv, 202.

[8] iii, 469.

[9] iv, 471, 467.

swering " such dry questions as : How did everyone in Germany become what he is? " [1]   He demanded an " animated account of civil history, in which, uniform as it appears, no scene appears twice ".[2]

For the historians of his time Herder also had the message that the national group must be regarded as the determining factor of history.   Hence he warned the historians against the one-sidedness which would inevitably result from isolating facts and removing them from their natural environment.   He told them that " no occurrence in human affairs stands isolated "; every occurrence " is rooted in the spirit of the times and nationalities and is to be considered only as the dial whose hands are moved by internal springs.[3]

Hence every nationality must be considered solely in its place with everything that it is and has; deliberate isolation, rejection of individual phases and customs will not result in history.   To gather such collections one steps into a charnel-house, into a lumber-room and wardrobe of the nationalities, but not into the living creation, into that great garden in which the nationalities grew like plants and of which they are a part; in which everything — air, earth, water, sun, light, even the caterpillar which crawls upon the plants and the worm which destroys them—belongs to it.[4]

Hence great deeds also were to Herder inexplicable except on the basis of a thorough study of the time and nationality in which they were performed.

A history of the opinions, of the practical principles of the nationalities as they exercised dominion, perpetuated themselves and quietly produced the greatest results—this history written

[1] iv, 467.
[2] xiii, 387.
[3] xiv, 448.
[4] xviii, 248.

with a clear moral sense in conscientious accord with the facts and witnesses would be the real key to the history of deeds.[1]

In summary, living in an age unhistorical in thought, Herder endeavored to turn the thoughts of his countrymen to the past, especially to their national past. Over against the tendency of the writers of the Enlightenment to believe that everything must be measured by the standards of their age, Herder advanced the idea that every age and every nationality has within itself the standard of its own perfection. The past, he told his age, can be understood only by approaching it sympathetically and "by feeling one's way" into it; it can never be understood by abstract reasoning. In his plea for a sympathetic approach to history Herder included the Middle Ages, which the Enlightenment regarded as the darkest and most barbarous period of history. He touched upon this idea in most of his varied writings. In general, Herder urged his countrymen to study the history of their nationality, to immerse themselves in their national past. To Herder, however, history was not merely a summary of political events or of the deeds of great men. Under the term history he grouped every manifestation of the national soul, including language, literature, art and religion. In urging the German people to acquaint themselves with the past, he stressed specifically those figures which had been prominent in the history of German culture. He likewise requested his countrymen to write the history of the German people. So that the writings might portray the true spirit of the German nationality, Herder demanded accuracy. It must be the primary concern of the historian to picture everything as it was. Finally, the historian must regard a nationality as a unit, thereby guarding against

[1] xvii, 321.

one-sidedness which would result from isolating facts and removing them from their natural environment.

* * * * * * * *

In attempting to evaluate Herder's influence through his insistence upon the study of the national past, one must keep in mind that Herder was not the first writer of eighteenth-century Germany who manifested an interest in the national past. Gottsched, Bodmer, Breitinger and others had, in a sense, been interested in the German literature of the ages preceding them. Hagedorn was one of the first to manifest an interest in the *Minnesänger,* and Gleim, Michaelis, Lange and others followed in his footsteps. About the middle of the eighteenth century Justus Möser drew up a plan for the publication of the works of all the German poets who had written prior to the sixteenth century. But he contributed nothing toward carrying out the plan. In 1758 Lessing wrote an introduction to Gleim's *Preussische Kriegslieder* and for this introduction collected some of the old German battle-songs and camp-songs. A brief glance, however, at the work of these men will show that their efforts to arouse an interest in the national past were not constant and did not rest on a definitely nationalist or strictly historical purpose.[1]

An eighteenth-century German poet whose influence in awakening interest in the German past must not be overlooked is Friedrich Gottlieb Klopstock (1724-1803). Although some of his works appeared before Herder began his literary activity, most of them were published contemporaneously with the writings of the latter. As a patriot Klopstock sought nourishment for his patriotism in the deeds and achievements of the early Germans and much of the

[1] Scherer, W., *Jacob Grimm*, 2nd ed. (Berlin, 1885), p. 31 *et seq.*; Möser, *Werke*, vol. viii, p. 201.

material on which he exercised his poetic talent was taken from early German history. In his poems and *Bardiete* he glorified the victories of Arminius, the " liberator " of Germany, representing him as a shining example of true devotion to his fatherland and to his people. Among others he extolled the heroic love of Thusnelda and celebrated Henry the Fowler as a great national hero.[1] In many of his odes and in his dramatic poems German deities take the place of the Greek and Roman gods. By his rejuvenation of the old Teutonic gods Klopstock endeavored to build a new German Olympus and to excite in the German people of his time an interest in Germanic mythology as an antidote to the foreign influence.[2]

Klopstock's motives, however, in turning to the remote German past were not solely patriotic. His interest in early German history might be ascribed to a fusion of romantic, personal and patriotic motives. He found nothing in contemporary Germany on which he wished to exercise his poetic talent. The personality of Frederick II repelled him and because of the political and religious division of Germany it was difficult, if not impossible, to find a subject which would have a general appeal among the German people. He, therefore, went to early German history which he regarded as the age of German greatness and German liberty. But genuine as his interest in this period may have been, his portrayal of it was unhistorical and confusing. His heroes are not living palpable beings, and the mythology which he incorporated in his odes and dramatic poems has a distinct Greek flavor. The outward appearance of the Teutonic warriors is genuine enough, but they speak in would-be Grecian voices.[3] This,

[1] *Werke*, Kürschner's *Deutsche Nationallitteratur*, vol. xlvii, pp. 60, 84, 111, 124, 141.

[2] *Ibid.*, pp. 115, 129, 131, 135.

[3] Scherer, *op. cit.*, p. 40.

it seems, detracted much from Klopstock's influence. Goethe said, " By emulation of the ancients, especially Tacitus, he sees himself constantly forced into narrower limits and as a result he becomes obscure and unpalatable ".[1] Klopstock's writings, it seems, did not have the same stimulating influence as the writings of Herder. Goethe said to Eckermann in 1826 that because of the remoteness of Arminius, Klopstock's " presentation had remained without effect and without popularity ".[2] And yet Klopstock did succeed in drawing attention to German antiquity. His influence in this respect upon Herder was not negligible. Klopstock's odes introduced into German literature if not Nordic mythology, at least the nomenclature of Nordic deities.

Although Herder was not the first German writer to become interested in the national past he was the first whose interest in the past was constant. Moreover, this interest rested, at least in large part, on definite nationalist motives. When Herder told his countrymen that each age and each nationality has within itself the standard of its perfection, when he proclaimed the idea of historical continuity, when he urged them to study the history of their nationality, and also to write history, it was one of his chief aims, if not his primary aim, to make them realize their relationship to the past. He sought to make them aware of the continuity of their past and present and future, to point out the relationships between those living, those who had gone before, and those who were to come. In contrast to the division of the German people and the drab political affairs of his time, he continually reminded the German people of their common

[1] *Werke*, Cotta ed., vol. xxiii, p. 66. See also *Von und an Herder*, vol. i, p. 324; *Herders Briefe an Hamann*, p. 194.

[2] *Gespräche mit Goethe in den letzten Jahren seines Lebens* (Leipzig, 1837), vol. i, p. 246.

past and of the heritage which must be preserved if German culture was to continue to exist.   Only by remaining true to themselves and to their antecedents, he told them, could they look forward to a great future.   The German people, he believed, had lost the true spirit of their nationality and could regain it only by a study of their national past.   Only in the past, he said in effect, could they find the true German national spirit unsullied by the culture of other nationalities.[1] In the poem *An die Deutschen* he wrote:

> Our fathers, O Germany, my sorrow,
> Were not as we now are.
> Read the honorable customs of the past
> And impress them on the heart of your youth.[2]

In the *Humanitätsbriefe* we read, " If any science is a study of humanity, an instrument of the most genuine patriotic spirit, it is history ".[3]   Briefly, in the national past Herder saw inspiration for a new national spirit and a new cultural life, and to this national past, the spring of national sentiment, Herder wished to lead the German people, so that they might refresh themselves by clear draughts and then go onward to a great future.

By iterating and reiterating the importance of becoming historically-minded Herder contributed perhaps more, both directly and indirectly, than any of his contemporaries toward making the German people conscious of their past.   The historical interest of many writers who came after him can be traced either to the direct or indirect influence of Herder. According to Kurt Breysig, " The historical sense of the period following Herder goes back to him ".[4]   Much of the

---

[1] i, 367 *et seq.*; v, 561, 624; xvi, 192.

[2] xxvii, 128.

[3] xvii, 259.

[4] " Die Historiker der Aufklärung ", in *Die Zukunft*, vol. xxiii (1898), p. 349.

interest which Herder excited manifested itself in research, inquiry and investigation. The interest in the national past which is reflected, for example, in Goethe's *Götz von Berlichingen* is due in part to the influence of Herder.[1] Fichte, it seems, borrowed the idea of historical development from Herder.[2] Freiherr vom Stein, whose interest in history was stimulated by the reading of Herder's writings and who seems to have been profoundly impressed by Herder's ideas on historical development and organic growth, was directly responsible for the organization of the *Gesellschaft für ältere deutsche Geschichtskunde* (1819) and launched the movement for the collection and publication of the sources of German history which were published under the title *Monumenta Germaniae Historica*.[3] By elaborating the idea of organic development with the aid of his wide learning Herder familiiarized the writers of his time with the evolutionary view of culture. At the point where Herder left off Friedrich and August Wilhelm Schlegel took up the idea and by them and by others who followed it was applied in detail to the different branches of German culture.[4] Herder's idea to the organic development of the group was further developed by Schelling and applied to the state by Hegel.[5] In general, Herder's philosophy of history and his entire manner of viewing his-

[1] Goethe's *Werke*, Cotta, vol. xxiii, p. 239.

[2] See Gelpcke, E., *Fichte und die Gedankenwelt des Sturm und Drang* (Leipzig, 1928), p. 238.

[3] See Botzenhart, E., *Die Staats- und Reformideen des Freiherrn vom Stein* (Tübingen, 1927), p. 232 *et seq.*; Kluckhohn, *Die deutsche Romantik*, p. 129; Gamble, W. M. T., " The Monumenta Germaniae Historica: Its Antecedents and Motives ", in *Catholic Historical Review*, vol. iv (1925), pp. 202-33.

[4] See Schmidt, *Herder und A. W. Schlegel*, p. 41; Silz, *Early German Romanticism*, p. 5.

[5] See Stadelmann, R., *Der historische Sinn bei Herder* (Halle, 1928), p. 80.

tory were to have the most decisive influence on Hegel.[1] Herder's interest in the past was a direct inspiration to the Grimms, and was responsible in a large degree for their interest in Germanic languages and literatures.[2] Even at a later time Wilhelm Scherer named Herder as one of the German writers who had filled him with enthusiasm for the German past.[3]

In his emotional appeals to the past glory of the German people Herder was the direct forerunner of the romanticists who contributed much to the rise of a national sentiment by their glorification of certain phases of the national history of the German people. Walking in the path which Herder had opened the romanticists did not grow weary of pointing to the high estate of Germany in the Middle Ages and of comparing it with the Germany of their time, thereby stimulating an interest in German history, especially in the history of German literature and of the German language, both of which were powerful influences in the rise of a national sentiment in Germany. The Middle Ages soon replaced Greek and Roman times as the ideal age of the romanticists. The older German literature was regarded by them as free from all foreign influences and therefore characteristically German. Herder's organic-genetic conception of culture as the expression of the national soul led the romanticists to place the beginning of this national development in the Middle Ages. They saw the Middle Ages as the heroic age of the German nationality.[4] That Herder was a forerunner

---

[1] See Kronenberg, M., *Geschichte des deutschen Idealismus*, vol. ii (Munich, 1909), p. 667.

[2] Lichtenstein, *op. cit.*, p. 516. See Wilhelm Grimm, *Kleinere Schriften*, vol. i, pp. 175, 278; vol. iv, p. 439.

[3] Rothacker, *Einleitung in die Geschichtswissenschaften*, p. 209.

[4] See Salomon, G., *Das Mittelalter als Ideal in der Romantik* (Munich, 1922), p. 46 *et seq.*

of the romanticists in this respect was stated as early
as 1804 by Brinckmann in a letter to Friedrich Jacobi.   He
wrote, " Did not Herder study and praise the folk songs, the
legends, the poets of the Middle Ages when the authors of
the *Athenaeum* were still children ".[1]   " If it is true ",
Kieser writes, " that romanticism has unlocked again the
enchanted castle of the German past, so that it could trace the
peculiar paths of the German national soul in the Middle
Ages—then it was our Herder who led the way.   After him
came Arnim and Brentano and the Grimm brothers ".[2]

The interest which Herder manifested in the national past
was soon shared by an ever-growing number of his countrymen.   Friedrich Schlegel wrote in 1800, " The spirit of our
old heroes of German art and science must remain ours.
The German artist has no distinctive national character at
all if he has not the character of an Albrecht Dürer, Keppler,
Hans Sachs, Luther and Jacob Böhme ".[3]   Again,

There is but one thing lacking—that the Germans make further
use of these materials, that they go back to the sources of their
own language and literature and liberate the former power and
noble spirit which, unrecognized up to now, lie dormant in the
documents of the national past from the Song of the Niebel-
ungen to Flemming and Weckherlin.[4]

Novalis wrote, " The present cannot be understood without
the past.   We carry the burdens of our fathers even as we
have received benefits from them, and thus men live in fact

[1] Cited in Stöcker, *Zur Kunstanschauung des achtzehnten Jahrhunderts,*
p. 93.

[2] Kieser, H., " Herders nationale Bedeutung ", in *Deutsch-evangelische
Blätter,* vol. xvi (1889-90), p. 797.   See also Schmidt, *Herder und A. W.
Schlegel,* p. 43.

[3] *Seine prosaischen Jugendschriften,* ed. by J. Minor, vol. ii (Vienna,
1906), p. 302.

[4] *Ibid.,* p. 352.

in the past and in the future ".[1]   In 1803-04 August Wilhelm Schlegel gave a series of addresses in Berlin on the history of German poetry and in them compared the *Niebelungenlied* with the *Iliad* of Homer.   In 1803 Ludwig Tieck published his collection of *Minnelieder aus dem schwäbischen Zeitalter*.   This collection was widely read and helped to stimulate an interest in the German literature of the past.   In the introduction to this collection Tieck not only proclaimed the merits of the German literature of the Middle Ages, but glorified medieval life in general.[2]   In 1806, the year of Jena, Arnim and Brentano's *Des Knaben Wunderhorn,* a collection of old German ballads, was published.   Of this collection Görres said that it " recalled to German minds the true spirit of their nationality ".[3]   In the following year Friedrich Heinrich von der Hagen published his high German edition of the *Niebelungenlied.*   Shortly after its appearance the historian Johannes von Müller wrote to von der Hagen, " The reception of your work is a proof to me of the still inherent sense of nationality which is the only thing upon which we can rest our hopes ".[4]   Jacob and Wilhelm Grimm soon added their contributions.   In 1811 Jacob Grimm published his first work entitled *Ueber den altdeutschen Meistersang,* and this was followed in the years 1812-15 by the *Kinder und Hausmärchen* and 1816-18 the *Deutsche Sagen* of the brothers Grimm.   In his lectures of 1812 Friedrich Schlegel said:

[1] Cited in Poetsch, A., *Studien zur frühromantischen Politik und Geschichtsauffassung* (Leipzig, 1907), p. 64.

[2] *Ausgewählte Werke*, ed. by Witkowski, vol. iv (Leipzig, 1902), pp. 1-22.

[3] Cited in Vaupel, R., *Stimmen aus der Zeit der Erniedrigung* (Munich, 1923), p. xxxii.

[4] Hagen, F. H. von der, *Sämmtliche Werke* (Tübingen, 1814), vol. xviii, p. 161.

Important it is above all things for the entire future development, nay for the entire spiritual existence of a nationality that a nationality have grand old national memories which mostly lose themselves in the dark periods of its early origin. To preserve these is the paramount duty of poetry. Such national memories, the most glorious inheritance that a nationality can have, are a gift which nothing else can replace.[1]

Literary journals were founded for the avowed purpose of reviving an interest in the past. Such a periodical, for example, was the short-lived *Zeitung für Einsiedler*, founded in 1808 under the editorship of Arnim. Among those who contributed to it were Brentano, Tieck, Görres, the Schlegels, Uhland, Hölderlin, the brothers Grimm and others.[2] In 1812 Friedrich Schlegel founded his *Deutsches Museum* and designated as the primary purpose of this periodical " that it assist in bringing to light the multifold treasures of our old language, history, and art; and not only for the learned and for a few lovers, but generally accessible and understandable for all, so that the whole German language, art and knowledge might be imbued with a new life from the original source ".[3] These collections of literature, lectures and periodicals were instrumental, in some degree, in stimulating the popular imagination and in arousing a romantic interest in the past which in turn quickened the spirit of nationality.

Finally, if we accept the dictum of Wegele, the inception of modern historiography can be traced directly to the ideas of Herder.[4] Niebuhr and Ranke, for example, were directly

---

[1] *Sämmtliche Werke*, vol. i (Vienna, 1846), p. 11.

[2] See Körner, J., " Die Renaissance des germanischen Altertums ", in *Zeitschrift für den deutschen Unterricht*, vol. xxvii (1913), p. 22 *et seq.*

[3] *Sämmtliche Werke*, vol. ii, p. 272. Cited in Körner, *op. cit.*, p. 26.

[4] Wegele, F. X., *Die Geschichte der deutschen Historiographie seit dem Aufleben des Humanismus* (Leipzig, 1885), p. 977.

influenced by ideas which Herder expressed.[1] Preuss writes regarding the age of Herder:

German historiography may well call to mind with proud satis-faction to what extent at that time, at the threshold of the nine-teenth century, the historical mode of thought and its offspring, the newly discovered knowledge of the development and inner relation of great historical events, had become potent factors in awakening and strengthening patriotic feeling.[2]

Was not Herder the first German of his age in his endeavors to stimulate historical-mindedness? Was he not the first German to develop the idea of organic growth and also the idea that each age and each nationality has its measure within itself? If, then, it is true that the remembrance of a com-mon past is a poten factor in stimulating national feeling, Herder was indubitably in this respect a powerful factor in stimulating the rise of a national sentiment in Germany.

[1] See Fueter, E., *Geschichte der neueren Historiographie* (Munich and Berlin, 1911), p. 467; Siegel, C., *Herder als Philosoph* (Stuttgart, 1907), p. 14.

[2] *Die Quellen des Nationalgeistes der Befreiungskriege*, p. 35.

CHAPTER VIII

Herder's Place in the History of Nationalism

Herder was neither a political theorist nor primarily interested in practical politics. Political theories and practical politics interested him only as aids in promoting the development of national characteristics. The culture of the national group was his chief interest. "The culture of a national group", he said, "is the flower of its existence".[1] The development of this culture was for Herder the most direct means of approximating the goal of humanity. Again, Herder regarded the nationality as a natural organization, but the states which he knew appeared artificial to him. Nature, which was for him the deciding factor, had, as he believed, created nationalities, but not states.[2] Herder's nationalism, therefore, was rather cultural than political.

And yet it is not surprising that Herder took no specific interest in politics, for interest in political affairs was at low ebb in Germany during the larger part of the eighteenth century. Political matters, it seems, were generally regarded as something outside the ken of everyone except the princes, diplomatists and officials of the governments. The *Wochen* and *Monatsschriften* were full of literary news of the day, but of political affairs of the time they said hardly a word. To Gottsched, who was the acknowledged leader in the literary circles of Germany for several decades in the first half

---

[1] xiv, 147.
[2] xviii, 137.

of the century, political interests were so completely foreign that a diligent searcher has found only two lines which have a political content in the 4700 letters and 22 volumes of Gottsched's literary remains.[1]

Political disinterestedness seems to have been common to most of the greater German writers of the second half of the century.   Goethe, for example, lived through the stirring times of the French Revolution and Napoleon, but only seldom, and then mostly in a cursory fashion, did he refer to the important political events of his time.   Judging from his published works he was hardly more moved by contemporary political events than if he had lived on another continent. Also in the correspondence of Schiller with his friend Körner political events are seldom mentioned.   Wilhelm von Humboldt, in a letter to Goethe from Paris near the end of the eighteenth century, said, " As you know, I do not concern myself with political matters ".[2]   What a wealth of literature such names as Wolff, Gellert, Klopstock, Lessing, Richter, Voss, Wieland, Kant, Schiller, Schelling and Jacob Grimm call up before our minds, but of all these not one was profoundly interested in the political events of the time.[3] It was, then, quite in accord with the spirit of his age in Germany that Herder should ignore political questions whilst attaching much importance to questions of culture.

This political apathy was due to a number of causes growing out of the absolutism of the time.   First, in the absolute states of eighteenth-century Germany there was little, if any,

[1] Jastrow, *Geschichte des deutschen Einheitstraumes*, p. 81.

[2] Cited in Sydow, E. von, *Die Kultur des deutschen Klassizismus* (Berlin, 1926), p. 23.

[3] See Klüpfel, K., *Die deutschen Einheitsbestrebungen in ihrem geschichtlichen Zusammenhang* (Leipzig, 1853), p. 286; Collier, P., *Germany and the Germans* (New York, 1914), p. 39; Biedermann, *op. cit.*, vol. ii, pt. ii, pp. 53, 219.

room for the man outside of official circles to participate in the government. The political life of the time was monopolized by the absolute rulers who concentrated all the power in their own hands, exercising it through officials and soldiers. Political activity for the princes who delegated their power to officials as they pleased, and political passivity for the rest of the citizens of the state, generally speaking, characterized the political life of eighteenth-century Germany. This condition of affairs tended to discourage any popular interest in political affairs.[1]

Secondly, the political condition of Germany, as a whole and also in many of the states, was so wretched that the better minds turned with disgust from the consideration of political matters to literature, aesthetics and philosophy, and the people in general, after experiencing the futility of inveighing against the political conditions of the time, settled down to contemptuous indifference to public affairs. Excepting officials, those who took an active interest in the Holy Roman Empire were so few in number that Wieland. let alone having seen them, had not even heard of them.[2] In a letter to Johannes Müller, Friedrich Jacobi wrote concerning the political situation of his time:

I cannot sympathize with you in the matter of your German patriotism. We are a poor people and I cannot see how conditions can be improved. Common sense is disappearing from our political organization and all its arrangements are becoming so senseless, so absurd, so ludicrous that one would gladly take leave with a ' Lord permit us to pass into the swine '.[3]

Although it would be going too far to say that Jacobi's senti-

---

[1] See Mitscherlich, W., *Der Nationalismus Westeuropas*, p. 184.

[2] *Sämmtliche Werke*, Göschen ed., vol. xxi, p. 252.

[3] Cited in Wenck, *Deutschland vor hundert Jahren*, vol. i, p. 166.

ments were common to the German people of his time, the
political resignation expressed in his lines seems to have
been widespread. According to Biedermann, it was even
considered cultured and refined for a person to be uncon-
cerned about and uninterested in public affairs.[1]

Thirdly, the writings of the time were strictly censored.
What we understand by the words freedom of the press was
unknown at that time, and the absolute princes of the German states did not permit the expression of political ideas
that were not in harmony with their tenets. Religious and
social matters could be discussed within certain limits, but
discussion of political matters except on the basis of the ideas
of the ruling princes was forbidden. Offenders against the
censorship were prosecuted in such a way as to make others
afraid to discuss politics.[2] Hence the discussion of politics
was made difficult, if not impossible, for those who might
have taken an interest in them. Herder himself was re-
strained by the strict censorship of his time. " If the tone
of our books were more republican ", he wrote, " I should
be able to state many a thing more clearly which I now perhaps speak of darkly or bravely in parables and allusions ".[3]
Herder's position as a preacher also forced restraint upon
him.

Nevertheless, Herder gave expression at different times,
though mostly in a fragmentary manner, to his political
ideas. Essentially they were in harmony with the ideas of
the Enlightenment. The state, according to Herder, is not
an end in itself, but it is simply the means for furthering

[1] *Deutschland im achtzehnten Jahrhundert*, vol. i, pt. i, p. 68.

[2] See Kapp, F., " Berliner geschriebene Zeitungen aus dem vorigen
Jahrhundert ", in *Deutsche Rundschau*, vol. xxi (1879), p. 107 *et seq.*;
Wenck, *op. cit.*, vol. i, p. 75 *et seq.*

[3] i, 528. See also xvii, 25, 85; xviii, 356, 554; *Von und an Herder*,
vol. i, p. 164.

the happiness of the group.[1] " The welfare of the group is united in the state ", Herder said.[2] It is, therefore, the duty of the state to establish a harmony of the different powers of the group and to give direction to its endeavors.[3] In his prize essay *Von Einfluss der Regierungen* he discussed the question of the relation of the state to the intellectual life of a national group in great detail. The welfare of a national group, he said in effect, is dependent upon its government. If the government degenerates, " education will also degenerate and with it intellectual pursuits, freedom, courage of a national group, everything ".[4] Contrariwise, the more a government cherishes wisdom, kindness and true humanity, so much the more will the intellectual life be animated by this spirit to pursue the same course. All golden ages of science prove that no example is as stimulating as that set by the government. Hence it is not the best omen that in Germany the government and the intellectual life are so foreign to each other.[5]

Although Herder's political ideas are, in their larger outlines, confined within the limits of the eighteenth century, he anticipated the political nationalism of the nineteenth century in at least one respect, and that is, in endeavoring to make the state and the nationality coterminous. In the *Ideen* he wrote :

The most natural state is *one* nationality with one national character. This it retains for ages, and this is most naturally formed when it is the object of its native princes; for a nationality is as much a plant of nature as a family, only with more

---

[1] See ix, 401 ; iii, 54 ; xiii, 340 ; i, 15.

[2] xiv, 224.

[3] ix, 375, 397.

[4] ix, 313.

[5] ix, 357 *et seq.*

branches. Nothing therefore appears so indirectly opposite to
the end of government as the unnatural enlargement of states,
the wild mixing of all kinds of people and nationalities under
one scepter. The human scepter is far too weak and slender
for such incongruous parts to be engrafted upon it. Glued
together indeed they may be into a fragile machine, termed a
machine of state, but it will be destitute of inner life and mutual
sympathy of the parts. Kingdoms of this kind, which make
ponderous the name of father of the fatherland to the best of
potentates, appear in history like symbols of the monarchies in
the vision of the prophet, where the head of the lion is combined with the tail of the dragon, and the wing of the eagle with
the paw of the bear, in one unpatriotic figure of a state. Like
Trojan horses such machines move against one another, guar-
anteeing one another's immortality, though, without a national
character, there is no life in them, and nothing but the curse of
fate can condemn to immortality the forced union; for the very
politics which produced them are those that play with men and
nationalities as with inanimate substances. But history sufficiently shows that these instruments of human pride are
formed of clay, and, like all other clay, will crumble to pieces
or dissolve.[1]

On this basis he vehemently opposed wars of conquest
and imperialism. Providence, he wrote,

has wonderfully separated nationalities not only by woods and
mountains, seas and deserts, rivers and climates, but more
particularly by languages, inclinations and characters, so that
the work of subjugating despotism might be rendered more
difficult, that all the four quarters of the globe might not be
crammed into the belly of a wooden horse. No Nimrod has
yet been able to drive all the inhabitants of the world into one
park for himself and his successors.[2] A kingdom consisting of
a single nationality is a family, a well-regulated household; it

[1] xiii, 384-85. Italics are Herder's.
[2] xiii, 341.

reposes on itself, for it is founded by nature, and stands and falls by time alone. An empire formed by forcing together a hundred nationalities, and a hundred and fifty provinces, is no body politic, but a monstrosity.[1]

After the death of Alexander the nationalities of his empire

quarreled among each other, and contended together for a long time, until each had established his nest on the spoils of victory. This has been the case with every state formed by such extension and speedy conquest, and supported only by the mind of the conqueror. The nature of the various nationalities and countries soon reclaims its rights.[2]

At times Herder went so far as to wish for political unity in Germany. In the *Fragmente* he stated that above everything else Germany needed an active unity and one capital, such as a true fatherland has.[3] He was sounding a warning to the German people, it seems, when he wrote in the *Ideen*, " The defective politics of the neighboring nations alone gave Rome her advantage; separately they were attacked, and separately they were conquered. . . . No nationality whose state is well regulated can perish even though it is conquered ".[4] In the *Humanitätsbriefe,* he wrote :

Truly our fatherland is to be pitied because it has no common voice, no common meeting place where we can hear one another. Everything in it is divided, and many a thing tends to maintain this division: religion, sects, dialects, provinces, governments, customs and laws. The cemetery seems to be the only place where common discussion and common acknowledgement will be permitted us.[5]

[1] xiv, 52.

[2] xiv, 139-40. See also xviii, 235.

[3] i, 141, 249, 290.

[4] xiv, 313.

[5] xvii, 35.

In 1780 Herder expressed his patriotic wish in a poem addressed to Joseph II:

> Imperial lord of nine and ninety princes,
> And subjects, countless as the ocean's sand;
> Thou head of all, O give us what we thirst for,
> A German fatherland,
>
> And one law and one beautiful language,
> And one honest religion.
> Complete the most worthy cause of your people
> Upon the throne of Rudolph,
>
> So that Germany's sons may love one another like brothers,
> And German customs and knowledge,
> Driven from the thrones for so long a time,
> May together with the strength of our fathers
>
> Return, so that the propitious times
> Which Frederick sees in the distance,
> And did not hasten, may encompass you
> And be your eternal song.[1]

Although this poem was not published until 1817, Herder sent a copy of it together with his prize essay *Vom Einfluss der Regierungen* to Emperor Joseph II upon his accession to the throne.[2]

Since the possibilities for a unified German state were remote, Herder confined his activities to criticism of the political *status quo,* endeavoring thereby to arouse the German people from their political lethargy. In the diary of his journey to France he wrote with a kind of resignation, "We are living in a century of experience, of police, of politics, of convenience, in which we must think as the

[1] xxix, 551.
[2] See xviii, 526.

others " and " in which we are forbidden by religion, politics, the tone of society, etc., to think as we wish ".[1]   In *Auch eine Philosophie* he spoke of the German states as " inverted pyramids " and said that the states of Germany were so completely under the control of the monarchs that they did not serve the purpose of their existence.   " This ", he added ironically, " has fostered the development of that highest virtue of the individual, resignation ".[2]   Civil wars, he stated, have not ceased because the subjects are possessed " of virtue, of the freedom of the Greeks, of the patriotism of the Romans, of the piety of the Orient ", but because they do not have all these and are " thin swaying branches ".[3] As a form of government the democratic government of Athens seems to have been his ideal, but he did not directly hold it up as a model for his time.[4]   Yet one cannot think on the basis of the foregoing statements what Herder might have said if the censorship had not been so strict.

In summary, Herder's age was unpolitical and in this sense Herder himself was a child of his age.   His interest was centered chiefly upon culture.   Nevertheless, he anticipated the nineteenth century in at least two respects.   First, Herder regarded the national state, in other words, the state which embraces the members of one nationality, as the most natural state.   This idea is a long way on the road to the theory of self-determination which the nineteenth-century nationalists preached so vigorously.   This was perhaps the most fruitful element in Herder's political views.   Secondly, Herder voiced the desire, though not always in so many words, for a unified German state.   Whilst others were

[1] iv, 455.

[2] v, 549.

[3] v, 556.

[4] i, 497; iv, 455; xiv, 121 *et seq.*; ix, 365.

working to strengthen their respective German states, Herder looked above the political division of his time to a Germany that would be united politically as well as culturally. He did not, however, present a positive plan for the building of this state. Besides stating his wish for a German national state, his work in behalf of its establishment consisted chiefly in his criticism of the absolute states which divided the Germany of his time.

*   *   *   *   *   *   *   *

Herder was indubitably one of the first, if not the first, of the writers of modern Europe to develop a comprehensive philosophy of nationalism. Living in an age in which nationalities were regarded as obstacles to the development of pure humanity, Herder conceived the nationality as the essential factor in the development of humanity. He expressed the idea which Ranke later restated in the words, " The idea of humanity, God gave it expression in the different nationalities ".[1] Again, as the eighteenth century asserted the individuality of man, and emphasized the importance of his separatism, so Herder, much as Mazzini did at a later time,[2] urged that only in his social context is man important. Upon the mind of his age Herder endeavored to impress the idea that the welfare of the individual is inseparably bound up with the welfare of the group, that the individual can attain his highest self-development only in the life of the group as a whole. To the individualism of the eighteenth century Herder opposed the collectivism of the nineteenth. In his philosophy of history mankind was no longer an aggregation of human beings, but a number of sharply separated national groups. The great theme

[1] Cited in Kaerst, J., *Das geschichtliche Wesen und Recht der deutschen nationalen Idee* (Munich, 1916), p. 21.

[2] See Venturi, E. A., *Joseph Mazzini* (translation of the *Duties of Man*) (London, 1875), p. 301.

" man " was no longer treated in such a way as to center on the individual, but on the national group as an individuality. Although the individual ego was not overlooked, it was regarded but as an aspect of the national ego. In short, Herder propounded a philosophy of history in which the emphasis shifts from the individual to the nationality.

In the conception of nationality which Herder gave to his age determinism is a prominent factor. Herder did not after the manner of the Enlightenment regard nationality as a fiction of the mind, as a linking together of a large number of human beings into an artificial unity. A nationality, as he saw it, was a natural organic entity, and each organism the product of a growth regulated by natural law. Each nationality, had, in a sense, developed as nature had prescribed. The individual, therefore, was not free to choose his own path; nature had chosen it for him. To picture, then, a world without definite divisions into nationalities was to misinterpret the whole meaning of creation. In this respect Herder was the precursor of such men as Fichte, Mazzini, Palacky, Kossuth, Kollar, Obradovic and others who regarded the nationality as the product of an irresistible natural force which was ceaselessly at work molding the members of a group into a compact unit.[1] Fichte, for example, wrote in 1807, " The distinction between the Prussians and the other Germans is artificial, founded on institutions established arbitrarily or by chance. The distinction between the Germans and other European nationalities is founded on nature ".[2]

Moreover, Herder's conception of nationalty was almost religious in character. His determinism was a divine de-

---

[1] See Jaszi, O., *The Dissolution of the Habsburg Monarchy* (Chicago, 1929), p. 248. For Mazzini see *Life and Writings of Joseph Mazzini* (London, 1891), vol. iii, p. 27 *et seq.*

[2] *Nachgelassene Werke*, vol. iii (Bonn, 1835), p. 232.

terminism. For him an immanent deity who governed according to an eternal plan was the directing force of the world. Herder spoke of the laws of nature as "the thoughts of the Creator" and "the language of God in nature".[1] Each nationality was to him a part of the divine plan in history. In the development of each nationality he saw the unfolding of the divine will. Into the order established by the divine will, Herder said in effect, the individual must fit himself if he desires the highest self-development, for otherwise he is destined to sterility. In the degree in which the individual ceases to be the mouthpiece of the group, in that degree will his work be without effect and without originality. Also in this respect he was the forerunner of men like Fichte, Schleiermacher, Schenkendorf and others. Fichte restated the idea in the words, "A nationality is the totality of human beings continually living together in society and constantly perpetuating themselves both bodily and spiritually, and this totality is subject to a certain specific law through which the divine develops itself".[2] Schleiermacher wrote:

Every nationality is destined through its peculiar organization and its place in the world to represent a certain side of the divine image. . . . For it is God alone who directly assigns to each nationality its definite task on earth and inspires it with a definite spirit in order to glorify himself through each one in a peculiar manner.[3]

Herder was also unquestionably one of the first, if not the first, in modern times to regard the nationality as a cultural organism. No one before Herder, it seems, developed the

---

[1] xiv, 245.

[2] *Werke*, vol. v (Leipzig, 1910), p. 492.

[3] Cited in Vaupel, *Stimmen aus der Zeit der Erniedrigung*, p. xxxiv. For Schenkendorf see his *Sämmtliche Gedichte* (Berlin, 1837), p. 268.

idea as extensively as he. A survey of his works will show that he was occupied with this thought throughout life. Montesquieu had in his *Esprit des lois* (1748) ascribed the difference in the laws to the differences of national character. This thesis seems to have influenced Herder profoundly.[1] Winckelmann, in his *Geschichte der Kunst des Altertums* (1764), had regarded Greek art as a natural growth and had endeavored to show how climate, national character, religion, politics and customs, in fact, all the conditions of Greek civilization had combined to produce its art. In Greek life as a whole he found the causes of the growth and decay of Greek art, thereby introducing the idea of organic and historical development.[2] Herder took this idea and applied it to culture as a whole. For Herder not only art, but also poetry, philosophy, language, religion, briefly, all culture was the expression of group life. He regarded the culture of each nationality as an organism and each branch of culture as an organic part of the larger organism. After Herder many came to regard all the various phenomena of culture as the expressions of the national or folk soul, and this soul was spoken of as being analogous to the individual soul. This view was held, for example, by many of the romanticists and by the historical school of law.[3]

Again, Herder was probably the first to preach the doctrine that culture must be national in regard to both form and content. Instead of a culture prepared according to a formula he asked for an original and spontaneous culture built on national foundations. He regarded the national

---

[1] For the influence of Montesquieu on Herder see, for example, i, 21; iv, 149, 150; also LB, vol. ii, p. 488; vol. i, pt. 3a, pp. 380, 391.

[2] Vols. v and vi of *Sämmtliche Werke* (Donauöschingen, 1825). See especially vol. vi, p. 323 *et seq.*

[3] See Kluckhohn, *Die romantische Schule*, p. 130 *et seq.*

character of culture not only as preferable, but as essential. For his countrymen he had the specific message that they must cease imitating the culture of other nationalities and must develop their innate faculties and national propensities if they desired to become a factor in the development of humanity at large.   This mission of national self-development which Herder established for the nationality soon came to stand as the supreme symbol of nationality and gave a decided impetus to the idea of nationality.[1]   It was, in a sense, the idea which Mazzini expressed in the words, " Each nationality has its special mission, which will contribute towards the fulfillment of the general mission of humanity. That mission constitutes its nationality.   Nationality is sacred ".[2]

Herder was also the first great modern champion in Germany of the doctrine of tradition.   Herder's traditionalism, however, was not of the type later sponsored in France by Bonald (1754-1840) who desired to turn back the wheels of time in order to return to a social order of the past.[3] Change as such was not to Herder as to Bonald a synonym of evil.[4]   It was not change in itself, but change to unnatural principles that Herder abhorred.   Progress to Herder meant advance along lines in accord with the innate abilities of the members of a nationality.   German progress, as Herder saw it, lay in developing the peculiar gifts and propensities of the German people.   To Herder a nationality represented historical values; it represented to him the idea of continuity, of a definite relationship between the living, the dead and those who were to come.   The

[1] See, for example, Fichte's *Reden* and Jahn's *Deutsches Volkstum.*

[2] *Life and Writings of Joseph Mazzini*, vol. iii (London, 1891), p. 33.

[3] See Laski, H. J., *Authority in the Modern State* (Yale University Press, 1919), p. 128.

[4] *Ibid.*, p. 137.

fatherland, he wrote, " has descended from our fathers; it arouses the remembrance of all the meritorious who went before us, and of all the worthy ones whose fathers we shall be ".[1] Although individuals pass on, the nationality as such remains, and to keep the continuity unbroken, Herder urged his countrymen to develop those abilities and characteristics which are typically German. In words like those of Maurice Barrès (1862-1923) at a later time in France, Herder counselled his countrymen " to walk in the spiritual footsteps of the fathers ".[2] Therein alone he saw salvation for the German people. He, therefore, begged them not to desert their native traditions in order to build upon those of another nationality, but to cherish the customs and traditions of the fathers and to build upon them. The true spirit of a nationality, Herder told his age, is to be found especially in the native language and in the literary monuments of the national past. The native language, Herder said, " is filled with the life and blood of our forefathers ".[3] In the literature of a nationality, he told them, its whole soul is revealed.[4] These must be cherished above all if a nationality is to reach its fullest development.

It is, then, not too much to say that by opening the door of the past Herder became, in a sense, the founder of historical nationalism in Germany. After Herder urged his countrymen to seek the true spirit of their nationality in the past, it became the task of his contemporaries, and also of those who came after, to delve into the national past for the

[1] xvii, 311.

[2] For Barrès see Guerard, A. L., *Five Masters of French Romance* (London, 1916), p. 215 *et seq.*; Curtius, E., *Maurice Barrès und die geistigen Grundlagen des französischen Nationalismus* (Bonn, 1921), p. 130 *et seq.*

[3] ii, 248.

[4] i, 262; ii, 160; ix, 318.

purpose of searching out the national characteristics of the German people.   The interest in the past which began when Herder endeavored to stimulate a love of the national heritage undoubtedly served to intensify national sentiment and also to make national consciousness more acute.   During the Napoleonic period tradition became a cohesive factor of the German people at large.[1]

In general, the principle of nationality, first developed by Herder, served as a moral basis in the struggle of the German people for freedom from foreign domination, and tended to draw them together into a more compact group. In the words of von Sybel:

Our people, though politically torn asunder, remembered and realized the bond of mental unity and affiliation which existed between them.   Holsteiners and Swabians, Franks and Saxons, felt themselves associated with each other in the same mental struggle, in the same *Sturm und Drang,* in the rejection of everything artificial and conventional, and in the passionate endeavor after pure nature—the source of all strength and beauty.[2]

After Herder writers tended to devote themselves more and more to the discussion of the principle of nationality. Under the pressure of Napoleonic rule in Germany this principle became a dynamic force which contributed in no small degree to the awakening of national feeling.   Schleiermacher, Wilhelm von Humboldt, Fichte, Jahn, Schelling, Ernst Moritz Arndt and others developed the idea in their writings.   Fichte, speaking of the ancient Germans, said:

[1] See Preuss, *Die Quellen des Nationalgeistes der Befreiungskriege, passim*; Verschoor, *Die ältere deutsche Romantik und die Nationalidee, passim.*

[2] Sybel, H. von, *The Founding of the German Empire,* translated by M. L. Perrin (New York, 1890), vol. i, p. 25.

Freedom to them meant that they remain Germans, that they continue to settle their affairs independently and in an original manner, that they, in accordance with this same spirit, move forward in their development, and that they also transmit this independence to their posterity. All those blessings which the Romans offered them meant slavery to them, because they would have had to become something that was not German.[1]

Arndt became the unflinching champion of the principle of nationality which he recognized as the bond of German unity.[2] " Freedom ", he wrote, " is where you may live according to the laws and customs of your fathers and where no foreign master will order and drive you ".[3] Heinrich von Kleist considered himself a part of the national organism. National life became a concrete ideal to him.[4] It was the idea of nationality which fired the imagination of the German youth when Germany was trampled on by Napoleon. In response to the call to liberate Germany from the Napoleonic rule the sons of Saxony and Prussia, enemies in the Seven Years' War, flocked alike to the standards. The feeling of cultural unity, real or imaginary, moved them to stand together in an effort to free Germany and save German culture.[5] " Never ", writes von Sybel, " had so many hearts thrilled at the thought of being German ".[6]

More than this, the idea of nationality soon began to influence political thought. Herder had regarded the national state as a means for the development of the national charac-

[1] *Werke*, vol. v (Leipzig, 1910), p. 500.

[2] See Coar, J. F., *Studies in German Literature in the Nineteenth Century* (New York, 1903), p. 54.

[3] Cited in Joseph, *Nationality*, p. 88.

[4] See Coar, *op. cit.*, p. 27.

[5] See Meinecke, F., *Das Zeitalter der deutschen Erhebung* (Leipzig, 1906), p. 1 *et seq*.

[6] von Sybel, *op. cit.*, p. 37.

shaken off the chains of slavery you will enjoy the possession of your picturesque lands from the Adriatic Sea to the Carpathian Mountains, and from the Don to the Muldaw, and in them you will celebrate your ancient festivals of peaceful industry and trade.[1]

In the *Humanitätsbriefe* he wrote:

Has a nationality anything more precious than the language of its fathers? In this language dwell its whole world of tradition, history, religion and principles of life, its whole heart and soul. To rob a nationality of its language or to degrade it, is to deprive it of its most precious possession. . . . Truly, as God tolerates all the different languages in the world, so also should a ruler not only tolerate, but honor the various languages of his nationalities. . . . The best culture of a nationality . . . . cannot be forced by a foreign language. It thrives best and, I should like to say, only on the native soil of the nationality and in the language which the nationality has inherited and which continues to transmit itself. With its language one takes away the heart of a nationality; and is it not a matter of great concern to many nationalities—Hungarians, Slavs, Rumanians, etc.,—to plant the seeds of wellbeing for the most distant future in accordance with their mode of thought and in the way that is most characteristic of them and most dear to them?[2]

Herder's statements were sympathetically received by the Slavs. His prophetic announcement of the future importance of the Slavic peoples was of no small moment in stimulating a Slavic consciousness. In harmony with Herder's statements concerning the Slavs, native writers pictured them as democratic, peaceful and industrious in contrast to the militaristic Germans. Herder's slavophil ideas were reprinted both in the original and in translation, and used

[1] xiv, 280.
[2] xvii, 58-59.

as the nucleus for further writings. Before the nineteenth century was many decades old collections of Slavic folk literature inspired in large part by Herder's statements made their appearance and were presented to the Slavic peoples as a sacred heritage of the past. Indirectly Herder became an unusually important phenomenon in Slavic literature, next to Jan Kollár perhaps the most important of the time.[1] In 1808 the linguist Bartholomew Kopitar, who was profoundly influenced by Herder, published his *Grammatik der slavischen Sprache in Krain, Kärnten und Steiermark*. This grammar was a pioneer in the field and of the utmost importance in the development of the Serbian literary language.[2] Kopitar wrote in his grammar, "How happy it must make the Slavs to know that their language is studied and praised by the greatest men of Germany".[3] In 1822 Jean Kollár (1793-1852) preached two sermons in Budapest in which he developed the slavophil ideas which Herder had expressed in the *Ideen*. In general Herder's glorification and idealization of the Slavs formed the basis of the gospel of Pan-Slavism which Kollár preached. In lofty and spirited sonnets he called to the scattered Slavs to unite and to fulfill the mission for which, according to Herder, they had been destined. He urged the Slavs to take over the leadership of the world from the decaying Teutons and Latins. Kollár's ideal was, like Herder's, cultural, not political. Herder's influence on Kollár manifested itself also in the latter's estimation of the *Volkslied*. Besides writing an introduction to the collections of Safarik, Kollár published two volumes of folk songs (1834-35).[4] In 1822 Francis

---

[1] See Karasek, J., *Slavische Literaturgeschichte* (Leipzig, 1916), vol. i, p. 170.

[2] See Fischel, *op. cit.*, p. 126.

[3] *Grammatik*, p. 459. Cited in Fischel, p. 42.

[4] For the influence of Herder on Kollár see Murko, *op. cit.*, p. 145

Ladislaw Celakovsky, an enthusiastic disciple of Herder, published a collection of folk songs, gathered from all the Slavic peoples, which was to be a Slavic counterpart of Herder's *Stimmen der Völker*. From Herder he adopted the idea that the true spirit of a nationality is inherent in its folk poetry.[1] The Czech linguist Joseph Dobrowsky (1753-1829) was inspired to do much of his work by the hopes which Herder held out for the future of the Slavs. Hoping to inspire others, Dobrowsky reprinted Herder's rosy-hued prophecy regarding the Slavic peoples in *Slawien,* a periodical founded for the purpose of stimulating an interest in the literature, language, and history of the Slavs.[2] Moved by Herder's writings and example Paul Joseph Safarik (1795-1861) published a collection of Slavic folk songs in the years 1823-27. In 1826 he also published in German his *Geschichte der slavischen Sprache und Literatur.*[3] Francis Palacky (1798-1876), the greatest of Slav historians and a potent force in stimulating a Bohemian national consciousness, was profoundly influenced by Herder. Among his favorite authors Herder held the first place. From Herder he learned that the study of history is an effective means of arousing patriotism and of quickening the national conscience. It was due at least in part to this influence that Palacky devoted himself to the study and writing of history and became the great historian of his people.[4] The political program which he elaborated for the peoples

et seq.; Máchal, J., " Die böhmische Literatur ", in *Die osteuropäischen Literaturen* (Berlin and Leipzig, 1908), p. 190; Jakubec and Novak, *op. cit.,* p. 184; Fischel, *op. cit.,* p. 107 *et seq.*

[1] See Jakubec, J., " Die literarische Wiedergeburt des böhmischen Volkes ", in Tobolka, Z. V., *Das böhmische Volk* (Prague, 1916), p. 55.

[2] See Fischel, *op. cit.,* pp. 37, 81.

[3] See Tobolka, *op. cit.,* p. 53.

[4] *Ibid.,* p. 65 *et seq.*

under Austrian rule was based on Herder's idea of nationality.[1]

Herder's influence reached also to Russia and Poland. His collection of folk songs gave impetus to the collections of folk literature in Russia.[2] In his *Geschichte der politischen Ideen in Polen seit der Teilung* (1795-1914) W. Feldman writes, "Among all the Slavic peoples there developed at that time an ideology of which Herder may be regarded as the most outstanding creator".[3] Casimir Brodzinski (1791-1835), for example, loved Herder as "his friend" and incorporated many of Herder's ideas, specifically the idea that literature must be characteristic of a nationality, in a work entitled *Ueber die Klassizität und den Romantismus* (1818). He also proclaimed the importance of national traditions and of popular elements for literature.[4] Fischel says regarding Herder's influence upon the Slavs:

Upon the emotional life and the aesthetic-cultural development of larger circles as well as upon the intensification of the national idea among the Slavs Johann Gottfried Herder was to have the most far-reaching influence. He is justly called ' the real father of the renaissance of the Slavic peoples '. . . . Herder, the panegyrist of the Slavs, whom they can justly style *praeceptor Slavorum,* was the creator of their philosophy of culture. They saw the course of their historical development up to the present with his eyes, they drew from his promises the certainty of their future high destiny.[5]

[1] See Oncken, H., "Deutsche geistige Einflüsse in der europäischen Nationalbewegung des neunzehnten Jahrhunderts ", in *Deutsche Vierteljahrschrift für Literaturwissenschaft und Geistesgeschichte,* vol. vii (1929), p. 613; Masaryk, T., *Russland und Europa* (Jena, 1913), vol. i, p. 260; Fischel, p. 280.

[2] See Masaryk, *op. cit.,* vol. ii, p. 330.

[3] (Munich and Berlin, 1917), p. 141. Cited in Oncken, *op. cit.,* p. 612.

[4] See Karasek, *op. cit.,* vol. i, p. 170.

[5] *Op. cit.,* p. 45.

But Herder's influence went beyond the Slavic peoples. In his *Ideen* Herder had regarded the Hungarians as a people in an advanced stage of decline.[1] Anxiously Hungarian patriots asked themselves whether or not Herder's statement was true. Soon a number of men arose to save the Hungarian people and Hungarian culture from extinction, and a great revival of interest in their native language and literature, and in politics, took place. This interest in the native language and literature, and in politics, was a definite influence in exciting a national spirit in Hungary.[2] Furthermore, the enthusiasm for the native literature which was manifest in Finland in the nineteenth century was in part evoked by Herder's statements regarding folk literature.[3] Herder's writings, we are told, also had a lasting influence on Mazzini's thought.[4] Mazzini, according to Vossler, had a copy of Quinet's French translation of the *Ideen* (1825-27) probably as early as 1827-28. With Herder the Italian prophet had in common the romantic or, in the last analysis, religious mode of thought. From Herder, Vossler tells us, Mazzini seems to have adopted the view that history is an orderly development with a set purpose, that a divine providence is guiding the destiny of the nationalities, that in the events of history an eternal plan is recognizable. As Herder had seen a spiritual unity in Germany, so Mazzini saw a national unity in Italy despite the outward division of his time. In 1843 Mazzini wrote:

One and all, like Herder, we demand of the instinct of our

[1] xiv, 269.

[2] See Riedl, F., "Die ungarische Literatur", in *Die osteuropäischen Literaturen*, p. 284 *et seq.*

[3] See Setälä, E., "Die finnische Literatur", in *Die osteuropäischen Literaturen*, p. 320.

[4] See Vossler, O., *Mazzinis politisches Denken und Wollen* (Berlin, 1927), pp. 32-42.

conscience a great religious Thought which may rescue us from doubt, a social faith which may save us from anarchy, a moral inspiration which may embody that faith in action, and keep us from idle contemplation.[1]

The nationalism, however, which Herder advocated was not the narrow nationalism of the later nineteenth century. Herder's nationalism was in its essence humanitarian; it was built around the principle of the essential unity of mankind as a whole. Hence his nationalism is free from the reproaches which may be brought against nationalism of the violent and exclusive type. He did not, like later nationalists, endeavor to inculcate in the minds of his countrymen an absolute faith in their superiority over all other nationalities. The foundation of his nationalism was human brotherhood, and not *Deutschland über Alles*. The glorification of nationality was to him not the ultimate goal. In urging the German people to cultivate their nationality, he was driven by the desire of having them fulfill their mission to mankind as a whole. He stressed the development of national characteristics and the spontaneous action of the national soul because he believed that both were necessary to the perfection of the nationality, and because he believed that the perfection of the various nationalities was requisite to the perfection of mankind. The final justification of national existence lay for him in the contribution of the national group to humanity at large.

Herder's nationalism was, therefore, not heavily freighted with war. In its essence it was non-aggressive.

Must one fatherland [he wrote] necessarily rise up against another, nay against every other fatherland which binds together its members with the same ties? Has not the earth room for us all? Does not one land lie quietly next to the

[1] *Life and Writings of Joseph Mazzini*, vol. iv, p. 57.

other? Cabinets may cheat one another, and political machines may be moved against one another until one shatters the other. Not so do *fatherlands* move one against another; they lie quietly side by side and, like families, assist each other. *Fatherlands against fatherlands* in bloody battle is the worst barbarism of the human language.[1] National glory is a deceiving seducer. When it reaches a certain height, it clasps the head with an iron band. The inclosed sees nothing in the mist but his own picture; he is susceptible to no foreign impressions.[2]

National pride he considered ridiculous, proposterous, per-nicious.[3] He regarded it as " the most harmful disease in history ", as the substance of which wars of conquest are made.[4] Whereas wars of conquest entail violation of the individuality of the national group which is attacked it is in the highest degree harmful. Moreover, wars of conquest involve in the end the ruin of the aggressor. This is illus-trated by the fate of Rome which fell, " a fearful monu-ment to the end that everywhere awaits the thirst of con-quest, whether in great or little states ".[5]

Herder also protested vigorously against national exclu-siveness. He wrote:

Let us contribute to the honor of our nationality to the utmost of our ability; let us defend it when it is wronged, but to extol it *ex professo*—that I consider self-praise without effect. It is the apparent plan of nature that as one human being, so also one generation, and also one nationality learn, learn incessantly, from and with the others until all have comprehended the difficult lesson: ' No nationality has been solely designated by God as the chosen people of the earth; above all we must seek the

---

[1] xvii, 319. Italics are Herder's.

[2] xviii, 208.

[3] xxxii, 519.

[4] xxiii, 214; xvii, 230.

[5] xiv, 186.

truth and cultivate the garden of the common good '. Hence no nationality of Europe may separate itself sharply, and foolishly say, ' With us *alone*, with us dwells *all* wisdom '.[1]

It was not his goal to make the German nationality self-contained. " Love of nationality ", he told his countrymen, " should not prevent us from recognizing the good which can only be effected by the progress of ages and nationalities ".[2] " To the German it is no disgrace to learn from other nationalities." [3] Although he was vehemently opposed to the imitation of other nationalities, he wished his countrymen to learn from the example of others, to emulate their great achievements. He told them that a nationality which refuses to learn from others will be one-sided and incomplete in its development.[4] He wished his countrymen to assimilate whatever they could profitably derive from the achievements of foreign thought and culture without impeding the action of the national soul and the expression of their innate abilities. His conception of nationality pointed toward toleration and mutual enrichment. His message in brief was: Each nationality has its peculiar duty to perform for the common good of mankind, and its special contributions to make to the common fund of civilization. Let us, therefore, be German, not because the German is superior to all other nationalities, but because we are Germans and cannot well be anything else, and because we can contribute to humanity at large only by being German.

But Herder's visionary mind, it seems, did not perceive the antagonism between theory and practice. Before many decades passed the cosmopolitan element was discarded and

[1] xvii, 211-12, Italics are Herder's.

[2] xviii, 137.

[3] xvii, 212.

[4] iv, 472, 477.

national success and advantage accentuated. For Fichte humanity was still the content of German culture, but men like Arndt, Jahn and Stein discarded the idea as " an empty luxury of the mind ".[1] Since the World War has shown the folly of the narrow, selfish nationalism of some nations and the violent, militaristic nationalism of others, it is but natural that at the present time there should be a revival of interest in Herder and his humanitarian nationalism.

[1] See Schultheiss, F., *Geschichte des deutschen Nationalbewusstseins,* vol. i (Munich and Leipzig, 1893), p. 40 *et seq.*

BIBLIOGRAPHY

SOURCES

Adelung, J. C., *Versuch einer Geschichte der Kultur des menschlichen Geschlechts* (Leipzig, 1782).

Arndt, E. M., *Gedichte*, vol. iv (Leipzig, 1892).

Eckermann, J. P., *Gespräche mit Goethe in den letzten Jahren seines Lebens*, 2 vols. (Leipzig, 1837).

Fichte, J. G., *Werke*, 6 vols. (Leipzig, 1908-12).

——, *Nachgelassene Werke*, vol. iii (Bonn, 1835).

Goethe, J. W., *Sämmtliche Werke*, Cotta, Jubiläums-Ausgabe, vols. xxiii, xxiv, xxv, xxxvi, xxxviii (Stuttgart and Berlin, 1902-12).

Grimm, W., *Kleinere Schriften*, edited by G. Hinrichs, vol. i (Berlin, 1881).

Hagen, F. H. von der, *Sämmtliche Werke*, vol. xviii (Tübingen, 1814).

Hamann, J. G., *Schriften*, edited by F. Roth, vol. iii (Berlin, 1822).

Herder, J. G., *Aus Herders Nachlass*, edited by H. Düntzer and F. G. von Herder, 3 vols. (Frankfort, 1856-57).

——, "Aus Herders letztem Lebensjahre: Ungedruckte Briefe" (edited by W. Deetjen), in *Jahrbuch der Goethe-Gesellschaft*, vol. xiv (1928), pp. 117-29.

——, *Briefe an Hamann*, edited by O. Hoffmann (Berlin, 1889).

——, *Briefwechsel mit Caroline Flachsland*, edited by H. Schauer, 2 vols. (Weimar, 1927-28).

——, *Briefwechsel mit Nicolai*, edited by O. Hoffman (Berlin, 1887).

——, *Sämmtliche Werke*, edited by B. Suphan, E. Redlich, et al., 33 vols. (Berlin, 1877-1913).

——, *Von deutscher Art und Kunst* (Hamburg, 1773).

——, *Von und an Herder*, edited by H. Düntzer and F. G. von Herder, 2 vols. (Leipzig, 1861-62).

——, *Outlines of a Philosophy of the History of Man*, translated by T. Churchill, 2nd ed., 2 vols. (London, 1803).

Herder, Caroline, *Erinnerungen aus dem Leben Johann Gottfried von Herders*, edited by J. G. Müller, 2 vols. (Tübingen, 1820).

——, *Herders Reise nach Italien: Briefwechsel mit seiner Gattin*, edited by H. Düntzer and F. G. von Herder (Giessen, 1859).

——, *Herders Lebensbild*, edited by H. Düntzer, 3 vols. (Erlangen, 1846). Materials on Herder's life collected by Caroline Herder.

Hardenberg, F. von (Novalis), *Schriften,* edited by J. Minor, vol. ii (Jena, 1907).

Humboldt, W. von, *Gesammelte Schriften,* edited by A. Leitzmann and B. Gebhardt, vols. iv and vii (Berlin, 1908).

Jacobi, F. H., *Auserlescner Briefwechsel,* edited by F. Roth, 2 vols. (Leipzig, 1825-27).

Klopstock, F. G., *Werke,* 4 vols. in 3 (Deutsche National-Litteratur, vols. 46-48) ... (Berlin and Stuttgart, 1884).

Leibniz, G. W., *Werke,* edited by Onno Klopp, 9 vols. (Hanover, 1864-84).

——, *Unvorgreifliche Gedanken,* edited by G. Schmarsow (Strassburg, 1877).

Lessing, G. E., *Sämmtliche Schriften,* Lachmann-Muncker edition, 23 vols. (Stuttgart, 1886-1924), especially vols. i, viii, x, xii and xiii.

Logau, F. von, *Sinngedichte* (Leipzig, 1870).

——, *Sinngedichte,* edited by C. W. Ramler and G. E. Lessing (Leipzig, 1759).

Mazzini, Giuseppe, *Life and Writings,* 6 vols. (London, 1890-91), especially vols. iii and iv.

Möser, Justus, *Sämmtliche Werke,* edited by F. Nicolai, 8 vols. (Berlin, 1798).

——, *Ueber die deutsche Sprache und Litteratur,* edited by C. Schüddekopf (Berlin, 1902).

Moser, F. K. von, *Beherzigungen* (Frankfort, 1761).

——, *Der Herr und der Diener* (Frankfort, 1761).

——, *Mannigfaltigkeiten,* 2 vols. in one, (Zurich, 1796).

——, *Neues Patriotisches Archiv,* 2 vols. (Mannheim and Leipzig, 1792-94).

——, *Von dem deutschen Nationalgeist* (Frankfort, 1766).

Opitz, M., *Aristarchus sive de contemptu linguae Teutonicae und Buch von der deutschen Poeterey,* edited by G. Witkowski (Leipzig, 1888).

Saupe, E. J., *Die Schiller-Goetheschen Xenien* (Leipzig, 1852).

Schenkendorff, M. von, *Sämmtliche Gedichte* (Berlin, 1837).

Scherer, W., *Kleine Schriften,* vol. ii (Berlin, 1893).

Schiller, J. C. F., *Werke,* edited by Bellermann, vol. xiii (Leipzig, 1897).

——, *Briefe,* edited by F. Jonas, 2 vols. (Stuttgart, 1893).

Schlegel, F., *Sämmtliche Werke,* vol. i (Vienna, 1846).

——, *Seine prosaischen Jugendschriften,* edited by J. Minor, 2 vols. (Vienna, 1906).

——, *Briefe an seinen Bruder August Wilhelm,* edited by O. Walzel (Berlin, 1890).

Stein, Freiherr vom, *Briefe und Schriften,* edited by K. Pagel (Leipzig, 1927).

Tieck, L., *Ausgewählte Werke,* edited by G. Witkowski, 4 vols. in one (Leipzig, 1902).

Wackenroder, W. H., *Werke und Briefe,* edited by F. von der Leyen, 2 vols. (Jena, 1910).

Weimarisches Herder-Album (Jena, 1845).

Wieland, C. M., *Sämmtliche Werke,* Göschen ed., vol. xxxi (Leipzig, 1858).

——, *Uebersetzungen,* vol. i (Berlin, 1909).

Winckelmann, J. J., *Sämmtliche Werke,* 12 vols. in 6 (Donauöschingen, 1825-29), especially vols. v and vi.

SECONDARY WORKS ON HERDER

Adler, F., *Herder and Klopstock* (New York, 1909).[1]

Adlhoch, O., "Herders Geschichtsphilosophie", in *Philosophisches Jahrbuch,* vol. vi (1893), pp. 312-20.

Andress, J. M., *Herder as an Educator* (New York, 1916).

Aron, E., *Die deutsche Erweckung des Griechentums durch Winckelmann und Herder* (Heidelberg, 1929).

Bächtold, J., *Aus dem Herderschen Hause* (Berlin, 1881).

Bärenbach, F. von. *Herder als Vorgänger Darwins und der modernen Naturphilosophie* (Berlin, 1877).

Barth, P., "Herder", in *Vierteljahrschrift für wissenschaftliche Philosophie,* vol. xxvii (1903), pp. 429-51.

Baumgarten, H., "Herder und Georg Müller", in *Preussische Jahrbücher,* vol. xxix (1872), pp. 23-51, 129-161.

Baumgarten, O., *Herders Anlage und Bildungsgang zum Prediger* (Halle, 1888).

Baumgarten, O., "Herders Stellung zum Rationalismus", in *Deutsch-Evangelische Blätter,* vol. xiv (1889), pp. 649-60.

Berger, A. E., *Herder und Winckelmann* (Halle, 1903).

Bittner, K., *Herders Geschichtsphilosophie und die Slawen* (Reichenberg, 1929).

Böhme, J., *Herder und das Gymnasium* (Hamburg, 1890).

Bojanowski, E. von, "Herder über Musik", in *Goethe-Jahrbuch,* vol. xxx (1909), pp. 56-66.

Braun, O., "Herders Ideen zur Kulturphilosophie", in *Historische Zeitschrift,* vol. cx (1912-13), pp. 292-326.

——, "Herders Kulturphilosophie", in *Zeitschrift für Philosophie und philosophische Kritik,* vol. cxliv (1911), pp. 165-81; vol. cxlv (1912), pp. 1-22.

Breul, K., "In Memory of J. G. Herder", in *Modern Language Quarterly,* vol. vii (1904), pp. 1-10.

---

[1] In addition to the secondary materials listed the author is indebted to an unpublished essay on Herder by Elizabeth P. MacCallum.

Bruntsch, M., "Der Geist von 'Sturm und Drang' in der Pädagogik des jungen Herder," in *Pädagogische Studien,* vol. xxv (1904), pp. 190-212, 241-64.

——, *Die Idee der Entwicklung bei Herder* (Crimmitschau, 1904).

Bürkner, R., *Herder, sein Leben und Wirken* (Berlin, 1904).

Castle, E., "Herder als Wiedererwecker des deutschen Volksliedes", in *Zeitschrift für die österreichischen Gymnasien,* vol. lv (1904), pp. 193-202.

Cunow, H., "Herders Geschichts und Staatsauffassung", in *Die neue Zeit,* vol. xxxvii (1919), pp. 348-55.

Denecke, A., "Lessing und Herder", in *Zeitschrift für den deutschen Unterricht,* vol. xii (1898), pp. 305-43.

Doerne, M., *Die Religion in Herders Geschichtsphilosophie* (Leipzig, 1927).

Döring, H., *Johann Gottfried von Herders Leben* (Weimar, 1829).

Ehrenberg, V., *Herders Bedeutung für die Rechtswissenschaft* (Göttingen, 1903).

Farinelli, Arturo, *Franche parole alla mia nazione, con aggiunto il discorso L'umanità di Herder e il concetto della "razza" nella storia dello spirito* (Torino, 1919).

Fritz, G., "Neuere und neueste Herderschriften", in *Monatshefte der Comeniusgesellschaft,* vol. xiv (1905), pp. 233-40.

Gemmingen, O. von, *Vico, Hamann und Herder* (Leipzig, 1918).

Genthe, T., *Der Kulturbegriff bei Herder* (Jena, 1902).

Girgensohn, H., *Das Problem des geschichtlichen Fortschritts bei Iselin und Herder* (Erlangen, 1913).

Goebel, J. "Herder als Historiker und Philosoph", in *German-American Annals, new series,* vol. ii (1904), pp. 178-84.

Goeken, W., *Herder als Deutscher (Tübinger germanistische Arbeiten,* vol. i) . . . (Stuttgart, 1926).

Götz, H., "War Herder ein Vorgänger Darwins?", in *Vierteljahrsschrift für wissenschaftliche Philosophie und Soziologie,* vol. xxvi (1902), p. 391-422.

Grundmann, J., *Die geographischen und völkerkundlichen Quellen und Anschauungen in Herders "Ideen zur Geschichte der Menschheit"* (Berlin, 1900).

Günther, H., *Herders Stellung zur Musik* (Leipzig, 1903).

Hänsch, B. F., "Darstellung und Kritik der Gedanken Herders über die Muttersprache", in *Pädagogische Studien,* vol. xxiii (1902), pp. 337-49, 369-93.

Hänssel, O., *Der Einfluss Rousseaus auf die philosophisch-pädagogischen Anschauungen Herders* (Dresden, 1902).

Francke, O., *Herder und das Weimarische Gymnasium* (Hamburg, 1893).

Hatch, J. C., "Shaftsburys Einfluss auf Herder", in *Studien zur vergleichenden Literaturgeschichte,* vol. i (1901), pp. 68-119.

Hauffe, G., *Herder in seinen "Ideen zur Philosophie der Geschichte der Menschheit"* (Leipzig, 1890).

Haussmann, J. F., "Der junge Herder und Hamann", in *Journal of English and Germanic Philology*, vol. vi (1907), pp. 604-48.

Hayes, C. J. H., "Contributions of Herder to the Doctrine of Nationalism", in *American Historical Review*, vol. xxxii (1927), pp. 719-36.

Haym, R., *Herder nach seinem Leben und seinen Werken dargestellt*, 2 vols. (Berlin, 1877-85).

H. D., *Die Herder-litteratur in Deutschland; Vollständiger Katalog von 1769 bis 1851* (Cassel, 1852).

Headtrom, B., "Herder and the Theory of Evolution", in *Open Court*, vol. xliii (1929), pp. 596-601.

Hillebrand, K., "Herder", in *North American Review*, vol. cxv (1872), p. 104-38, 235-87; vol. cxvi (1873), pp. 389-424.

Hoffart, E., *Herders "Gott"* (Halle, 1918).

Horn, J., *Herders Stellung zu Friedrich dem Grossen* (Leipzig, 1928).

Jacoby, G., *Herder als Faust* (Leipzig, 1911).

——, "Herder und Schopenhauer", in *Jahrbuch der Schopenhauer-Gesellschaft*, vol. vii (1918), pp. 156-211.

Jonetz, A., *Ueber Herders nationale Gesinnung* (Brieg, 1895).

Joret, C., *Herder et la renaissance littéraire en Allemagne au 18e siécle* (Paris, 1875).

Karsten, G. E., *Herder und das Volkslied*, in *Washington University Bulletin*, vol. iii (1905), pp. 101-22.

Kayser, E., *Rousseau, Kant, Herder über den ewigen Frieden* (Leipzig, 1916).

Keller, L., *Herder und die Kulturgesellschaften des Humanismus* (Berlin, 1904).

Koch, M., "Herders Führerstellung in der Entwicklung der deutschen Litteratur", in *Jahresbericht der schlesischen Gesellschaft für vaterländische Kultur*, vol. lxxxi (1904), pp. 96-109.

Koch, W., "Der junge Herder und Russland", in *Preussische Jahrbücher*, vol. clxviii (1917), pp. 54-66.

Koeppen, W., *Herders Reisetagebuch von 1769* (Greifswald, 1926).

Kohlbrugge, J. H., "Herders Verhältnis zur modernen Naturanschauung", in *Naturwissenschaften*, vol. i (1913), pp. 1110-1116.

Kohlschmidt, W., *Herder-Studien* (Berlin, 1929).

Krapp, L., "Herders Bedeutung für unsere Zeit", in *Historisch-politische Blätter für das katholische Deutschland*, vol. i (1903), pp. 911-24.

Kröhnert, O., *Herder als Politiker und deutscher Patriot* (Gumbinnen, 1905).

Kronenberg, M., *Herders Philosophie nach ihrem Entwicklungsgang und ihrer historischen Stellung* (Heidelberg, 1889).

Kühnemann, E., *Herder*, 3rd edition (Munich, 1927).

——, *Herders Persönlichkeit in seiner Weltanschauung* (Berlin, 1893).

——, "Herder, Kant, Goethe", in *Logos*, vol. ii (1912), pp. 265-302.

——, "Herder und das deutsche Wesen", in *Der Kunstwart*, vol. xvii (1903), pp. 381-89.

——, "Herder und seine Geschichtsphilosophie", in *Deutsche Monatsschrift für das gesamte Leben der Gegenwart*, vol. iii (1903), pp. 338-51.

Kunz, F., *Bekämpfung und Fortbildung Lessing'scher Ideen durch Herder* (Teschen, 1887).

Laas, E., "Herders Einwirkung auf die deutsche Lyrik von 1770-1775", in *Die Grenzboten*, vol. xxx (1871), pp. 534-48, 577-84, 609-18, 654-62.

Lamprecht, K., "Herder und Kant als Theoretiker der Geschichtswissenschaft", in *Jahrbücher für Nationalökonomie und Statistik*, series 3, vol. xiv (1897), pp. 161-203.

Langer, L., "Herder und das Volkslied", in *Ueber Land und Meer*, vol. xci (1904), p. 260.

Lauchert, F., "Die Anschauungen Herders über den Ursprung der Sprache", in *Euphorion*, vol. i (1894), pp. 747-71.

Lehmann, R., *Die deutschen Klassiker: Herder, Schiller, Goethe* (Leipzig, 1921).

——, "Herders Humanitätsbegriff", in *Kant-Studien*, vol. xxiv (Berlin, 1919), pp. 242-60.

——, "Herder und Hamannn", in *Preussische Jahrbücher*, vol. lxv (1890), pp. 266-72.

Lichtenstein, E., "Die Idee der Naturpoesie bei den Brüdern Grimm und ihr Verhältniss zu Herder", in *Deutsche Vierteljahrsschrift für Literaturwissenschaft und Geistesgeschichte*, vol. vi (1928), pp. 513-47.

Lindau, H., "Herder", in *Nord und Süd*, vol. cvii (1903), pp. 290-318.

Lovejoy, A., "Herder, Eighteenth-century Evolutionist" in *Popular Science*, vol. lxv, pp. 327-36.

Lutz, E., *Herders Anschauungen vom Wesen des Dichters und der Dichtkunst in der ersten Hälfte seines Schaffens* (Erlangen, 1925).

Martin, E., "Herder und Goethe in Strassburg", in *Jahrbuch des Historisch-litterarischen Zweigvereins der Vogesen-Clubs*, vol. xiv (1898), pp. 106-23.

Matthias, T., "Der Politiker Herder nach der ursprünglichen Fassung seiner Humanitätsbriefe", in *Neues Jahrbuch für das klassische Altertum*, vol. vi (1900), pp. 401-26.

May, W., "Herders Anschauungen der organischen Natur", in *Archiv für die Geschichte der Naturwissenschaften und der Technik*, vol. iv (1913), pp. 8-39, 89-113.

Nevinson, H. W., *A Sketch of Herder and His Times* (London, 1884).

Noll, R., "Herders Verhältniss zur Naturwissenschaft und dem Entwicklungsgedanken", *Archiv für die Geschichte der Philosophie*, vol. xxvi (1913), pp. 302-38.

Nunns, T., "Herder as Sponsor of Folksong", in *Temple Bar*, vol. cxi (1897), 527-39.

Posadzy, L., *Der entwicklungsgeschichtliche Gedanke bei Herder* (Posen, 1906).

Regli, A., *Iselins Geschichte der Menschheit, eine Vorarbeit zu Herders "Ideen"* (Munich, 1920).

Reinke, J., *Herder als Uebersetzer altdeutscher Gedichte* (Münster, 1902).

Sapir, E., "Herders Ursprung der Sprache", in *Modern Philology*, vol. v (1907), pp. 109-42.

Saunders, T. B., "Herder", in *Hibbert Journal*, vol. ii (1904), pp. 681-702.

Schmidt, G., *Herder und August Wilhelm Schlegel* (Berlin, 1917).

Schulz, K., *Die Vorbereitung der Geschichtsphilosophie Herders im achtzehnten Jahrhundert* (Greifswald, 1926).

Schütze, M., "The Fundamental Ideas in Herder's Thought", in *Modern Philology*, vol. xviii (1920-21), pp. 65-78, 289-302; vol. xix (1921-22), pp. 113-30, 361-82; vol. xxi (1923-24), pp. 29-48, 113-32.

See, Henri, "La philosophie de l'histoire de Herder", in *Revue de Synthèse Historique*, vol. xlviii (1929), pp. 21-36.

Sembritzki, J., "Trescho und Herder", in *Altpreussische Monatsschrift*, new series, vol. xli (1904), pp. 531-70.

Siegel, C., *Herder als Philosoph* (Stuttgart, 1907).

Simpson, G. R., *Herder's Conception of "Das Volk"* (Chicago, 1921).

Smith, J. F., "Herder as Theologian", in *Theological Review*, vol. ix (1872), pp. 179-96, 437-57.

Stadelmann, R., *Der historische Sinn bei Herder* (Halle, 1928).

Stavenhagen, K., *Herder in Riga* (*Abhandlungen des Herder-Instituts zu Riga*, vol. i), (Riga, 1925).

Steig, R., "Wilhelm Grimm und Herder", in *Vierteljahrschrift für Literaturgeschichte*, vol. iii (1890), pp. 573-98.

Stephan, H., *Herders Philosophie* (Leipzig, 1906).

——, *Herder in Bückeburg und seine Bedeutung für die Kirchengeschichte* (Tübingen, 1905).

Sturm, W., *Herders Sprachphilosophie* (Breslau, 1917).

Suphan, B., "Herder als Schüler Kants", in *Zeitschrift für deutsche Philologie*, vol. iv (1873), pp. 225-37.

——, "Herders Volkslieder", in *Zeitschrift für deutsche Philologie*, vol. iii (1872), pp. 458-75.

Tronchon, H., *La fortune intellectuelle de Herder en France* (Paris, 1920).

Tumarkin, A., *Herder und Kant* (Bern, 1896).

Unger, R., "Zur neueren Herderforschung", in *Germanisch-romanische Monatsschrift*, vol. i (1909), pp. 145-68.

Vesterling, H., *Herders Humanitätsprincip* (Halle, 1890).

Warda, A., "Kleine Beiträge zur Jugendgeschichte J. G. von Herders", in *Altpreussische Monatsschrift,* vol. xl (1903), pp. 508-20.

Wedel, M., *Herders Eintritt in die deutsche Literaturkritik* (Berlin, 1927).

Wegener, T., *Herders Forschungen über Sprache und Poesie* (Potsdam, 1875).

Wenderoth, O., "Der junge Quinet und seine Uebersetzung von Herders Ideen", in *Romanische Forschungen,* vol. xxii (1908), pp. 311-98.

Willmann, O., "Herders Bedeutung für das deutsche Bildungswesen", in *Hochland,* vol. i (1903), pp. 316-21.

Witte, J. H., *Die Philosophie unserer Dichterheroen,* vol. i (Bonn, 1880).

Wolf, H., "Die Genielehre des jungen Herder", in *Deutsche Viertel-jahrsschrift für Literaturwissenschaft und Geistesgeschichte,* vol. iii 1925), pp. 400-30.

Wolf, R., *Herder und Karoline Flachsland* (Bartenstein, 1884).

Wolfram, A., "Schiller und Herder", in *Euphorion,* vol. xxviii (1927), pp. 35-54.

General Secondary Aids

Arnold, F., *Das deutsche Volkslied* (Prenzlau, 1907).

Babbitt, I., *Rousseau and Romanticism* (Boston, 1919).

Barker, Ernest, *National Character and the Factors in Its Formation* (New York and London, 1927).

Bartels, A., *Geschichte der deutschen Literatur* (Leipzig, 1924).

Bassenge, E., *Der nationale Gedanke in der deutschen Geschichte* (Leipzig, 1921).

Baumgarten, H., *Wie wir wieder ein Volk geworden sind* (Leipzig, 1870).

Behrens, F. W., *Deutsches Ehr- und Nationalgefühl in seiner Entwicklung durch Philosophen und Dichter, 1600-1815* (Leipzig, 1891).

Benfey, T., *Geschichte der Sprachwissenschaft und orientalischen Philologie in Deutschland* (Munich, 1869).

Berger, A. E., *Friedrich der Grosse und die deutsche Litteratur* (Bonn, 1890).

——, "Volksdichtung und Kunstdichtung", in *Nord und Süd,* vol. lxviii (1894), pp. 76-96.

Biedermann, K., *Deutschland im achtzehnten Jahrhundert,* 2 vols. in 3 (Leipzig, 1867-80).

——, *Deutschlands trübste Zeit oder der dreissigjährige Krieg in seinen Folgen* (Berlin, 1862).

——, *Geschichte des deutschen Einheitsgedankens* (Wiesbaden, 1894).

Blochmann, E., "Die deutsche Volksdichtungsbewegung in Sturm und Drang und Romantik", in *Deutsche Vierteljahrsschrift für Literaturwissenschaft und Geistesgeschichte,* vol. i (1923), pp. 419-52.

Boehn, M. von, *Deutschland im achtzehnten Jahrhundert*, 2 vols. (Berlin, 1922).

Botzenhart, E., *Die Staats- und Reformideen des Freiherrn vom Stein* (Tübingen, 1927).

Braitmaier, F., *Geschichte der poetischen Theorie und Kritik von den Diskursen der Maler bis auf Lessing*, 2 vols. (Frauenfeld, 1888).

Breul, K., *The Romantic Movement in German Literature* (Cambridge, Eng., 1927).

Breysig, Kurt, "Die Historiker der Aufklärung", in *Die Zukunft*, vol. xix (1897), pp. 295-305, 343-55.

Brüggemann, F., "Der Kampf um die bürgerliche Welt- und Lebensanschauung in der deutschen Literatur des achtzehnten Jahrhunderts", in *Deutsche Vierteljahrsschrift für Literaturwissenschaft und Geistesgeschichte*, vol. iii (1925), pp. 94-127.

Buchholz, G., "Ursprung und Wesen der modernen Geschichtsauffassung", in *Deutsche Zeitschrift für Geschichtswissenschaft*, vol. ii (1889), pp. 17-37.

Cassirer, E., *Freiheit und Form* (Berlin, 1916).

Coar, J. F., *Studies in German Literature in the Nineteenth Century* (New York, 1903).

Collier, P., *Germany and the Germans* (New York, 1914).

Crueger, J., *Die erste Gesammtausgabe der Nibelungen* (Frankfort, 1884).

Curtius, E., *Maurice Barrès und die geistigen Grundlagen des französischen Nationalismus* (Bonn, 1921).

Day, Clive, *History of Commerce* (New York, 1916).

DeQuincey, Thomas, *Essays on Philosophical Writers and Other Men of Letters* (Boston, 1854).

DeStael-Holstein, Baroness, *Germany,* translated by O. W. Wight, 2 vols. (New York, 1861).

Dietze, H., *Geschichte des deutschen Handels* (Leipzig, 1923).

Dilthey, W., *Gesammelte Schriften,* vol. ii (Leipzig, 1914).

Dittmann, F., *Der Begriff des Volksgeistes bei Hegel* (Leipzig, 1909).

Drüner, H., "Der nationale und der universale Gedanke bei dem Freiherrn vom Stein", in *Historische Vierteljahrsschrift,* vol. xxii (1924-25), pp. 28-69.

Eichler, F., *Das Nachleben des Hans Sachs* (Leipzig, 1904).

Erhard, H. A., *Geschichte des Wiederaufblühens wissenschaftlicher Bildung*, 3 vols. (Magdeburg, 1827-32).

Richard, E., *History of German Civilization* (New York, 1911).

Feldmann, W., "Modewörter des achtzehnten Jahrhunderts", in *Zeitschrift für deutsche Wortforschung,* vol. vi (1904/5), pp. 345-50.

Fester, R., *Rousseau und die deutsche Geschichtsphilosophie* (Stuttgart, 1890).

Fischel, A., *Der Panslawismus bis zum Weltkrieg* (Berlin, 1919).

Fischer, Kuno, "Goethes Faust", in *Deutsche Rundschau*, vol. xiii (1877), pp. 54-98.

Flint, R., *The Philosophy of History in Europe*, vol. i (New York, 1875).

Francke, Kuno, *A History of German Literature as Determined by Social Forces* (New York, 1911).

Frederking, A., "Unsere Muttersprache unter Fremdherrschaft", in *Wissenschaftliche Beihefte zur Zeitschrift des allgemeinen deutschen Sprachvereins*, no. 14/15 (1898), pp. 148-66.

Fueter, E., *Geschichte der neueren Historiographie* (Munich and Berlin, 1911).

Gelpcke, E., *Fichte und die Gedankenwelt des Sturm und Drang* (Leipzig, 1928).

Gervais, E., *Die antike und die französische Tragödie: Die Nachahmung beider von Gottsched und seinen Schülern* (Hohenstein, 1864).

Gooch, G. P., *Germany and the French Revolution* (London, 1920).

Guerard, A. L., *Five Masters of French Romance* (London, 1916).

Guhrauer, G. E., *Gottfried Wilhelm, Freiherr von Leibniz*, 2 vols. (Breslau 1846).

Günther F., *Die Wissenschaft vom Menschen* (Gotha, 1906).

Hagenbring, P., *Goethes Götz von Berlichingen* (Halle, 1911).

Hayes, C. J. H., *Essays on Nationalism* (New York, 1926).

——, *Historical Evolution of Modern Nationalism* (New York, 1931).

Haym, R., *Die romantische Schule* (Berlin, 1872).

——, *Wilhelm von Humboldt* (Berlin, 1856).

Heinemann, E., *Zur Geschichte der Staatsanschauungen in Deutschland während des achtzehnten Jahrhunderts* (Bonn, 1915).

Heinemann, K., *Die deutsche Dichtung* (Leipzig, 1914).

Hempel, P., *Die Kunst Friedrichs von Logau* (Berlin, 1917).

Hettner, H., *Geschichte der deutschen Literatur im achtzehnten Jahrhundert*, edited by G. Witkowski (Leipzig, 1929).

Heubaum, A., *Geschichte des deutschen Bildungswesens seit der Mitte des 17. Jahrhunderts* (Berlin, 1905).

Heyck, E., *Die geschichtliche Berechtigung des deutschen Nationalbewusstseins* (Munich, 1897).

Hibben, J. G., *The Philosophy of the Enlightenment* (New York, 1910).

Hillebrand, J., *Die deutsche Nationalliteratur seit dem Anfange des achtzehnten Jahrhunderts*, 2 vols. (Hamburg and Gotha, 1850-51).

Hillebrand, K., *German Thought from the Seven Years War to Goethe's Death* (New York, 1880).

Gamble, W. M. T., "The *Monumenta Germaniae Historica:* Its Antecedents and Motives", in *Catholic Historical Review*, vol. iv (1925), pp. 202-33.

Hirt, H., *Geschichte der deutschen Sprache* (Munich, 1919).

Hodermann, R., "Universitätsvorlesungen in deutscher Sprache", in *Wissenschaftliche Beihefte zur Zeitschrift des allgemeinen deutschen Sprachvereins*, no. viii (1895), pp. 99-116.

Höffding, H., *A History of Modern Philosophy*, 2 vols. (London, 1908).

Huber, J., *Das Verhältnis der deutschen Philosophie zur deutschen Erhebung* (Berlin, 1871).

Jakubec, Jan, "Die literarische Wiedergeburt des böhmischen Volkes", in Tobolka, Z., *Das böhmische Volk* (Prague, 1916).

Jakubec, Jan, and Novák, A., *Geschichte der cechischen Litteratur* (Leipzig, 1913).

Janson, F., *Fichtes Reden an die deutsche Nation* (Berlin and Leipzig, 1911).

Japp, A. H., *German Life and Literature* (London, 1880).

Jastrow, I., *Geschichte des deutschen Einheitstraumes und seiner Erfüllung*, 4th edition (Berlin, 1891).

Jaszi, O., *The Dissolution of the Habsburg Monarchy* (Chicago, 1929).

Jenisch, D., *Vergleichungen der Sprachen Europas* (Berlin, 1796).

Joachimsen, P., *Vom deutschen Volk zum deutschen Staat* (Leipzig, 1916).

Jördens, K. H., *Lexikon deutscher Dichter und Prosaisten*, vol. iv (Leipzig, 1809).

Joseph, B., *Nationality: Its Nature and Purpose* (New Haven, 1929).

Kaemmel, O., *Der Werdegang des deutschen Volkes*, 4 vols., 4th edition (Berlin and Leipzig, 1921).

Kaerst, J., *Das geschichtliche Wesen und Recht der deutschen nationalen Idee* (Munich, 1916).

Kapp, F., "Berliner geschriebene Zeitungen aus dem vorigen Jahrhundert", in *Deutsche Rundschau*, vol. xxi (1879), pp. 107-22.

Karasek, J., *Slavische Literaturgeschichte*, 2 vols. (Leipzig, 1916).

Kiefl, F. X., *Leibniz und die religiöse Wiedervereiningung Deutschlands* (Regensburg, 1925).

King, B., *Mazzini* (London, 1911).

Kircher, E., *Volkslied und Volkspoesie in der Sturm- und Drangzeit* (Strassburg, 1902).

Klenze, C. von, *From Goethe to Hauptmann* (New York, 1926).

Kluckhohn, P., *Persönlichkeit und Gemeinschaft: Studien zur Staatsauffassung der deutschen Romantik* (Halle, 1925).

——, *Die deutsche Romantik* (Leipzig, 1924).

Klüpfel, K., *Die deutschen Einheitsbestrebungen in ihrem geschichtlichen Zusammenhang dargestellt* (Leipzig, 1853).

Koch, M., *Nationalität und Nationallitteratur* (Berlin, 1891).

Korff, H. A., *Der Geist der Goethezeit*, vol. i (Leipzig, 1923).

Körner, J., "Die Renaissance des germanischen Altertums", in *Zeitschrift für den deutschen Unterricht*, vol. xxvii (1913), pp. 1-30.

Köster, A., *Die deutsche Literatur der Aufklärungszeit* (Heidelberg, 1925).

Kronenberg, M., *Geschichte des deutschen Idealismus*, 2 vols. (Munich, 1909).

Kühnemann, E., *Aus dem Weltreich deutschen Geistes* (Munich, 1914).

Lamprecht, K., "Entwicklung der deutschen Geschichtswissenschaft vornemlich seit Herder", in *Beilage zur Allgemeinen Zeitung*, no. 83 (Munich, 1898), pp. 2-8.

Laski, J. H., *Authority in the Modern State* (New Haven, 1919).

Laurent, F., *La philosophie de l'histoire* (Paris, 1870).

Lehmann, M., *Freiherr vom Stein* (Berlin, 1920).

Lenz, M., "Deutsches Nationalempfinden im Zeitalter unserer Klassiker", in *Jahrbuch der Goethegesellschaft*, vol. ii (Leipzig, 1915), pp. 265-300.

Levy, Paul, "Geschichte des Wortes Volkslied", in *Acta Germanica*, vol. vii (Berlin 1911), pp. 301-492.

Lévy-Bruhl, L., *L'Allemagne depuis Leibnitz* (Paris, 1890).

Lewin, E., *The Germans and Africa* (New York, 1915).

Lohre, H., *Von Percy zum Wunderhorn* (Berlin, 1902).

Luden, H., *Christian Thomasius nach seinen Schicksalen und Schriften* (Berlin, 1805).

Machal, Jan, "Die böhmische Literatur", in *Die osteuropäischen Literaturen*, edited by A. Bezzenberger *et al.*, (Berlin and Leipzig, 1908).

Mackie, J. M., *Life of Godfrey William Leibnitz* (Boston, 1845).

Malye, J., "Leibniz théoricien du nationalisme allemand", in *L'Acropole*, vol. i (1920), pp. 442-58.

Martin, E., "Zur Geschichte der deutschen Sprache", in *Wissenschaftliche Beihefte zur Zeitschift des allgemeinen deutschen Sprachvereins*, no. xxi (1902), pp. 1-11.

Masaryk, T. G., *Russland und Europa*, 2 vols. (Jena, 1913).

Matthias, A., *Geschichte des deutschen Unterrichts* (Munich, 1907).

Meier, J., *Kunstlied und Volkslied in Deutschland* (Halle, 1906).

Meinecke, F., *Das Zeitalter der deutschen Erhebung, 1795-1815* (Leipzig, 1906).

——, *Weltbürgertum und Nationalstaat*, 6th edition (Munich and Berlin, 1922).

Mentz, G., "Friedrich der Grosse und die deutsche Sprache", in *Zeitchrift für deutsche Wortforschung*, vol. i (1901), pp. 194-226.

Merz, J. T., *Leibniz* (Edinburgh, 1884).

Meyer, Hans (editor), *Das deutsche Volkstum*, 2nd rev. ed. (Leipzig, 1903).

Milberg, E., *Die deutschen moralischen Wochenscriften des achtzehnten Jahrhunderts* (Meissen, 1880).

Mitscherlich, W., *Der Nationalismus Westeuropas* (Leipzig, 1920).

——, "Der Nationalismus und seine Wurzeln", in *Jahrbuch für Gesetz gebung*, vol. xxxvi (1912), pp. 1285-1320.

Mollenhauer, K., *Justus Mösers Anteil an der Wiederbelebung des deutschen Geistes* (Braunschweig, 1896).

Murko, M., *Deutsche Einflüsse auf die Anfänge der böhmischen Romantik* (Graz, 1897).

Oncken, H., "Deutsche geistige Einflüsse in der europäischen National-bewegung des neunzehnten Jahrhunderts", in *Deutsche Vierteljahrsschrift für Literaturwissenschaft und Geistesgeschichte*, vol. vii (1929), pp. 607-27.

Paul, H., *Grundriss der germanischen Philologie*, 3 vols. in 4 (Strassburg, 1891-93).

Perry, T. S., *From Opitz to Lessing* (Boston, 1885).

Pertz, G. H., *Das Leben des Ministers Freiherrn vom Stein*, 6 vols. in 7 (Berlin, 1849-55).

Pfleiderer, E., *Leibniz als Patriot, Staatsmann, und Bildungsträger* (Leipzig, 1870).

Pietsch, P., "Leibniz und die deutsche Sprache", in *Wissenschaftliche Beihefte zur Zeitschrift des allgemeinen deutschen Sprachvereins*, no. 19/20 (1907-8), pp. 265-356.

Poetzsch, A., *Studien zur frühromantischen Politik und Geschichtsauffassung* (Leipzig, 1907).

Preuss, G. F., *Die Quellen des Nationalgeistes der Befreiungskriege* (Berlin, 1914).

Prutz, R. E., *Geschichte des deutschen Journalismus*, vol. i (Hanover, 1845).

Radl, E. M., *Geschichte der biologischen Theorien*, 2 vols. (Leipzig, 1909-13).

Ratzel, F., *Anthropogeographie*, 2nd ed., 2 vols. (Stuttgart, 1899-1912).

Raumer, K. von, *Geschichte der Pädagogik*, vol. i (Langensalza, 1897).

Raumer, R., von, *Geschichte der germanischen Philologie* (Munich, 1870).

Reichel, E., *Gottsched der Deutsche* (Berlin, 1901).

Benner, B., *Die nationalen Einigungsbestrebungen F. K. von Mosers* (Königsberg, 1919).

Reuter, H., "Schleiermachers Stellung zur Idee der Nation und des nationalen Staates", in *Theologische Studien und Kritiken*, vol. xxi (1918), pp. 439-504.

Riedl, F., "Die ungarische Literatur", in *Die osteuropäischen Literaturen* (Berlin and Leipzig, 1908).

Rose, J. H., *Nationality in Modern History* (New York, 1916).

Rosenkranz, K., *Neue Studien*, vol. i (Leipzig, 1875).

Rosenstein, I., "Friedrich Karl von Moser", in *Preussische Jahrbücher*, vol. xv (1865), pp. 229-58.

Rothacker, E., *Einleitung in die Geschichtswissenschaften* (Tübingen, 1920).

Rühs, F., *Historische Entwickelung des Einflusses Frankreichs und der Franzosen auf Deutschland und die Deutschen* (Berlin, 1815).

Saintsbury, G., *A History of Criticism and Literary Taste in Europe,* vol. i (New York, 1904).

Salomon, G., *Das Mittelalter als Ideal in der Romantik* (Munich, 1922).

Schäfer, D., *Deutsche Geschichte,* 7th ed., 2 vols. (Jena, 1919).

Schaumkell, E., *Geschichte der deutschen Kulturgeschichtsschreibung von der Mitte des achtzehnten Jahrhunderts bis zur Romantik* (Leipzig, 1905).

Scherer, W., *Jacob Grimm,* 2nd ed. (Berlin, 1885).

Scherer, W., and Walzel, O., *Geschichte der deutschen Literatur,* 3rd ed. (Berlin, 1921).

Schmalenbach, H., *Leibniz* (Munich, 1921).

Schmidt, J., *Geschichte des geistigen Lebens in Deutschland von Leibnitz bis auf Lessings Tod,* 2 vols. (Leipzig, 1862-64).

Schultz, H., *Die Bestrebungen der Sprachgesellschaften des achtzehnten Jahrhunderts* (Göttingen, 1888).

Schultz, W., " Das Erlebnis der Individualität bei Wilhelm von Humboldt ", in *Deutsche Vierteljahrsschrift für Literaturwissenschaft und Geistesgeschichte,* vol. vii (1929), pp. 654-81.

Schultheiss, F. G., *Geschichte des deutschen Nationalbewusstseins,* vol. i (Munich and Leipzig, 1893).

Setälä, E., " Die finnische Literatur ", in *Die osteuropäischen Literaturen* (Berlin and Leipzig, 1908).

Silz, W., *Early German Romanticism* (Harvard Univ. Press, 1929).

Silvers, J. von, *Humanität und Nationalität* (Berlin, 1869).

Skene, A. von, *Entstehen und Entwicklung der slavisch-nationalen Bewegung in Böhmen und Mähren im neunzehnten Jahrhundert* (Vienna, 1893).

Sokolowsky, R., *Der altdeutsche Minnesang im Zeitalter der deutschen Klassiker* (Dortmund, 1906).

Sperber, H., *Geschichte der deutschen Sprache* (Berlin, 1926).

Steinhausen, G., *Der Aufschwung der deutschen Kultur vom achtzehnten Jahrhundert bis zum Weltkrieg* (Leipzig and Vienna, 1920).

Steinthal, H., *Der Ursprung der Sprache,* 4th ed. (Berlin, 1888).

Stephan, G., *Die häusliche Erziehung in Deutschland während des achtzehnten Jahrhunderts* (Wiesbaden, 1891).

Stern, A., *Der Einfluss der französischen Revolution auf das deutsche Geistesleben* (Stuttgart, 1928).

Stettiner, P., *Der Tugendbund* (Königsberg, 1904).

Stöcker, H. H., *Zur Kunstanschauung des achtzehnten Jahrhunderts* (Berlin, 1904).

Stötzner, P., " Christian Thomas und sein Verdienst um die deutsche Sprache ", in *Zeitschrift des allgemeinen deutschen Sprachvereins,* vol. iii (1888), pp. 86-90.

Strauss, D. F., *Gesammelte Schriften,* vol. x (Bonn, 1878).

Strich, F., *Die Mythologie in der deutschen Literatur von Klopstock bis Wagner,* 2 vols. (Halle, 1910).

Sugenheim, S., *Frankreichs Einfluss auf und Beziehungen zu Deutschland von 1517-1789,* 2 vols. (Stuttgart, 1845-56).

Suphan, B., *Friedrichs des Grossen Schrift über die deutsche Litteratur* (Berlin, 1888).

Suter, J., *Das Volkslied und sein Einfluss auf Goethes Lyrik* (Aarau, 1897).

Sybel, H. von, *The Founding of the German Empire,* transl. by M. L. Perrin, vol. i (New York, 1890).

Sydow, E. von, *Die Kultur des deutschen Klassizismus* (Berlin, 1926).

Tietz, J., *Die geschichtliche Entwickelung des deutschen Nationalbewusstseins* (Hanover, 1880).

Tobolka, Z. V., *Das böhmische Volk* (Prague, 1916).

Trevelyan, G., *The Life and Letters of Lord Macaulay,* 2 vols. (New York, 1877).

Uden, K. F., *Ueber die Erziehung der Töchter des Mittelstandes,* 2nd ed. (Stendal, 1796).

Unger, R., *Hamann und die Aufklärung,* 2 vols. (Jena, 1911).

Vaughan, C. E., *The Romantic Revolt (Periods of European Literature,* vol. x), (Edinburgh and London, 1907).

Vaupel, R., *Stimmen aus der Zeit der Erniedrigung (Der deutsche Staatsgedanke,* vol. viii), (Munich, 1923).

Venturi, E. A., *Joseph Mazzini* (London, 1875).

Verschoor, A. D., *Die ältere deutsche Romantik und die Nationalidee* (Amsterdam, 1928).

Vorländer, K., *Von Machiavelli bis Lenin: Neuzeitliche Staats- und Gesellschaftstheorien* (Leipzig, 1926).

Vossler, O., *Mazzinis politisches Denken und Wollen (Beiheft 11 der historischen Zeitschrift),* (Munich, 1927).

Wackernell, J. E., *Das deutsche Volkslied* (Hamburg, 1890).

Wagener, H. F., *Das Eindringen von Percys Reliques in Deutschland* (Heidelberg, 1897).

Waldberg, M. von, *Goethe und das Volkslied* (Berlin, 1889).

Walzel, O. F., *Deutsche Romantik,* 5th ed. (Berlin, 1926).

Warstat, W., "Deutsches Leben in Riga zu Herders Zeit", in *Die Grenzboten,* vol. lxxxvi (1917), pp. 272-80.

Weech, F. von, "Der Versuch der Gründung eines Instituts für den Allgemeingeist Deutschlands", in *Preussische Jahrbücher,* vol. xxi 1868), pp. 690-97.

Wegele, F. X., *Geschichte der deutschen Historiographie seit dem Aufleben des Humanismus* (Leipzig, 1885).

Weise, O., *Unsere Muttersprache,* 2nd ed. (Leipzig, 1895).

Weissenfels, R., *Goethe im Sturm und Drang*, vol. i (Halle, 1894), pp. 31-37, 224-33.

Wenck, W., *Deutschland vor hundert Jahren,* 2 vols. (Leipzig, 1887).

Wenderoth, O., " Der junge Quinet und seine Uebersetzung von Herders ' Ideen ' ", in *Romanische Forschungen,* vol. xxii (1908), pp. 311-98.

Windelband, W., *Geschichte der neueren Philosophie,* 6th ed., 2 vols. (Leipzig, 1919).

Wirth, M., *Die deutsche Nationaleinheit in ihrer volkswirtschaftlichen, geistigen und politischen Entwickelung an der Hand der Geschichte beleuchtet* (Frankfort, 1859).

Witkowski, G. (editor), *Goethes Faust,* 2 vols. (Leipzig, 1908).

Wundt, M., *Fichte* (Stuttgart, 1927).

INDEX

Adelung, J. C., Herder's influence on, 175
Anthropology, Herder urges development of, 108-109
Arminius, 192, 230
Arndt, E. M., on the German language, 173; 254; 255; idea of a national state, 256; 266
Arnim, A. von, Herder's influence on, 207; 235; 236; 237
Aufklärung, see Enlightenment
Augustus the Strong, predilection for French culture, 25

Babbitt, Irving, on Herder, 194
Barrès, M., 253
Bebel, H., a German patriot, 11
Bodmer, J. J., 217, 229
Boie, H. C., and Herder, 203
Boineburg, J. C. von, 36
Bonald, L., 252
Bopp, F., Herder's influence on, 106, 174
Breitinger, J. J., 229
Brentano, C., Herder's influence on, 207; 235; 236
Brodzinski, Casimir, Herder's influence on, 261
Bürger, G. A., Herder's influence on, 207-208

Calixtus, G., efforts to unite confessions, 19
Carl Friedrich of Baden and Herder, 114, 128-129
Celakovsky, F. L., Herder's influence on, 260
Celtis, K., a German patriot, 11
Comparative literature, H e r d e r urges study of, 107
Comparative philology, H e r d e r urges development of, 105
Cosmopolitanism in eighteenth-century Germany, 31-32, 96-97
Culture and nationality, 84-89, 115-127, 149-160, 180-212, 249-252

Dante, 199

Dobrowsky, J., Herder's influence on, 260

Education, as a factor in the development of national peculiarity, 91; in eighteenth-century Germany, 160-167
Eichendorf, J. K. von, 211
Enlightenment, the, and the idea of nationality, 100; and history, 213-219; Herder and, 95-97, 214-217

Fichte, J. G., Herder's influence on, 102, 175; develops ideas stated by Herder, 137, 233; on German nationality, 249; 250; 254-255; idea of a national state, 256, 266
Finnish nationality, Herder and, 262
Flachsland, Caroline, 68; marries Herder, 71-72; i n f l u e n c e on Herder, 202, 203
Folk literature, 195-212
Folk songs, 196-212; Herder's collection of, 202-203; Goethe collects, 210
Forster, G., 103
Fragmente, effect of, 190-191
Frederick the Great, on Gallomania, 24; love of French culture, 26; lack of knowledge of German literature, 27; criticism of German literature, 47; Herder and, 62-64; 230
Frederick III of Brandenburg, founds Berlin Academy, 39
French, use of in eighteenth-century G e r m a n y, 20-22, 163-166; Herder's opposition to the imitation of the, 119, 185
French books in Germany, 153
Fruchtbringende Gesellschaft, purpose of, 28-29

Gallomania, in Germany, 22-27; Herder's opposition to, 119, 164, 185

283

ST. MARY'S COLLEGE OF MARYLAND LIBRARY
ST. MARY'S CITY, MARYLAND

34652

DUE

DEC 16 1977

PRINTED IN U.S.A.